CAR AND DRIVER

ON MOPAR

1968–1975

Reprinted From
Car and Driver Magazine

ISBN 0 948207 50 7

Published By
Brooklands Books with permission of Car and Driver

CAR AND DRIVER

Titles in this series

CAR AND DRIVER ON BMW 1955-1977
CAR AND DRIVER ON BMW 1977-1985
CAR AND DRIVER ON COBRA, SHELBY & FORD GT 40 1963-1984
CAR AND DRIVER ON DATSUN Z 1600 & 2000 1966-1984
CAR AND DRIVER ON CORVETTE 1956-1967
CAR AND DRIVER ON CORVETTE 1968-1977
CAR AND DRIVER ON CORVETTE 1978-1982
CAR AND DRIVER ON FERRARI 1955-1962
CAR AND DRIVER ON FERRARI 1963-1975
CAR AND DRIVER ON FERRARI 1976-1983
CAR AND DRIVER ON MOPAR 1956-1967
CAR AND DRIVER ON MOPAR 1968-1975
CAR AND DRIVER ON PONTIAC 1961-1975
CAR AND DRIVER ON SAAB 1956-1985

Distributed By

Car and Driver
3460 Wilshire Blvd,
Los Angeles,
California 90010

Brooklands Book Distribution Ltd.
Holmerise, Seven Hills Road,
Cobham, Surrey KT11 1ES,
England

CAR AND DRIVER

CAR AND DRIVER

Car and Driver is a living, breathing entity. Although some of our older editions may be a bit cranky and occasionally stiff-legged, they do live on for an eternity (if only on our shelves). We do love to share our previous work, but it's obviously not possible to crank up the printing presses on a whim. Instead, we've produced this series of books, each of which encompasses virtually everything said about a particular subject during a given period in Car and Driver.

We hope you enjoy these collections. They have not been edited or updated in any way, so this is vintage Car and Driver at its finest (we think).

Printed in Hong Kong

Dodge Charger

It looks like the Chrysler Corporation is flat out
in the automobile business again.

Last year, we applauded Plymouth for building what we thought was the best looking Detroit car of 1967, the Barracuda. A remarkable feat, considering the Chrysler Corporation's odd, unstable styling history which, since the Airflow, has been marked by committee-styled cars which, aside from lacking integrity of design, have oscillated between being far out to the point of vulgarity and being timid to the point of sterility—a seemingly endless series of overcompensations for each preceding year. With this background, we were pleasantly surprised by the '67 Barracuda, but quite prepared to wait years before Chrysler came up with a worthy successor. We conjured a picture of designers and stylists lying about their studios, spent from their Barracuda effort, and barely able to create

so much as a new bumper for 1968.

Imagine, therefore, our surprise—again pleasant—when we saw Dodge's new Charger. Working with Chrysler Corporation's 117-in. wheelbase "B" series body/chassis, the designers that we'd imagined were worn out have not only achieved far more than a face-lift, they have easily surpassed the mark of excellence set less than a year ago.

The only 1968 car which comes close to challenging the new Charger for styling accolades is the new Corvette, which is remarkably similar to the Charger, particularly when viewed from the rear quarter. But, we give the honors to the Charger for several reasons. First, the Corvette, being a smaller car in both seating capacity and wheelbase, has a much easier time attaining

the desired sporty image. Second, Dodge stylists have shown that they can create a car in the current idiom with originality, combining just the right amount of tasteful conformity with that novelty and freshness which attracts attention. Originality takes guts in Dodge's position as the smaller division of the number three automaker, but the Charger's aerodynamic wedge theme is not only distinctly new but it is very like the new breed of wind-tunnel tested sports/racing cars which are just now making their debut in the 1967 Can-Am series. Third, while the Charger is a vast improvement over its predecessor, the 1968 Corvette is anticlimactic after the Mako Shark show cars which preceded it.

Chrysler Corporation, then, is flat-out in the automobile business again. The Marlin-

Dodge stylists have shown that they can create a car in the current idiom with originality, combining just the right amount of tasteful conformity with that novelty which attracts attention.

like Charger of the past (really a Coronet with a hastily added fastback roof), and the similarly makeshift Barracuda were grim reminders of the Corporation's close call with financial disaster in the early Sixties. But the belt-tightening policies of Lynn Townsend—Chrysler's chief executive since 1961, and more recently Board Chairman—combined with his intense efforts to improve and increase the Corporation's manufacturing facilities seem to be paying off. The 1967 Barracuda and the new Charger, each with its own distinctive sheet metal now, are evidence of Chrysler's increasing strength and ability to meet both the financial and creative challenge of the specialty car age.

Specialty cars are conceived from a significantly different planning philosophy than that of the bread-and-butter cars which Detroit used to build exclusively. Bread-and-butter cars are built with the primary intention of offending no potential buyer, rendering the cars largely featureless and unexciting. Specialty cars, on the other hand, are built to please specific groups of customers. We like the more positive philosophy behind the specialty car, and the Charger is chock-full of features with obvious appeal for the performance-minded enthusiast.

The aerodynamic appearance of the Charger (it's as aerodynamically slippery as it looks, according to Chrysler's engineers) is accented by a rear spoiler combined with a truncated rear end for a Kamm effect—a design approach which has become almost mandatory in modern racing cars. The Charger takes on the nose-down appearance common to both NASCAR and NHRA, and the bulging rear fenders should accommodate the racing tires used in both drag and stock car racing with a minimum of rework. The greenhouse, following the sharply curved sideglass, slants steeply towards the center of the car, very reminiscent of Le Mans Ferraris, particularly when viewed from the rear. A tunnel-type backlight is used instead of a pure fastback (a styling feature fast going out of fashion from over-use). The smaller rear window of the tunnel roof also gives much less distortion to rear vision than a steeply slanted fastback window.

Further visual performance identity is achieved by the use of a racing-style gas filler cap mounted high on the left rear quarter, and quasi fog/driving/parking and turn signal lights mounted low in the front bumper. Matte black paint is used extensively in the grille and around the tail lights. Full wheel cut-outs, fat tires on 6-inch rims, and simulated engine compartment exhaust vents in the hood (which also house turn signal indicator lights, like the Mustang GT) and at the leading edge of the doors complete the Charger's complement of visually "in" features.

The interior of the Charger carries the GT theme further, with bucket seats, map pockets in the doors, and a well-padded dash with a full complement of instruments set in a matte black background. The tachometer and speedometer are directly in front of the driver while the smaller engine instruments are to the right of the driver, but angled towards him.

With all this performance image going for the Charger, we just had to order an engine to go with it—and when you're talking a Chrysler product, the performance engine is the Hemi. There just isn't more honest horsepower available off the showroom floor than you get from this bright orange monster. While there are larger displacement engines to be had (Dodge offers a 440 cu. in. V-8 option for the Charger for less money than the 426 cu. in. Hemi), none of them can be had with two 4-barrel carburetion.

The Hemi, despite its high performance carburetion, comes very close to meeting smog control regulations without any modifications, hence, has had only minor alterations to the carburetor and distributor calibrations to meet the new laws. The carburetors feed the hemispherical combustion chambers through huge ports and 2.25-in. intake valves with thin (.309-in.) stems, all calculated to put as much fuel/air mixture in the Hemi as possible. The exhaust system is as efficient, with 1.94-in. valves, thin stems, and cast headers leading to a 2.5-in. dual exhaust system.

The rest of the Hemi is just as tough, with cross-bolted caps for three of its five main bearings; a specially heat-treated, forged steel crankshaft; big, husky connecting rods; forged domed pistons; solid lifters and heavy duty pushrods; and a dual-breaker distributor—in short, a racing engine. And that's what it was originally designed for.

The only 1968 car which comes close to challenging the new Charger for styling accolades is the new Corvette, itself remarkably similar to the Charger, particularly when viewed from the rear.

When Chrysler decided to sell the Hemi as an option, they found it was cheaper to carry over the racing parts into production, in most cases, than to tool up for cheaper, street parts. For all-out competition, about all you need is the high compression pistons (same basic design, but more pop-up), a longer duration camshaft, and a set of tubular headers. For stock car racing, there is a very special "ram-tuned" intake manifold and a giant Holley 4-bbl. carb.

Our "street" Hemi was more than powerful enough for any use an ordinary citizen might find. Rated conservatively at 425 hp and 490 lbs./ft. of torque, the Hemi propelled the Charger through the quarter-mile traps at just over 105 mph, covering the distance in 13.5 seconds—not bad for 4346 lbs. test weight and a "cooking" engine. The drag racers buy a 500-lb. lighter 2-door sedan, and do some of the tuning we mentioned above, to go through the traps at close to 130 mph—just in case you had any doubts about our engine being in street tune.

Some of you may have had a Hemi before, and may have experienced some problems with it, particularly in the area of oil consumption. For 1968 the Hemi has undergone some changes to fix this problem and to insure against some others. New valve stem oil seals have cured the oil consumption problem, an oil pan windage tray has permitted the addition of an extra quart of oil to the sump to make sure that the oil pick-up never sucks air, and a fuel vapor separator has been added to the fuel line to prevent vapor lock (which can make hot starts difficult). A slightly longer duration camshaft is also new. Although the peak rating hasn't changed since 1967, the new cam improves the shape of the power curves. We suspect, however, that the camshaft and the windage tray are responsible for the Charger's extra one mph at the end of the quarter-mile, compared to the Plymouth Hemi Satellite we tested in April, 1966.

The Satellite we tested was a 4-speed manual, and we remarked at the time that we'd rather have had an automatic, so we ordered our Charger with one. We were right; the automatic is the plan. Driving through the special high-stall-speed torque convertor which comes with the Hemi, you can either shift manually, winding the Hemi right out to 6500 rpm, or leave it in Drive, where the TorqueFlite shifts for you at

(Text continued on page 9
Specifications overleaf)

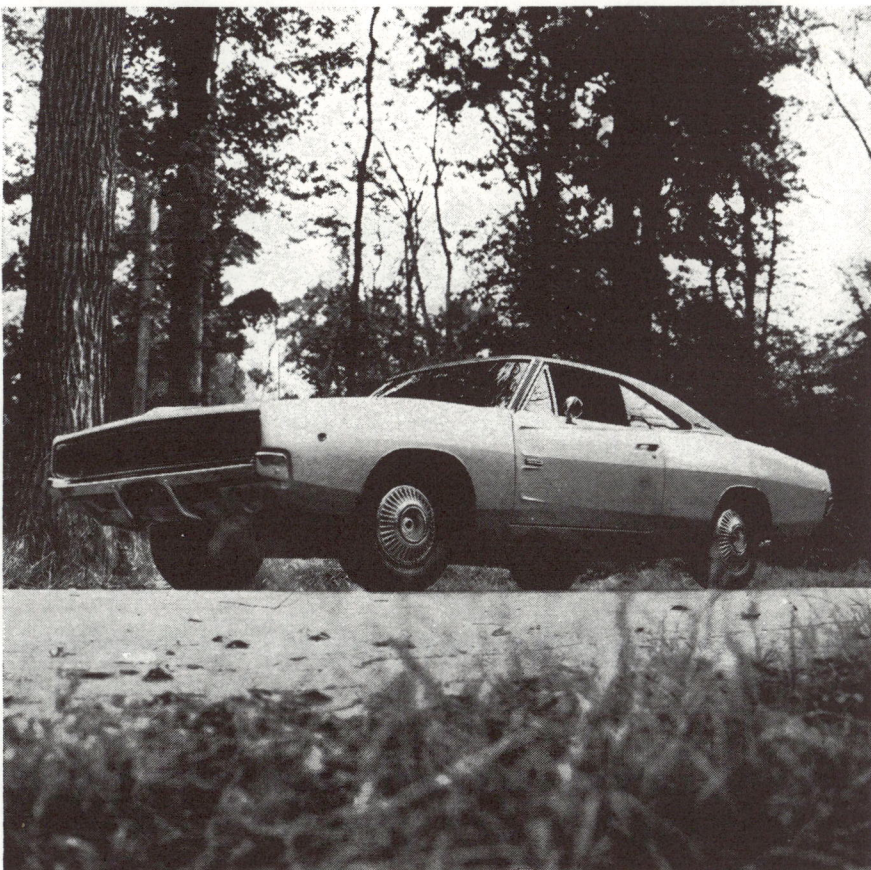

DODGE CHARGER

Manufacturer: Dodge Division
Chrysler Corporation
7900 Joseph Campau
Detroit, Michigan

Number of dealers in U.S.: 3128

Vehicle type: Front-engine, rear-wheel-drive, 4-passenger sports sedan with all-steel integral body/chassis

Price as tested: NA
(Prices for the 1968 models had not been released by the manufacturer at press time)

Options on test car: Hemi engine, automatic transmission, power steering, power disc brakes, HD suspension, limited-slip differential, 15-in wheels and tires, sports console, floor-mounted gearshift, AM radio, vinyl roof, rear window de-fogger, special paint

ENGINE
Type: Water-cooled V-8, cast-iron block and heads, 5 main bearings
Bore x stroke . . . 4.25 x 3.75 in, 108.2 x 95.2mm
Displacement . . . . 426 cu in, 6981 cc
Compression ratio . . . . 10.25 to one
Carburetion . . . . 2 x 4-bbl Carter
Valve gear . . . . Pushrod-operated overhead valves, mechanical lifters
Power (SAE) . . . . 425 bhp @ 5000 rpm
Torque (SAE) . . . . 490 lbs/ft @ 4000 rpm
Specific power output . . . . 0.99 bhp/cu in, 61.1 bhp/liter
Max. recommended engine speed . . . 6500 rpm

DRIVE TRAIN
Transmission . . . . 3-speed automatic
Max. torque converter ratio . . . . 2.1 to one
Final drive ratio . . . . 3.23 to one

Gear	Ratio	Mph/1000 rpm	Max. test speed
I	2.45	9.7	63 mph (6500 rpm)
II	1.45	16.5	107 mph (6500 rpm)
III	1.00	24.0	139 mph (5800 rpm)

DIMENSIONS AND CAPACITIES
Wheelbase . . . . 117.0 in
Track . . . . F: 59.5 in, R: 59.2 in
Length . . . . 208.0 in
Width . . . . 76.6 in
Height . . . . 53.2 in
Ground clearance . . . . 5.7 in
Curb weight . . . . 4035 lbs
Test weight . . . . 4346 lbs
Weight distribution, F/R 55.5/44.5%
Lbs/bhp (test weight) 10.2
Battery capacity . . . . . . 12 volts, 78 amp/hr
Alternator capacity . . . . 445 watts
Fuel capacity . . . . 19.0 gal
Oil capacity . . . . 6.0 qts
Water capacity . . . . 18.0 qts

SUSPENSION
F: Ind., unequal-length wishbones, torsion bars, anti-sway bar
R: Rigid axle, semi-elliptic leaf springs

STEERING
Type . . . . Power-assisted recirculating ball
Turns lock-to-lock 5.3
Turning circle . . . . 41 ft

BRAKES
F . . . . 11.0-in vented disc
R . . . . 10.0 x 2.5-in cast iron drum
Swept area . . . . 387.8 sq in

WHEELS AND TIRES
Wheel size and type . . . 6.0JK x 15-in, stamped steel wheel, 5-bolt
Tire make, size and type . . . . Goodyear F70-15, 2-ply nylon, tubeless
Test inflation pressures . . . F: 30 psi, R: 30 psi
Tire load rating . . . . 1280 lbs per tire @ 24 psi

PERFORMANCE
Zero to	Seconds
30 mph	1.7
40 mph	2.5
50 mph	3.5
60 mph	4.8
70 mph	6.0
80 mph	8.5
90 mph	10.0
100 mph	12.5

Standing ¼-mile . . . . 13.5 sec @ 105 mph
80–0 mph panic stop . . . . 274 ft (0.78 G)
Fuel mileage . . . . . . 9–12 mpg on premium fuel
Cruising range . . . . 171–228 mi

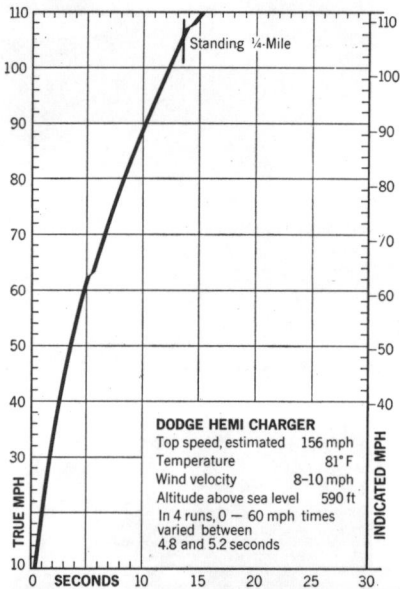

DODGE HEMI CHARGER
Top speed, estimated 156 mph
Temperature 81°F
Wind velocity 8–10 mph
Altitude above sea level 590 ft
In 4 runs, 0 — 60 mph times varied between 4.8 and 5.2 seconds

CHECK LIST

ENGINE
Starting . . . . Fair
Response . . . . Very Good
Vibration . . . . Good
Noise . . . . Fair

DRIVE TRAIN
Shift linkage . . . . Poor
Shift smoothness . . . . Good
Drive train noise . . . . Very Good

STEERING
Effort . . . . Excellent
Response . . . . Very Good
Road feel . . . . Poor
Kickback . . . . Excellent

SUSPENSION
Ride comfort . . . . Good
Roll resistance . . . . Very Good
Pitch control . . . . Very Good
Harshness control . . . . Fair

HANDLING
Directional control . . . . Very Good
Predictability . . . . Very Good
Evasive maneuverability . . . . Very Good
Resistance to sidewinds . . . . Very Good

BRAKES
Pedal pressure . . . . Very Good
Response . . . . Good
Fade resistance . . . . Very Good
Directional stability . . . . Good

CONTROLS
Wheel position . . . . Good
Pedal position . . . . Very Good
Gearshift position . . . . Very Good
Relationship . . . . Very Good
Small controls . . . . Very Good

INTERIOR
Ease of entry/exit . . . . Very Good
Noise level (cruising) . . . . Good
Front seating comfort . . . . Poor
Front leg room . . . . Very Good
Front head room . . . . Excellent
Front hip/shoulder room . . . . Very Good
Rear seating comfort . . . . Good
Rear leg room . . . . Good
Rear head room . . . . Very Good
Rear hip/shoulder room . . . . Very Good
Instrument comprehensiveness . . . Excellent
Instrument legibility . . . . Excellent

VISION
Forward . . . . Very Good
Front quarter . . . . Good
Side . . . . Excellent
Rear quarter . . . . Fair
Rear . . . . Good

WEATHER PROTECTION
Heater/defroster . . . . Excellent
Ventilation . . . . Excellent
Air conditioner . . . . —
Weather sealing . . . . Excellent

CONSTRUCTION QUALITY
Sheet metal . . . . Very Good
Paint . . . . Very Good
Chrome . . . . Very Good
Upholstery . . . . Very Good
Padding . . . . Very Good
Hardware . . . . Very Good

GENERAL
Headlight illumination . . . . Excellent
Parking and signal lights . . . . Excellent
Wiper effectiveness . . . . Excellent
Service accessibility . . . . Fair
Trunk space . . . . Very Good
Interior storage space . . . . Excellent
Bumper protection . . . . Very Good

CONTINUED FROM PAGE 7

about 5500 rpm. If you keep your foot in it that long, the 2-3 shift has you doing well over 90 mph. If you cool it, the automatic lets you drive the Hemi like the 230-hp, 318 cu. in. (standard equipment for the Charger). It would take a fairly sharp mother-in-law to suspect that you had anything but the most docile of powerplants underneath the hood.

We were prepared to not like the brakes on our Charger, as the brakes on Chrysler's "B" body cars have previously fallen short of our standards, but things have changed. We ordered the disc brake option, wanting all the stopping power we could get to go with the Hemi's go power, and found the brakes to be very satisfactory. Directional stability was good, and our stopping distances were right around 274 ft. (.78 G), a perfectly acceptable figure, considering the mass of the car. We did encounter fade once, early in our braking tests, which we attributed to "green fade," a phenomenon that new brake pads go through once before they settle down. Afterwards, we experienced no fade in five successive panic stops from 80 mph.

Handling was dominated by the Charger's inherent understeer characteristics, a function of both the massive Hemi engine in the front of the car and the large front anti-sway bar. The understeer tendency was strong enough that once the limit of adhesion was reached and the front end began to plow, only instant full throttle in the lower gears would get the rear end out. A gentle increase in throttle would only increase the amount of understeer. By anticipating breakaway, we could coax the Charger into a 4-wheel slide with a flick of the wheel and a simultaneous increase in throttle. This induced power-slide was fairly easy to control, but it took up a lot of the road. Generally, the Goodyear F70-15 tires gave good performance and allowed fairly fast cornering without breaking traction—the only way to go, on the street; other maneuvers we restricted to the test track. The Charger assumes a fair amount of body lean when cornering, despite the giant anti-sway bar, stiff springs, and heavy-duty shock absorbers—all of which come with the Hemi.

The Hemi Charger's ride, while harsh by most standards, will be called appropriately firm by most enthusiasts. There will be those who will argue that a Pontiac GTO or an Olds 4-4-2 handles as well without the attendant harshness. But both of these cars suffer from a certain amount of axle hop under hard braking and acceleration, something we didn't encounter with the Charger. It's all a question of how hard the rubber bushings are, and, in the case of the Charger, how many leaves the rear springs have. We'd rather suffer a harshness than axle hop, if a common solution to both problems can't be found. Much of the harshness we felt resulted from the 30 psi tire pressures that are recommended with the Hemi.

While we are discussing handling, we ought to point out that unless your Hemi Charger is going to be used strictly on the drag strip, power steering is a must, not only for it's ease of operation—you've got to be a weight lifter to park a manual steering Hemi—but also because of the faster steering ratio in the power unit. The manual steering has an overall ratio of 28.8-to-one while the power gear is 18.8-to-one—almost twice as fast.

Our main objections to the Charger were on the inside. The seats are terrible—they just don't do anything right. Our unhappiness concerned not so much the seat cushions themselves, but the position of the seat in the car and the angle between the seat proper and the seat back. The seat is very low, relative to the steering wheel, and the seat back—not adjustable—seems to be almost perpendicular to the seat cushion, forcing us to sit bolt-upright. The guys who design seats should have to sit in them while they work at their drawing boards.

We also didn't like the shift lever in the optional console we ordered. Not only is it ugly and out of place in the context of the rest of the Charger's interior, but the detent button is directly on top, making for an unnatural motion when shifting manually. Of the levers we've seen, the T-handle with the button on the side, like the Cougar and the Mustang, or the "goal-post" shifter used by Buick and Oldsmobile, where one squeezes the crossbar to release the detent, are both excellent. We'd settle for either in place of the Charger's (which is shared by all Chrysler console shifters).

With the exception of the rear quarters, vision from within the Charger is good, and we aren't prepared to sacrifice the attractive tunnel-roof wings for visibility. We do, however, recommend a right-hand outside mirror to compensate.

We don't care for (and didn't order) optional belt-like stripes around the rear quarters that Dodge is emphasizing this year. Stripes—like fastbacks—are out in any form; matte black anti-glare paint on the hood is in now, and a good design could be worked into the Charger's hood vent sculpturing.

The Chrysler Corporation is opposed to ventless door windows, on the grounds that there really isn't a practical flow-through ventilation system. So the Charger still has vent windows, and we suspect that Chrysler might just be right. Time will tell. We were glad to have them on our Charger, because air-conditioning is not available with the Hemi engine—it just won't fit.

To add frosting to the cake, the new Charger is 165 lbs. lighter than the old one, and while at this writing prices were as unavailable as peace in Vietnam, we suspect the new Charger will be cheaper than the old one. These days, when you get something better for less, snap it up. ●

Plymouth Road Runner

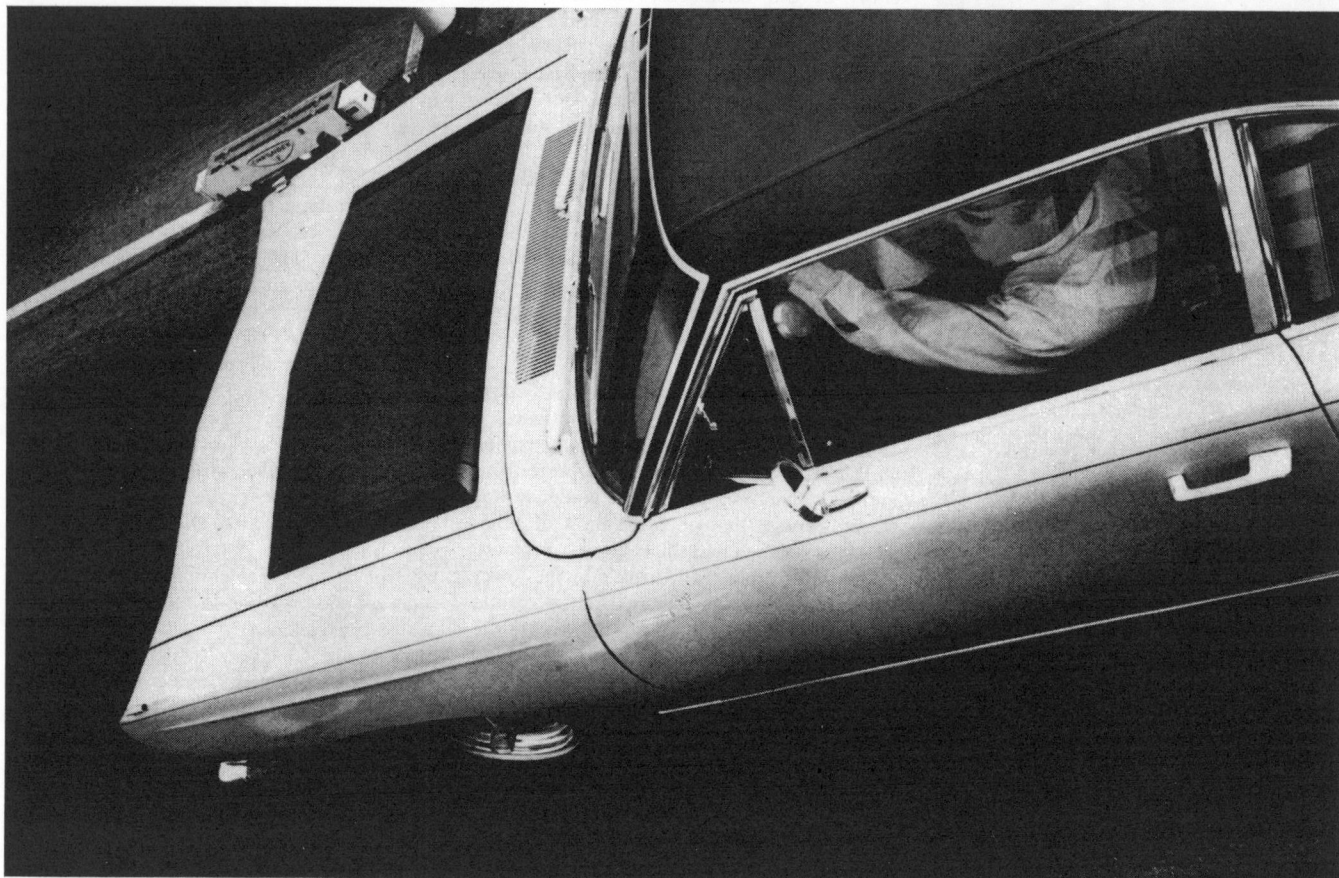

Some morning, Mr. Proud Owner of a Plymouth Road Runner, don't be surprised when you switch the ignition on and your car explodes. It's just our own Brock ("The Assassin") Yates taking his revenge. BOOM! There goes another Beep Beep.

You remember Ayn Rand's novel, *The Fountainhead*? The part where superman architect Howard Roark blows up the Cortlandt housing project? Roark had secretly designed the project for a weak, sniveling fellow architect named Keating on two conditions. One, Keating had to say it was his own design. Two, Cortlandt House had to be built exactly as Roark designed it. Well, the proles put the pressure on poor old Keating, he caves in, and Cortlandt House is built with all kinds of unspeakable alterations to Roark's original. Roark, who's a roaring egocentric, reckons that his contract has been violated, so he takes it upon himself to dynamite the partially

completed housing project. BOOM! There goes Cortlandt House.

You see, the Road Runner was Yates' idea, and Plymouth has made unspeakable alterations to the original. The difference is that Yates isn't the sorehead Roark was, no matter how closely he otherwise resembles him ("Howard Roark laughed. He stood naked at the edge of a cliff ... looking ... at her; it was not a glance, it was an act of ownership"), and Yates didn't have any kind of iron-clad arrangement with Plymouth, secret or otherwise, about how the Road Runner was to turn out. However, tumescent street racers, the fact remains that the Beep Beep was the Assassin's idea.

At least in the beginning.

A year ago, Yates proposed the idea of an economy street racer to Plymouth's top management. A stripped business coupe with a very big motor—either the Hemi

or the 440 Super Commando—as standard equipment. For members of the Propa PH set who play chicken with their insurance companies, there would be a detuned version, with a friendly little engine like the 318, to have teeny-races with pseudo-Super Cars like Buick's GS 350. The only options would be some low-cost drag racing hardware that would easily and cheaply convert the Road Runner into a competitive NHRA/AHRA stocker. Both versions would have all the props of a street racer, but none of the cost or ostentation of show-off equipment. The car would look like a perfectly innocent transportation module, with no visual identification, save for a set of "in" wheels, either mags or no hubcaps—standard. Something so that the street racers could spot each other, but nothing the fuzz would notice.

In an expansively McLuhanesque mood, Yates suggested that "his" econo-racer be

The kids who might buy and race Plymouth's Road Runner call it the Beep Beep, but whatever it's called it was originally Brock ("The Assassin") Yates' idea. Somewhere along the line, Plymouth made unspeakable alterations to the original. Yates is sore. BOOM! There goes another Beep Beep.

marketed only in cool primary colors, with an appropriately malicious-looking all-black vinyl interior, and, possibly, tinted glass all around—like a gas coupe—to further nail down the cool image that today's automotive youth craves. Yates specifically advised against hood scoops, racing stripes, chrome flashes, and razzle-dazzle trim.

The sticker price for the Assassin's street racer would be an irresistible $2800 or less, ready to roll.

The Plymouth guys said they loved the idea, but not right now. The '67 business coupe was too ugly to make it, they said, "but wait'll you see the '68 coupe—that's the perfect basis for your car," they said . . . and that was the last Yates heard of it.

Until his econo-racer appeared as the Road Runner.

The name Road Runner is all Plymouth's own, and we thought it was a stroke of genius until we found out that nobody calls it that. At least, not the people who count. The kids who might buy and race the Road Runner call it the Beep Beep, which was also Plymouth's idea. Reportedly, $50,000 of the Chrysler Corporation's hard-earned bucks went into trying to capture the "beep-beep" noise made by Warner Brother's TV cartoon character, Road Runner, for the car's horn. To us, the Road Runner's horn sounds more like the single note emitted by a Ford Econoline van, but then, we don't spend all that much time watching sub-teen cartoons.

As to Yates' econo-racer concept, we think the Road Runner misses the mark. In the first place, it's too many marketing ideas at once. Yates' original idea is embodied somewhere within, but it's mixed up with all the ballyhoo about the name, Road Runner, and the beep-beep horn. And somewhere along the line, the central theme of Yates' idea—that the car should be inconspicuous—got lost, and the Road Runner came out as a screaming advertisement to get caught by the police. The hood has a gigantic pair of non-functional bulges capped by a pair of non-functional air scoops, dead give-aways to the car's real role. On top of that, Plymouth is pushing a $17.55 cop-baiting option: a giant square of flat-black paint in the middle of the hood. Then there are medallions depicting

(Text continued on page 13; Specifications overleaf)

PLYMOUTH ROAD RUNNER

Manufacturer: Chrysler-Plymouth Division
Chrysler Corporation
Detroit, Michigan

Number of dealers in U.S.: 4000

Vehicle type: Front-engine, rear-wheel-drive, 5-passenger sports coupe, all-steel integral body/chassis

Price as tested: $3,753.40
(Manufacturer's suggested retail price, including all options listed below, Federal excise tax, dealer preparation and delivery charges; does not include state and local taxes, license or freight charges)

Options on test car: Vinyl roof ($78.75), paint stripe ($14.70), light package ($27.95), axle group ($87.50), AM radio ($60.25), power brakes ($43.75), power steering ($94.15), disc brakes ($72.95), bumper guards ($28.70), hood paint ($17.55), tinted glass ($41.50), custom sill moulding ($20.45), head rests ($43.90), remote outside mirror ($9.40), belt line mouldings ($13.20), deluxe lap belts ($11.00), foam front seat ($8.75), third rear seat belt ($6.80), front shoulder belts ($27.70), tachometer ($51.10), under coating ($16.10), styled wheels ($102.05), variable speed wipers ($5.20)

ENGINE

Type: Water-cooled V-8, cast iron block and heads, 5 main bearings
Bore x stroke..4.25 x 3.38 in, 108.0 x 85.9 mm
Displacement.............383 cu in, 6276 cc
Compression ratio.............10.0 to one
Carburetion...............1 x 4-bbl Carter
Valve gear......Pushrod-operated overhead valves, hydraulic lifters
Power (SAE)..........335 bhp @ 5200 rpm
Torque (SAE)......425 lbs/ft @ 3400 rpm
Specific power output........0.88 bhp/cu in, 53.4 bhp/liter
Max recommended engine speed....5400 rpm

DRIVE TRAIN

Transmission.....4-speed manual, all-synchro
Clutch diameter.....................11.0 in
Final drive ratio.................3.55 to one

Gear	Ratio	Mph/1000 rpm	Max. test speed
I	2.66	8.0	43 mph (5400 rpm)
II	1.91	10.8	58 mph (5400 rpm)
III	1.39	15.3	82 mph (5400 rpm)
IV	1.00	21.2	114 mph (5400 rpm)

DIMENSIONS AND CAPACITIES

Wheelbase..............................116 in
Track.............F: 59.5 in, R: 59.2 in
Length................................202.7 in
Width..................................76.2 in
Height.................................52.5 in
Ground Clearance........................6.6 in
Curb weight.........................3634 lbs
Test weight.........................3843 lbs
Weight distribution, F/R..........56.2/43.8%
Lbs/bhp (test weight)..................11.5
Battery capacity..........12 volts, 59 amp/hr
Alternator capacity.................445 watts
Fuel capacity.........................19.0 gal
Oil capacity...........................5.0 qts
Water capacity........................17.0 qts

SUSPENSION

F: Ind., unequal-length wishbones, torsion bars, anti-sway bar
R: Rigid axle, semi-elliptic leaf springs

STEERING

Type........Power-assisted recirculating ball
Turns lock-to-lock.......................3.5
Turning circle.......................42.8 ft

BRAKES

F..........................11.0-in vented disc
R..............10.0 x 2.5-in cast iron drum
Swept area.........................387.8 sq in

WHEELS AND TIRES

Wheel size and type.......6.0 x 14-in, styled stamped steel wheel, 5-bolt
Tire make, size and type....Goodyear F70-14, 2-ply nylon, tubeless
Test inflation pressures...F: 30 psi, R: 30 psi
Tire load rating......1280 lbs per tire @ 24 psi

PERFORMANCE

Zero to	Seconds
30 mph	2.2
40 mph	3.3
50 mph	5.1
60 mph	7.1
70 mph	8.8
80 mph	10.8
90 mph	13.6
100 mph	16.0

Standing ¼-mile.......15.0 sec @ 96 mph
80–0 mph panic stop.........242 ft (0.88 G)
Fuel mileage.....11–13 mpg on premium fuel
Cruising range...................209–247 mi

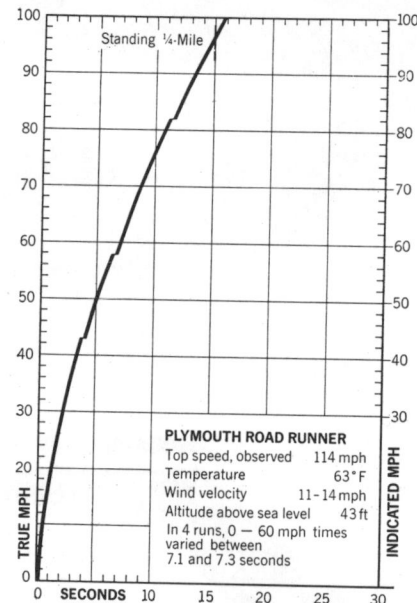

PLYMOUTH ROAD RUNNER
Standing ¼-Mile

Top speed, observed	114 mph
Temperature	63°F
Wind velocity	11–14 mph
Altitude above sea level	43 ft

In 4 runs, 0 — 60 mph times varied between 7.1 and 7.3 seconds

TRUE MPH / INDICATED MPH / SECONDS

CHECK LIST

ENGINE
Starting.........................Good
Response.....................Excellent
Vibration.....................Very Good
Noise............................Poor

DRIVE TRAIN
Shift linkage....................Poor
Synchro action...............Very Good
Clutch smoothness............Very Good
Drive train noise................Fair

STEERING
Effort.......................Excellent
Response.........................Fair
Road feel........................Poor
Kickback.....................Excellent

SUSPENSION
Ride comfort.....................Fair
Roll resistance..................Good
Pitch control................Very Good
Harshness control................Fair

HANDLING
Directional control..........Very Good
Predictability...............Very Good
Evasive maneuverability..........Good
Resistance to sidewinds..........Good

BRAKES
Pedal pressure...............Very Good
Response.........................Good
Fade resistance..................Good
Directional stability............Good

CONTROLS
Wheel position...................Fair
Pedal position...................Good
Gearshift position...........Very Good
Relationship.....................Good
Small controls...............Very Good

INTERIOR
Ease of entry/exit...........Very Good
Noise level (cruising)...........Good
Front seating comfort............Good
Front leg room...............Very Good
Front head room..............Excellent
Front hip/shoulder room......Very Good
Rear seating comfort.............Poor
Rear leg room....................Fair
Rear head room...............Very Good
Rear hip/shoulder room.......Very Good
Instrument comprehensiveness...Very Good
Instrument legibility............Fair

VISION
Forward......................Very Good
Front quarter....................Good
Side.........................Excellent
Rear quarter.....................Good
Rear.........................Very Good

WEATHER PROTECTION
Heater/defroster.............Very Good
Ventilation..................Excellent
Weather sealing..............Very Good

CONSTRUCTION QUALITY
Sheet metal..................Very Good
Paint............................Fair
Chrome...........................Good
Upholstery.......................Poor
Padding......................Very Good
Hardware.....................Very Good

GENERAL
Headlight illumination.......Excellent
Parking and signal lights....Excellent
Wiper effectiveness..........Excellent
Service accessibility............Good
Trunk space..................Very Good
Interior storage space...........Good
Bumper protection............Very Good

PLYMOUTH ROAD RUNNER

CONTINUED FROM PAGE 11

the goofy bird running around. Somehow, all the subtlety of the original got lost in the shuffle, replaced by styling gimmicks hardly less obvious than burning your draft card—and your driver's license—right in front of the Pentagon.

In defense of the flat-black paint option on the Road Runner's hood, we must say that it is much more "in" than racing stripes —a gimmick that has become outmoded on most racing cars, hence has lost much of its appeal as a dress-up option for high performance street cars. And, at least it's functional (anti-glare).

At least the Road Runner is economical. Or it *can* be economical. Our test car wasn't. We didn't order it; whoever did, loaded it with every accessory known to man (see specifications page), adding nearly a grand's worth of non-essentials to our test car's base price of $2870. Our complaint is that our test car sure didn't look like $3800.

As a drag strip performer, in perfectly stock street tune, the Road Runner is impressive, turning the quarter-mile in 15 seconds flat, at 96 mph. And that's with the standard engine, a special 383 that's only available in the Road Runner. This V-8 uses the intake manifolds, heads, and windage tray of the 440 Super Commando to raise the 383's horsepower to 335 at 5200 rpm. It apparently wasn't practical to make the 440 standard, but the souped-up 383 feels as strong as any stock 440 we've ever driven. The only optional engine is the *very* strong 425-horsepower, 426 cu. in. Hemi V-8. Adios, insurance.

Standard equipment on the Road Runner are such items as heavy-duty 11-inch drum brakes, stiff suspension and shocks, wide-oval F70-14 tires, and a 4-speed manual transmission. The only optional transmission is a beefed-up 3-speed automatic.

The only performance option on our test car was the $87.50 "axle group," consisting of a heavy-duty 3.55 ring and pinion, limited-slip differential, heavy-duty radiator and a viscous-drive fan. Our test car was also equipped with $116.70 power disc brakes. Drag racers don't like disc brakes because, (a) they're heavier, and (b) the pads rub on the discs, robbing horsepower. Curiously, when you order discs for the front wheels, the rear drums are an inch smaller in diameter. The brakes on our test car delivered commendably short stopping distances despite a lot of axle hop. The hop disappeared after the brakes warmed up, but fade was evident after our third successive panic stop from 80 mph.

The power steering seemed to be very slow and unresponsive. The car gets sideways with a wheel-spinning start, and the steering was so listless under this relatively innocent condition that we never wanted to toss the car into turns as hard as it would go to explore its ultimate cornering performance. It leans more than you'd expect, and understeers predictably. Quick steering would help immeasurably. The Dodge Charger (*C/D*, November), is more stiffly sprung, and not only handles better, it rides better than the Road Runner too.

There was an intramural difference of opinion about the shift linkage. The Editor, who babied it out of the hole and got the quickest elapsed time (15.0 seconds) found nothing to fault in the mechanism. The Technical Editor, an old drag racing hand, complained mightily about the weaknesses of the Inland shifter when forcing shifts, drag racing style. It's probably not up to the rigors of "board shifting."

The Road Runner's seating comfort was also a topic of considerable discussion among the staff. We have mentioned in the past that we do not care for Chrysler's bucket seat design, but we generally like the Road Runner's bench seat except for its position in the car. The driving position is the opposite of the lean-back-and-stretch-out-your arms pose affected by sports car buffs. You sit more or less bolt upright in the Road Runner's bench seat, practically on top of the controls, and there's no way of adjusting the position to anything other than the classic posture of a kid waiting for the count-down on the Christmas tree. The steering wheel is very large in diameter, and mounted very high, making the driver feel like an undersized teenager (a little applied psychology from the interior designers?). It's perfect for drag racing, but not for touring. So the seating comfort/driving position question boils down to the question of intent. If the Road Runner is to be considered as a basically drag racing oriented car, the seating package is OK, but if the car is to have more general appeal in the performance car market, we would recommend a re-evaluation of the driving position.

Plymouth scrapped Yates' notions for the interior. Instead of all-black, it's exceptionally cheap-looking two-tone vinyl; instead of simple Stewart-Warner gauges, there's a small, expensive ($51.10) tachometer. The tach is not only hard to read, but also redlined at 5000 rpm, 200 shy of the power peak and a good 500 below valve float. Like we said, the car doesn't look like $3800, an impression the raft of options, like pin-striping ($14.70), doesn't dispel.

No matter, Plymouth will probably sell more Road Runners than they ever imagined—and congratulate themselves for being right on target. All the hokey touches won't be lost on the masses, at least, which is probably what Plymouth had in mind when they "adapted" The Assassin's idea to their own purposes. We hear that the first recorded sale of a Road Runner was to a 44-year-old guy in the Midwest who bought it for his wife. No wonder Yates is sore. BOOM! There goes another Beep Beep. ●

Car and Driver Presents:

MINI TESTS

ON SELECTED

American Cars

Mini-Tests, as the name implies, are something less than the full-scale road tests we do throughout the year as a matter of course.

On the other hand, we discovered that when we answer the innumerable queries for consumer-type information on a car our readers are thinking of buying, we can generally give them a pretty clear idea of what the car is all about in a few well-chosen words. That's what a Mini-Test is: a short, sharp vignette that reveals some basic truth about each car. The *whole* truth about the cars we're interested in will be laid out before you as the year unfolds in our full-length road tests.

Mini-Tests differ in another way from our standard format: they include a short check list, but no detailed graph with all the figures attached. That's because a good number of the cars we drove were pre-production prototypes whose performance sometimes varies significantly from the cars which will eventually see the showroom floor.

When we decided to write the Mini-Tests on every basic make and model for sale in this country, we realized that there are only about 50 U.S. and 50 imported cars—for a nice, round total of 100. We're taking the '68 American cars this month and the foreign cars next month.

A word of warning, don't be put off by some apparent duplication in the American car section. It doesn't take much to see that a fire-breathing Montego 427 is quite a different animal from an economical Comet 302, even though the two cars look nearly identical.

You'll find no difficulty in discovering our likes and dislikes. We're evaluating the cars from *C/D's* point of view. We're enthusiasts, so are you. The result is that, when we test a basic-transportation kind of car, we'll concentrate more on how it handles than on how many miles per gallon it gets.

These 50 tests weren't intended to be our patented comparison tests, but we can't help noting that many of the American cars are alike. There may never have been a business as competitive as the automobile business, and, the way it is practiced in America, never one so imitative. If one auto-maker scores a success with a unique car (Mustang), it is axiomatic that the others will copy it (Barracuda, Camaro, Cougar, Firebird, Javelin). Moreover, there is probably more competition between divisions within the same corporation as between companies.

This intense competition—and the amazing technological similarity of most of these cars—has led to the most astonishing fact of all: there are no really bad cars made in America; some are just better than others.

Next month we'll test 50 foreign cars, and, as the technical differences lengthen and the option lists shorten, the qualitative differences between the cars will become more marked.

Chrysler Imperial

Chrysler Corporation, after several years of trying to build the Imperial as a unique car—with completely different sheet metal and chassis from the rest of the Chrysler line—last year gave up on the idea and returned the car to its original status of a super-appointed New Yorker. And, it's much better for the change: it rides better, it handles better and—surprisingly—it's put together better. Evidently Chrysler simply didn't have a sufficient engineering effort to make a going proposition of the Imperial's separate but unequal status.

By utilizing standard Chrysler components, the '68 Imperial became an infinitely more appealing car. Handling is significantly improved and gives the driver a much more tangible idea of how the car is meeting the road. The ride is not as soft as some of the luxury cars made by other manufacturers, but the small increase ·in harshness is more than compensated for by the extra confidence the driver has in being able to cope with emergency situations. Front disc brakes are standard on this two-and-a-half-ton vehicle—an uncommon policy in the luxury car field. The rococo Men's Club atmosphere of the interior may be a little stifling for your taste, but it's better than the Gemini I-style cockpits that some manufacturers feel is synonymous with luxury.

CHRYSLER IMPERIAL

Manufacturer: Chrysler-Plymouth Division
Chrysler Corporation
Detroit, Michigan

CAR AS TESTED
Engine . . . . 350-hp, 440 cu. in. V-8
Transmission . . . . 3-speed automatic
Steering . . . . Power-assisted
Suspension . . . . Standard
Brakes . . . . Disc F, Drum R

CHECK LIST

ENGINE
Throttle Response . . . . Fair
Noise Insulation . . . . Excellent

DRIVE TRAIN
Shift Linkage . . . . Very Good
Shift Smoothness . . . . Very Good

STEERING
Effort . . . . Very Good
Response . . . . Fair

HANDLING
Predictability . . . . Very Good
Evasive Maneuverability . . . . Fair

BRAKES
Directional Stability . . . . Good
Fade Resistance . . . . Good

INTERIOR
Ease of Entry/Exit . . . . Excellent
Driving Position . . . . Very Good
Front Seating Comfort . . . . Very Good
Rear Seating Comfort . . . . Very Good

GENERAL
Vision . . . . Very Good
Heater/Defroster . . . . Excellent
Weather Sealing . . . . Excellent
Trunk Space . . . . Very Good

Dodge Charger

Hey, this time the Dodge Brothers really did it. After struggling along with the old Charger—a car that reminded veteran sales types at Chrysler of the Airflow disaster—this year they really bowled a strike with a new and completely revamped model—and it swings!

The 1968 Charger has to be one of the most visually exciting cars on the market, anywhere, and we are here to tell you that it's every bit as good as it looks. Naturally if you're going to swing for a machine like the Charger, you go for the super motor, right? And that has to be the optional 426 Hemi, right? And with the Hemi comes a really complete handling package, including stiffer shocks and springs, big front disc brakes, etc., right? So without question, that's the hot set-up for the Charger, right?

The interior of the Charger is every bit as nice as the outside—discreet, rich-looking and functional. Round instruments tell you what's going on, and the pleated, unruffled vinyl seats make you think of the Orsi Brothers or Pininfarina or somebody.

Packed with the Hemi, the Charger goes like its looks imply it should. Here is a genuine 150-mph car that does everything an automobile should do, and well. Surely the Charger ranks among the best of this year's crop.

DODGE CHARGER

Manufacturer: Dodge Division
Chrysler Corporation
Detroit, Michigan

CAR AS TESTED
Engine . . . . 425-hp, 426 cu. in. V-8
Transmission . . . . 3-speed automatic
Steering . . . . Power-assisted
Suspension . . . . Heavy-duty
Brakes . . . . Disc F, Drum R

CHECK LIST

ENGINE
Throttle Response . . . . Very Good
Noise Insulation . . . . Fair

DRIVE TRAIN
Shift Linkage . . . . Poor
Shift Smoothness . . . . Good

STEERING
Effort . . . . Excellent
Response . . . . Very Good

HANDLING
Predictability . . . . Very Good
Evasive Maneuverability . . . . Very Good

BRAKES
Directional Stability . . . . Good
Fade Resistance . . . . Very Good

INTERIOR
Ease of Entry/Exit . . . . Very Good
Driving Position . . . . Good
Front Seating Comfort . . . . Poor
Rear Seating Comfort . . . . Fair

GENERAL
Vision . . . . Good
Heater/Defroster . . . . Excellent
Weather Sealing . . . . Excellent
Trunk Space . . . . Very Good

Dodge Charger

DODGE CHARGER

Manufacturer: Dodge Division
Chrysler Corporation
Detroit, Michigan

CAR AS TESTED
Engine ....425-hp, 426 cu. in. V-8
Transmission ....3-speed automatic
Steering ....Power-assisted
Suspension ....Heavy-duty
Brakes ....Disc F, Drum R

CHECK LIST

ENGINE
Throttle Response ....Very Good
Noise Insulation ....Fair

DRIVE TRAIN
Shift Linkage ....Poor
Shift Smoothness ....Good

STEERING
Effort ....Excellent
Response ....Very Good

HANDLING
Predictability ....Very Good
Evasive Maneuverability ....Very Good

BRAKES
Directional Stability ....Good
Fade Resistance ....Very Good

INTERIOR
Ease of Entry/Exit ....Very Good
Driving Position ....Good
Front Seating Comfort ....Poor
Rear Seating Comfort................Fair

GENERAL
Vision ....Good
Heater/Defroster ....Excellent
Weather Sealing ....Excellent
Trunk Space ....Very Good

Hey, this time the Dodge Brothers really did it. After struggling along with the old Charger—a car that reminded veteran sales types at Chrysler of the Airflow disaster—this year they really bowled a strike with a new and completely revamped model—and it swings!

The 1968 Charger has to be one of the most visually exciting cars on the market, anywhere, and we are here to tell you that it's every bit as good as it looks. Naturally if you're going to swing for a machine like the Charger, you go for the super motor, right? And that has to be the optional 426 Hemi, right? And with the Hemi comes a really complete handling package, including stiffer shocks and springs, big front disc brakes, etc., right? So without question, that's the hot set-up for the Charger, right?

The interior of the Charger is every bit as nice as the outside—discreet, rich-looking and functional. Round instruments tell you what's going on, and the pleated, unruffled vinyl seats make you think of the Orsi Brothers or Pininfarina or somebody.

Packed with the Hemi, the Charger goes like its looks imply it should. Here is a genuine 150-mph car that does everything an automobile should do, and well. Surely the Charger ranks among the best of this year's crop.

Dodge Coronet

DODGE CORONET

Manufacturer: Dodge Division
Chrysler Corporation
Detroit, Michigan

CAR AS TESTED
Engine ....290-hp, 383 cu. in. V-8
Transmission ....3-speed automatic
Steering ....Standard
Suspension ....Standard
Brakes ....Drum F, Drum R

CHECK LIST

ENGINE
Throttle Response ....Very Good
Noise Insulation ....Very Good

DRIVE TRAIN
Shift Linkage ....Very Good
Shift Smoothness ....Good

STEERING
Effort ....Fair
Response ....Very Good

HANDLING
Predictability ....Very Good
Evasive Maneuverability ....Very Good

BRAKES
Directional Stability ....Very Good
Fade Resistance ....Good

INTERIOR
Ease of Entry/Exit ....Good
Driving Position ....Good
Front Seating Comfort ....Very Good
Rear Seating Comfort ....Good

GENERAL
Vision ....Good
Heater/Defroster ....Excellent
Weather Sealing ....Very Good
Trunk Space ....Very Good

It really doesn't make a lot of sense. In the corporate scheme of things, Plymouths are supposed to be slightly smaller and less expensive than Dodges, but something went haywire somewhere. The Fury III is built on the same basic body as Dodge's Monaco and Polara, while the Dodge Coronet shares the same body with Plymouth's Belvedere. Now it would stand to reason that the Plymouths would dominate the cheaper intermediate field, and the Dodges the full-size field. But it ain't so; the Fury III decisively outsells the Polara and Monaco combined, while the intermediate Coronet is much more successful than the Belvedere.

Why the Coronet is so successful in what would appear to be a Plymouth market becomes obvious when the car is driven. The Coronet 500 hardtop, with the 383 cu. in. 4-bbl. engine and TorqueFlite automatic, is a right-sized, well-behaved sharply-appointed family car that drives a lot better than it looks. This is not to say the car isn't pretty, but its coke-bottle rear fenders showed up on GM cars two years ago, and, as always, the Dodges look a bit dated.

In stock trim, the Coronet is as roadable as any intermediate on the market, though its standard 318 cu. in. V-8 is a trifle weak-hearted for anyone with a normal pulse-rate. Forget the extra gas and get the 383.

Dodge Coronet R/T

We might as well get it over with; R/T stands for Road and Track, and all of us dim-bulb sporty car types know what *that* means, don't we? Well, the Dodge R/T is not a dim-bulb sporty car in any sense of the word, but rather a well-balanced intermediate designed to make the same scene with cars like the GTO, 396 Chevelle, Road Runner, *et cetera* (and we know what that is, too, don't we?).

The Dodge R/T is a jazzed-up Coronet carrying some trim options, stiffer suspension and, if the buyer is wise, the gargantuan 440 Magnum engine. This monster is rated at 375 horsepower and will go around acting like a Hemi until some rather exotic speed ranges are obtained.

Like all of the Dodge/Plymouth intermediates built on this common Chrysler B-body, the R/T has a rather high, padded instrument panel lip that hampers forward visibility and detracts somewhat from an otherwise workmanlike, if somewhat pedestrian, interior design job.

The Chrysler Corporation has produced some really hot intermediates in 1968, and because of a wide overlap in engine, transmission and suspension applications, it is very difficult to state that one is better or worse than another. It can be said that they arĕ collectively a good, solid bunch of performance machines.

Dodge Dart GTS

One of the company's press releases describes the Dodge Dart GTS as a "smooth-handling, corner-hugging road-gripper" which, apparently, means it's pretty good. The Dart GTS is, in fact, a tough little machine on curves and bends, thanks to springs and shocks that appear to be as stiff as any in the industry, but about the only big news involves a boffo trim package that includes, of all things, a set of "power bulges" on the hood and "bold bumblebee stripes" that wrap around the trunk. Yes, good things are happening in Hamtramck.

Unlike the Barracuda, the Dodge boys have had to take the basically unsporting Dart body shell and make it appear exciting.

The Dart is, and has been, an ordinary, middle-of-the-road, compact Detroit sedan, but Dodge has managed to inject it with enough romance so that its sales have been one of the industry's big success stories.

With the new 340 cu. in. "baby rumble-guts" engine on board, the Dart GTS becomes a fun car to drive, just like its cross-town cousin, the Barracuda, (which shares the same basic suspension and engine set-ups).

The body shape is pretty, if a bit boxy, and driver comfort is excellent, despite an immense steering wheel. It's a neat, well-executed car, bumblebee stripes not withstanding.

Dodge Monaco

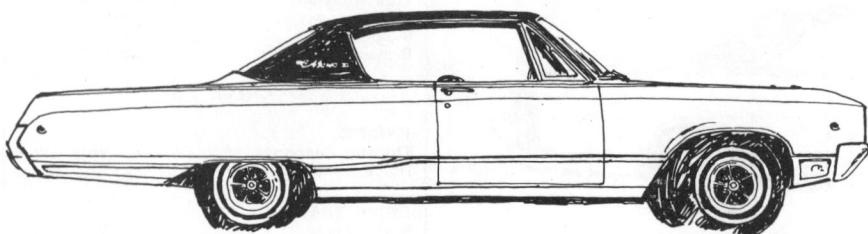

All of Chrysler Corporation's "full-size" cars (some read that "over-size") are built on a common body, so there is really very little to choose from when comparing the Plymouth Furys, the Dodge Polaras and Monacos, and the Chryslers. All of them use the same engines (318, 383 and 440) and the same old and much-revered TorqueFlight automatic transmission, and evaluation has to be reduced to differences in styling details and simple subjective reactions to one car versus another.

Our Dodge Monaco used the husky 440 cu. in. V-8 that is reserved for the 500-series Monaco which is also trimmed more luxuriously than Dodge's less opulent models.

The optional disc brakes are almost mandatory on this powerful 4100-lb. car. And don't be mislead, the Monaco *is* a large car —even gigantic by most enthusiasts' standards—but it is firmly suspended for its bulk, and control at normal speeds is not a problem. The car is ideally suited to turnpike use, what with its low noise level, long-legged gearing and powerful engine.

Monacos are available with adjustable power front seats, and they are recommended for anyone planning lengthy trips. Our Monaco had one of those standard seats that felt delightful at first sitting, but managed to wreck the base of the spine within a few hours.

Plymouth Barracuda

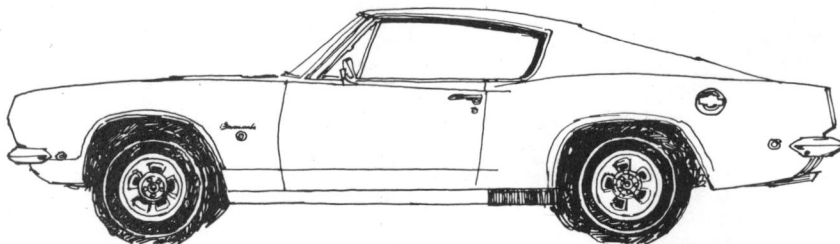

Hey, at long last, the Barracuda—the sporty car that refused to die—has gotten some, er, you know, *brio,* some guts, some *cojones.* After letting it putter through life with a feckless 273 cu. in. V-8, Plymouth finally stuffed the neat little machine full of its throbbing new 340 cu. incher that acts and sounds like a junior varsity Hemi.

The Plymouth people have known for some time that the Barracuda lacked the rough-and-tumble personality that would endear it to the enthusiast market, and several abortive corrections have been tried. First they installed a noisy muffler that succeeded only in infuriating the cops, then

last year they wedged in the big-car 383 4-barrel V-8 engine, but it was so massive that power steering wouldn't fit, and it took an NFL linebacker to park it.

But this year the 340 puts Plymouth right into the program. Now the Barracuda has plenty of performance (plus excellent handling), to run with the standard Mustangs and Camaros. The standard 'Cuda mill is a 318 this year, but forget about it; get the 340 or nothing.

The Plymouth stylists have managed to cunningly disguise the notchback and convertible Barracudas to look like Valiants, so only the original fastback has any truly distinctive lines.

Plymouth GTX

The GTX is Plymouth's jumbo street racer, complete with all the acceptable props—hood scoops, bucket seats, mag-type wheels, zoomie medallions and stripes—plus a very neat engine/chassis combo.

The standard GTX engine is the muscular Super Commando 440 cu. in. high-performance version. This massive, free-breathing powerplant is gutsy enough that it will make the GTX perform nearly as impressively as the optional, more expensive, slightly more temperamental Hemi. Coupled with the ultra-tough, ultra-flexible TorqueFlite 3-speed automatic (forget about 4-speed manual on a car like this unless you are a 32nd-degree drag racer),

the 440 will do all the tricks and keep running forever.

The Chrysler Corporation B-body, from which the GTX is derived, features as neatly articulated yet as conventional a suspension system as there is in the USA. The heavy-duty shocks and springs that come on the GTX make it one of the most agile intermediates in the business. Add to this a set of 11-inch disc brakes at the front and you've got plenty of stopping power for a car that will come out of the gate with the best of 'em, and cruise for hours at 80 mph.

It looks good, the interior is tasteful, if slightly uninspired, and the GTX is a load of civilized performance for the money.

PLYMOUTH GTX

Manufacturer: Chrysler-Plymouth Division
Chrysler Corporation
Detroit, Michigan

CAR AS TESTED

Engine .... 375-hp, 440 cu. in. V-8
Transmission .... 3-speed automatic
Steering .... Power-assisted
Suspension .... Heavy-duty
Brakes .... Disc F, Drum R

CHECK LIST

ENGINE
Throttle Response .... Very Good
Noise Insulation .... Fair

DRIVE TRAIN
Shift Linkage .... Very Good
Shift Smoothness .... Good

STEERING
Effort .... Excellent
Response .... Very Good

HANDLING
Predictability .... Very Good
Evasive Maneuverability .... Very Good

BRAKES
Directional Stability .... Excellent
Fade Resistance .... Very Good

INTERIOR
Ease of Entry/Exit .... Very Good
Driving Position .... Good
Front Seating Comfort.............. Good
Rear Seating Comfort............... Fair

GENERAL
Vision .... Very Good
Heater/Defroster .... Very Good
Weather Sealing .... Very Good
Trunk Space .... Very Good

Plymouth Fury III

That the Fury III is not America's sweetheart is a sad reflection on the taste and perception of the American public. This car, which is Plymouth's entry in the mass-class sweepstakes so handily dominated by the Chevrolet Impala and the Ford Galaxie, is a truly outstanding machine for the money.

It is tastefully styled, both inside and out, and feels taut and silent under even the nastiest road conditions. Comfort is impressive, although Plymouth has, to its everlasting credit, resisted the temptation of providing the kind of jello-bowl suspension that has become omnipresent on the big Chevys and Fords. Visibility is very good and the

driver can make it down the highway with a Fury III and honestly feel that he has some direct influence over what the machine is doing. No question, the Fury II and III (the latter has better trim) models are the best-handling cars in the so-called "volume" segment of the auto market.

The standard V-8 for the Fury is a fusty 318 cu. in., 2-bbl. V-8, and this, if anything, is a flaw in the appointment. Such an otherwise modern sedan needs more performance (with no sacrifice in economy) and one can only hope that a version of Chrysler's new 340 cu. in. V-8 will be offered in the future. In the meantime, spend a few extra bucks and get the optional 383.

PLYMOUTH FURY III

Manufacturer: Chrysler-Plymouth Division
Chrysler Corporation
Detroit, Michigan

CAR AS TESTED

Engine .... 230-hp, 318 cu. in. V-8
Transmission .... 3-speed automatic
Steering .... Power-assisted
Suspension .... Standard
Brakes .... Drum F, Drum R

CHECK LIST

ENGINE
Throttle Response .... Fair
Noise Insulation .... Very Good

DRIVE TRAIN
Shift Linkage .... Very Good
Shift Smoothness .... Very Good

STEERING
Effort .... Excellent
Response ..,.................. Very Good

HANDLING
Predictability .... Very Good
Evasive Maneuverability .... Good

BRAKES
Directional Stability .... Very Good
Fade Resistance .... Good

INTERIOR
Ease of Entry/Exit .... Very Good
Driving Position .... Good
Front Seating Comfort .... Very Good
Rear Seating Comfort .... Very Good

GENERAL
Vision .... Very Good
Heater/Defroster .... Excellent
Weather Sealing .... Very Good
Trunk Space .... Very Good

Plymouth Road Runner

The Road Runner was originally conceived as a stripped Plymouth Belvedere, stuffed full of enough horsepower to make it a showroom version of the de-chromed, super-cool Q-ships that Young America presently drives on the street.

The project has, by-and-large, been completed without compromise, although the stylists and product planners couldn't resist overstating the non-functional hood scoops. Within the context of this market, the name is a stroke of genius, and Plymouth will doubtlessly exploit it for all it's worth. The Road Runner is basically a Belvedere I, which is Plymouth's low-buck fleet special, equipped with a specially-tuned 383 cu. in., 4-bbl. V-8 and heavy-duty suspension. The result is the world's fastest club coupe. The interior trim is a bit sparse although improved upholstery is on the way. The car, like all Chrysler intermediates with heavy-duty suspension, handles very well, and the 383 gives it plenty of power for the street racing scene. However, if you are really serious about the whole thing, you'll spend the extra money for the fabled Hemi, which should put the Road Runner *right there* with the 427 Corvette.

This is the first car since the GTO to be aimed directly at American youth and it very probably is dead on target. But just wait till ol' Nader hears about it.

Plymouth Valiant Signet

Look again, that stark little sedan you just passed is "America's Economy King." Thanks to a long-sought, hard-fought win in the 1967 Mobil Economy Run, Plymouth is at last able to brag a bit about its drab Valiant. This is an important matter to Plymouth because sales have been dropping for the past few years, and unless something is done, the Valiant could turn into a massive pain in the assembly line.

Like the Corvair and the Falcon, the Valiant has been around since Detroit's automotive wizards discovered the compact car nearly a decade ago, and, like its aging compatriots, all attempts to market it as a semi-sporty car have long since disappeared over the horizon.

It is an "economy king" pure and simple, and if you are willing to subordinate all other standards of automotive performance for a few extra mpg, you can buy this cleanly-styled sedan with—now get this—a 115-hp Six and a 2.76-to-one rear axle ratio. Needless to say, this is the set-up that won the Mobil Run.

Without question, the most satisfactory engine for the Valiant is the 190-hp, 273 cu. in. V-8 coupled to a TorqueFlite or 4-speed transmission. This gives the Valiant Signet adequate power for short-haul driving, but then the question arises, mileage fans, how would it do in the Mobil Run?

Dodge Dart GTS

We figure that the "S" stands for sneaky.

GT-what *this* time? Suddenly we're like the tiny cartoon characters who are crouched sideways, hands and arms outstretched, ready for any manner and form of animal or device to leap out from the world to attack. Lately it's been a GT, and they've gone from A to Z so *naturally* it's been only a matter of time until the GTS came along.

Maybe GTS stands for something fairly obscure. Maybe GTSneaky for those Chrysler engineers who have made a modest sized 340 cubic inch V-8 put out more horsepower than even the insurance companies would believe. Or perhaps GTSuper for a car able to leap a wide variety of public roads in a single bound with only a polite grunt to mark its passing. Or even GTSilly which describes offering both 340 and 383 cubic inch engines when each produces substantially identical performance. According to Dodge it's GTSport which is descriptive to a degree that only ad men and product planners have mastered.

Dodge wants it GTSport, so GTSport it will be although the car is clearly conservative in the appearance department. The stylists have tried very hard to convey a racer impression by painting part of the grille black, fastening die-cast, incredibly remote facsimiles of intake stacks onto the hood and bolting GTS signs in strategic locations. The Dart defies their best efforts and manages to blend into the greenery as though it had been practicing. Funny thing, though—whenever we stopped at a gas station or parked it at some event that drew the youthful car culture we were immediately greeted by queries, "...uh, 340?" Offhand that may seem aboriginal, but in the lexicon of the young it was also remarkable in itself because nowhere on the Dart's exterior is there any mention of the engine. "How does it do against Road Runners?" Information gathering for the mandatory street racer classifying system. Then comes the astounding part. "It's only rated at 275 hp but really it puts out about 350." *They* were telling *us*. When it comes to finding out about cars those kids easily have the CIA covered. None of them want to spend their hard earned dollars for a sheep in wolf's clothing so the word gets through the underground pretty fast about who is building stones and

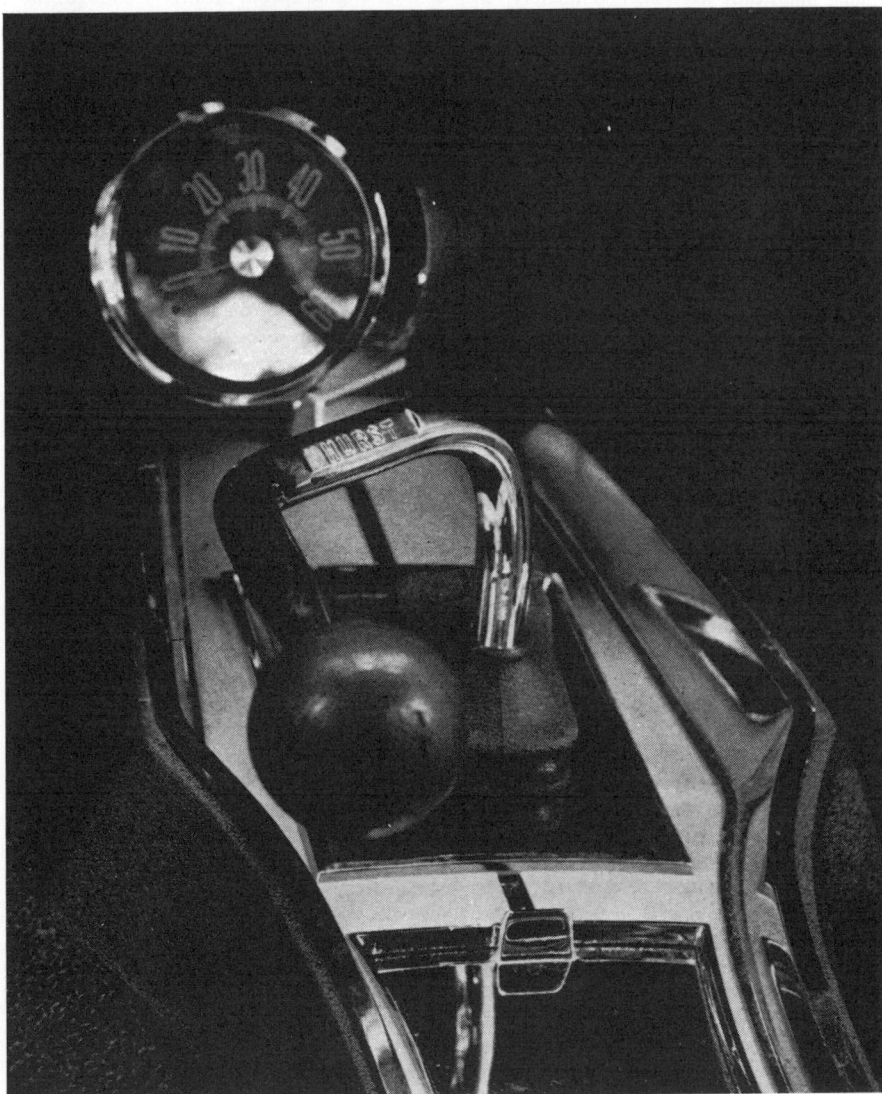

whose cars really can do the job.

The latest word from the underground is that the little Mopar 340 is the hot set-up. A giant killer from Hamtramck. We're believers.

In concept the 340 is just a big-bore version of the 273-318 series V-8s which have been quietly going about their duties under Plymouth and Dodge hoods for years. The 340's 4.04-inch bore is a monstrous hole when compared to the 3.63-inch bore of the 273 but the stroke remains the same at 3.31

inches. To make sure the 340 lives under the hard use that a high revving engine like this can expect, the bottom end consists of a heat-treated, forged steel crankshaft with stronger connecting rods of a new design. In the Chrysler engineers' eagerness to get horsepower out of their new little engine, not a single part that might restrict breathing escaped redesign. Starting with the cylinder heads, they simply threw the old ones out and started all over again. All of that resulted in very generous ports with 2.02-

21

inch intake and 1.60-inch exhaust valves. (For comparison they're exactly the same size as the high performance small-block Chevrolet valves.)

Then came the new low-restriction 2-level intake manifold and 4-bbl. Carter carburetor with air valve secondaries. To let everything out in the same style that it got in, the exhaust manifolds were also completely redesigned.

A little known fact about 340s is that the manual transmission version gets a different camshaft than the automatic—a cam with more lift and duration which should make more power although both engines remain rated at 275 hp.

Because the 340 was intended to be very effective in high speed ranges, no effort was spared to make sure that it didn't give away any horsepower when you're twisting it. For that reason things like a viscous-drive fan, dual-point distributor and a windage baffle in the crankcase to prevent the crankshaft from playing egg beater with the oil are all part of the package. Because of its 10.5 to one compression ratio, the 340 requires premium fuel, but that's par for the course in the high performance world. As we've already said, the intrepid Chrysler engineers bravely stuck their necks way out and rated this strong-hearted little engine at 275 hp at 5000 rpm. We'd be the last to accuse anyone of underrating but the underground isn't kidding when they say 340s shoot Darts down the road in a 350-hp fashion.

The test car was a 4-speed version with a 3.91 rear axle ratio which right away tells you that it wasn't built with top speed in mind. Still, you could hardly call it a serious drag strip car either since its option list included almost every weight adding device available on Darts—with the exception of air conditioning—which brought the curb weight up to 3480 pounds. Nothing that the 340 couldn't cope with, however, because standing quarter miles were a matter of 14.4 seconds at 99 mph. Nothing to be trifled with—and nobody has to be told *that* either. The engine willingly revs to 6000 rpm, the highest number on the tach, but the best times were obtained by shifting at 5500 rpm.

The real question is whether a 3.91 gear is unbearable on the street. We would have thought so, but after 2000 miles of both turnpike and city traffic driving we've concluded that the 340 and a 3.91 gear are admirably suited to each other. The benefits are obvious. The 340 tends to be slightly short on torque so the deep ratio helps to get through the weak spot in a hurry. It also makes the car very easy to drive. You can get launched without bogging—which is difficult to avoid with the standard 3.23 ra-

tio. The big surprise is that engine noise isn't objectionable in a 70 mph cruising situation. The hydraulic lifters are, of course, totally silent. The exhaust is quiet to the point of being almost overmuffled from the enthusiast point of view, but probably most important is the viscous-drive fan which significantly reduces cooling fan noise at high engine speed. Strangely enough, the only time noise ever becomes objectionable is at idle when the manifold heat valve sets up a ruckus that wouldn't even be tolerated in a Maytag. This clatter has been a characteristic of every 340 we've driven, which indicates that a little help is needed in the design department.

The last point in favor of the high numerical axle ratio, or at least not against it, is that fuel economy doesn't suffer appreciably. The Dart averaged over 14 mpg in a trip from Detroit to New York when cruising speeds were held in the 70-75 mph range wherever possible. The poorest tank average was 11 mpg which included the acceleration tests.

The big news for 4-speed fanciers is that Hurst shift linkage is once again standard equipment, thanks to a mid-year change. When Chrysler first introduced its beefy 4-speed transmission in 1964, the Hurst linkage was included as a standard part of the package. Everything was fine until the product planners, always on the lookout for some new, trick device, spotted a Ford with a reverse lock-out on its shifter. With lightning speed it was decided that reverse lockout triggers would be a part of every Chrysler 4-speed too. Black were the years between 1966 and 1968½—the years of the infamous wet-noodle shifter as it was known by the dissenters within Chrysler's engineering walls—the shifter that required readjustment after every hard shift. You know, the one with the buzzing reverse trigger.

Anyway, forget the past because once again Hurst has taken up residence in Dart consoles, supplying the solid and precise feeling that makes manual transmission cars fun to drive. Chrysler 4-speeds have always been of the high shift effort variety, higher than any other domestic box, and that hasn't changed. Trying to engage low gear when stopped is a task whose difficulty is exceeded only by trying to find reverse. As an apparent acknowledgment of the problem, a reverse indicator light under the instrument panel lights whenever the shift lever is pushed fully home in the R-slot. It doesn't make reverse any easier to *engage* but at least you know when you're there.

About here the shape of the shift lever

(Text continued on page 25;
Specifications overleaf)

The stylists did their best to make it stand out but the GTS blends into the greenery as though it had been practicing. It was up to the engineering department to make it stand out.

ACCELERATION standing ¼ mile, seconds

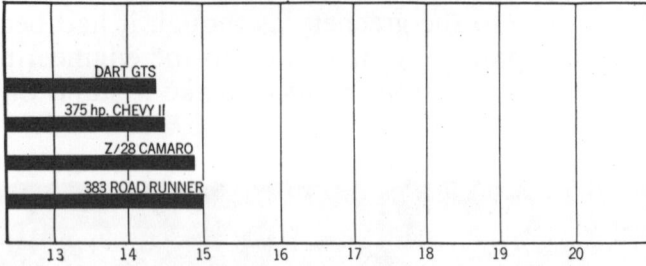

	13	14	15	16	17	18	19	20
DART GTS								
375 hp. CHEVY II								
Z/28 CAMARO								
383 ROAD RUNNER								

BRAKING 80-0 mph panic stop, feet

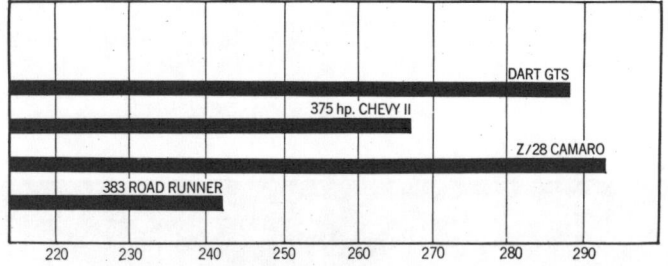

	220	230	240	250	260	270	280	290
DART GTS								
375 hp. CHEVY II								
Z/28 CAMARO								
383 ROAD RUNNER								

FUEL ECONOMY RANGE mpg

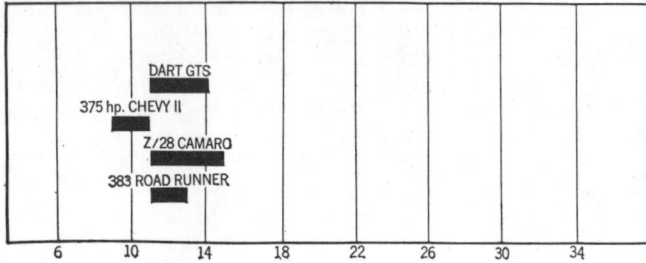

	6	10	14	18	22	26	30	34
DART GTS								
375 hp. CHEVY II								
Z/28 CAMARO								
383 ROAD RUNNER								

PRICE AS TESTED dollars x 1000

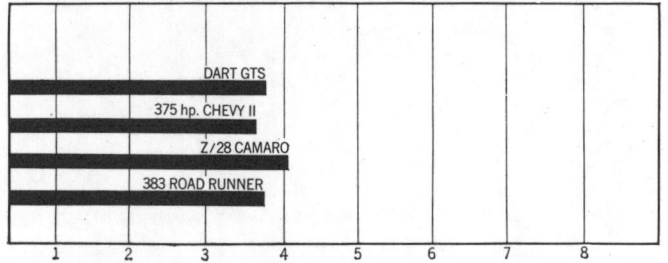

	1	2	3	4	5	6	7	8
DART GTS								
375 hp. CHEVY II								
Z/28 CAMARO								
383 ROAD RUNNER								

DODGE DART GTS

Manufacturer: Dodge Division
Chrysler Corporation
7900 Joseph Compau
Detroit, Michigan 48231

Vehicle type: Front-engine, rear-wheel-drive, 5-passenger, 2-door hardtop

Price as tested: $3795.30
(Manufacturer's suggested retail price, including all options listed below, Federal excise tax, dealer preparation and delivery charges; does not include state and local taxes, license or freight charges)

Options on test car:
Dart GTS including 340 cu. in. engine, paint stripe, 4-speed transmission, E70-14 tires ($3189.00), vinyl roof ($75.10), radio group ($182.45), light package ($22.15), power brakes ($41.75), disc brakes ($72.95), bumper guards ($25.30), console ($50.10), wood rim steering wheel ($25.95), tachometer ($51.10), undercoating and hood insulating pad ($16.10)

ENGINE
Type: V-8, water-cooled, cast iron block and heads, 5 main bearings
Bore x stroke..4.04 x 3.31 in, 102.7 x 84.0 mm
Displacement.................340 cu in, 5580 cc
Compression ratio.................10.5 to one
Carburetion.............1 x 4 bbl Carter AVS
Valve gear..Pushrod-operated overhead valves
Power (SAE)..........275 bhp @ 5000 rpm
Torque (SAE)..........340 lbs/ft @ 3200 rpm
Specific power output....0.81 bhp/cu in, 49.4 bhp/liter

DRIVE TRAIN
Transmission............4-speed, all-synchro
Final drive ratio...................3.91 to one

Gear	Ratio	Mph/1000 rpm	Max. test speed
I	2.66	7.1	39 mph (5500 rpm)
II	1.91	9.9	54 mph (5500 rpm)
III	1.39	13.6	75 mph (5500 rpm)
IV	1.00	18.9	114 mph (6000 rpm)

DIMENSIONS AND CAPACITIES
Wheelbase.........................111.0 in
Track................F: 58.1 in, R: 56.3 in
Length............................195.4 in
Width.............................69.7 in
Height.............................52.8 in
Ground clearance....................5.9 in
Curb weight.......................3480 lbs
Weight distribution, F/R........55.8/44.2%
Battery capacity..........12 volts, 48 amp/hr
Alternator capacity...............444 watts
Fuel capacity.....................18.0 gal
Oil capacity........................4.0 qts
Water capacity....................18.0 qts

SUSPENSION
F: Ind. upper wishbones, single lower arms with struts, torsion bars, anti-sway bar
R: Rigid axle, semi-elliptic leaf springs

STEERING
Type........Recirculating ball, power assisted
Turns lock-to-lock.........................3.5
Turning circle curb to curb............41.5 ft

BRAKES
F:........10.8-in vented disc, power assisted
R:.10 x 1.75-in cast iron drum, power assisted

WHEELS AND TIRES
Wheel size...........................14 x 5.5-in
Wheel type.............Stamped steel, 5-bolt
Tire make and size.........Firestone E70-14
Tire type................Tubeless, 4 P.R.
Test inflation pressures...F: 26 psi, R: 26 psi
Tire load rating.....1120 lbs per tire @ 24 psi

PERFORMANCE
Zero to	Seconds
30 mph	2.0
40 mph	3.2
50 mph	4.3
60 mph	6.0
70 mph	7.7
80 mph	9.9
90 mph	12.2
100 mph	14.5

Standing ¼-mile.........14.4 sec @ 99.0 mph
Top speed.........................114 mph
80-0 mph.......................288 ft (.74 G)
Fuel mileage...11–14.5 mpg on premium fuel
Cruising range...................198–256 mi

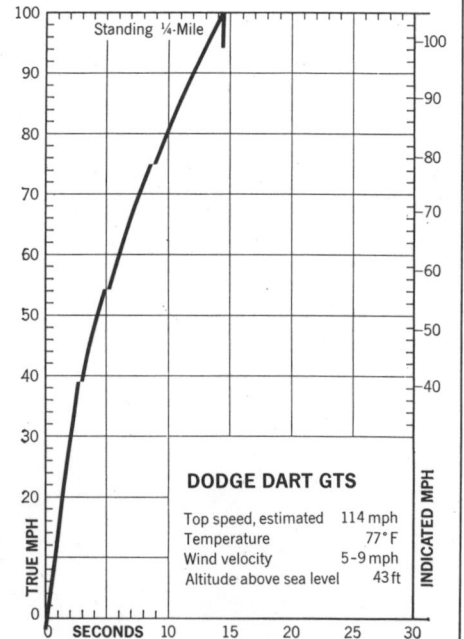

DODGE DART GTS
Standing ¼-Mile

Top speed, estimated	114 mph
Temperature	77°F
Wind velocity	5-9 mph
Altitude above sea level	43 ft

DODGE DART GTS

CONTINUED FROM PAGE 22

comes in for some comment. The stylists, with the stylists' eye for what's right, decided that it must come through the widest part of the console and right in the middle. That the hole in the console is a foot forward of the spot where the shifter comes through the floor is merely a problem for the engineering department. The result is a shift lever that looks as if Charles Atlas got mad at it, but fortunately function is in no way impaired.

Just when you conclude that Chrysler is really tuned in to the performance market you discover the tachometer, mounted on the console under the instrument panel. There can be no rational explanation for locating such an important instrument so far from the driver's line of sight. The tach's less-than-precision nature, particularly when cold—which allows the needle to waver over a 1000 rpm range on the dial when the engine is operating at a steady speed— plus the incredible location, makes it the biggest waste of $51.10 we've come across in some time.

Heavy duty suspension, which is standard equipment on the GTS, certainly rates high marks in the handling department. It has a modest understeering nature which most drivers will find very secure for any type of road driving. The only improvement we would suggest would be to control the movement of the rear axle which bounces around more than is comfortable on rough surfaces.

In the past we've been very critical of the power steering in Chrysler's small cars blaming the lack of road feel on the very low steering effort. As we drive more of these cars we've discovered that although the effort is approximately the same in all of them, the road feel varies widely from one car to the next. The problem actually results from a large amount of free-play encountered when reversing the direction of the steering wheel in some cars and is apparently a matter of quality control rather than a design fault. The accuracy of the steering in the test Dart was more than acceptable.

Only in braking does the Dart fall short of the ability expected of a high performance automobile. The power-assisted disc brakes respond predictably with very reasonable pedal effort to normal stopping demands, but when an emergency arises you're really in trouble. Any sort of maximum effort stop with the manual transmission car sends the rear axle into a violent hop and the disc/drum system is proportioned in such a way that straight line stops are out of the question. After an 80-0 panic stop the Dart was invariably broadside to the direction of travel, the only consolation being that in each stop it consistently turned in the same direction. Inside, the driver has the sensation of a violent, shaking doom which is reinforced by the screws coming loose and raining on his legs from under the instrument panel. The managing editor, who was stationed along the strip to measure braking distances, reported seeing daylight under the rear wheels on every hop. No wonder the Dart requires 288 feet (0.74G) to stop from 80 mph. How can it be expected to do any better when its wheels only touch the ground half of the time? It's true that the hop never gets started if the clutch is depressed at the time of brake application.

To meet government safety standards the lower portion of the Dart's instrument panel has been padded in such a way that it actually forms a shelf useful for storing cigarettes, parking meter change and other small necessities for travel. The Dart's instrumentation is easily readable and complete with the exception of a warning light which supplies oil pressure information. Chrysler products traditionally have more complete instrumentation than their competitors, and for that they deserve credit.

We found the Dart's driving position difficult to get used to. The seat is very low, creating the impression that the driver is sitting in a hole. The steering wheel is so high that you have to reach up for it and diminutive ladies have trouble seeing over —a kind of automotive equivalent to Ape-Hanger handlebars. It does make for plenty of headroom though, if you like to wear high hats while driving.

The Dart's interior is fully covered with vinyl which is easily cleanable and looks smart but is definitely lacking comfort in times of extreme temperature. To make matters worse, the seats are covered in a completely rib-free design which assures that every square inch of your backside contacts the unventilated surface. Cloth inserts in the seats would make a highly desirable option.

The interior ventilation provided in the Dart by traditional corner vent windows is complimented by two trap doors under the instrument panel—one on each side. The amount of air and its direction can be controlled by the position of the doors, which we think is a simple and effective system.

After more than 2000 miles in the GTS we find it to be an endearing machine which does exactly what it's supposed to do— brakes excluded, of course. The 340 engine is an eager performer and remarkably tractable considering its output. Easily the most exciting engine Chrysler has produced since the Hemi. The car is well constructed with a unit body free of shakes and groans even though road noise is present to a noticeable extent. Its greatest virtue is that it can cover great stretches of public roads with ease and yet never be boring. Even the picture editor, who we'd like to think didn't have a clue about anything but cameras, tries to get dibs on the Dart whenever he can. ●

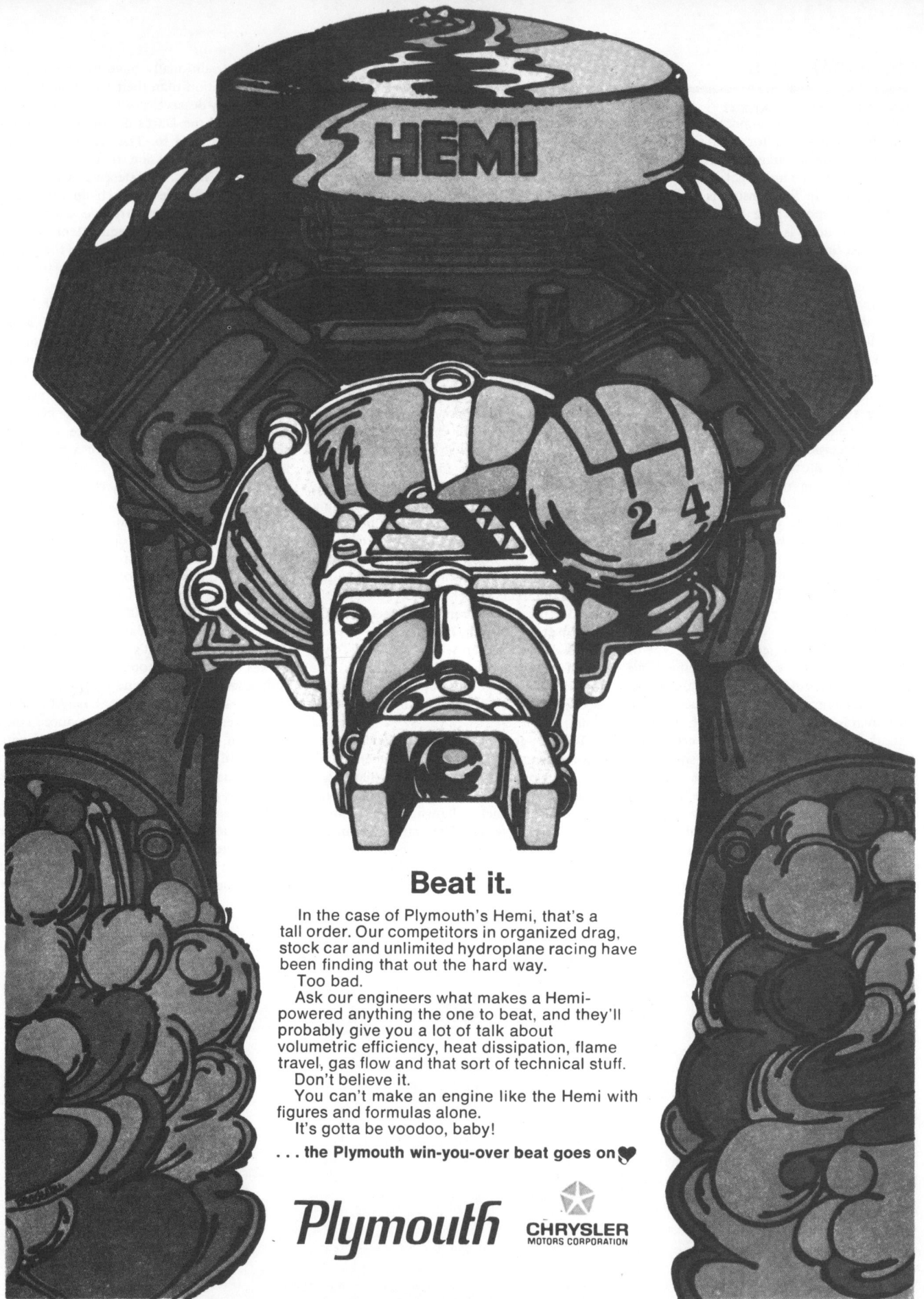

Beat it.

In the case of Plymouth's Hemi, that's a tall order. Our competitors in organized drag, stock car and unlimited hydroplane racing have been finding that out the hard way.

Too bad.

Ask our engineers what makes a Hemi-powered anything the one to beat, and they'll probably give you a lot of talk about volumetric efficiency, heat dissipation, flame travel, gas flow and that sort of technical stuff.

Don't believe it.

You can't make an engine like the Hemi with figures and formulas alone.

It's gotta be voodoo, baby!

. . . the Plymouth win-you-over beat goes on ♥

Plymouth

CHRYSLER
MOTORS CORPORATION

SIX ECONO-RACERS

CHEVELLE SS396 · COBRA · CYCLONE CJ · HEMI ROAD RUNNER · SUPER BEE · THE JUDGE

If you like the taste of whiskey you drink it on the rocks, right? Distilled. There's nothing very complicated about that. But what do you do if you really like the taste of automobiles? We'll tell you what. You pick one of Detroit's warhorses—the intermediates. The same machines that carry the corporate banners as Grand National stock cars and have traditionally filled out drag racing's super stock ranks. These are the Fairlanes and the Cyclones, the Belvederes and the Coronets and the Chevelles. You order your car with every go, stop, and turn part available, but nothing else. No candy coating to kill the flavor because the flavor is the thing. And you haven't pushed the price out of sight with tack-ons (not to be confused with tach-ons) which only serve to confuse the issue anyway. You've got yourself an Econo-Racer and it's sano.

Plymouth pioneered the idea. The division realized it wasn't doing its big engines any favors by stuffing them into cars already overweight with gadgets and glitter and after much introspection it produced the Road Runner. Road Runner logic forthwith became impossible to argue with—as all of Detroit discovered—when, in the first year, 19.8% of the intermediate-size Plymouths were Road Runners. Dodge, which is always somewhere on the same lap with Plymouth, joined the movement with the Super Bee. A kind of inverse kinky name, but no less a real car.

With the introduction of its 1969 models, the Ford Motor Company admitted that Econo-Racers were the name of the game and laid *its* cards on the table—a Cobra for the Ford Division and a Cyclone CJ from Lincoln-Mercury. It wasn't bluffing either—no less than the 428 Cobra Jet engine as standard equipment in each.

All the elements of a genuine automotive battle. With a thunderhead like

27

this on the horizon and all of the enthusiasts crying for rain, we tend to get very solemn about duty and all and act as a catalyst. In this case that means a comparison test which happens to be one of our specialties.

We would definitely expect an entry from Plymouth, Dodge, Ford and Mercury since they had already declared themselves to be in the market. But what about GM, which almost never admits a competitive urge? Anyone with the ego to bill itself as the "Number 1 Team," as does Chevrolet, could reasonably be expected to have an Econo-Racer on its order form. As we suspected, Chevrolet offers its SS396 package on the 300 Deluxe 2-door coupe—which fits the description regardless of what Chevrolet chooses to call it. Pontiac, too, was pushing The Judge over the horizon and suddenly *Pontiac* couldn't be overlooked either.

A moment here, if you will. It is vital to a meaningful comparison test that every

car have substantially equal equipment. To make things simple we asked for the base engine with the optional functional hood scoops on every car—with one exception, the Road Runner. Since the Super Bee and the Road Runner are mechanically identical it didn't make sense to have both of them with the standard 383, so we asked for the only other option—the 426 Hemi—in the Road Runner.

To keep everything even, each car was ordered with F70 tires, an axle ratio as close as possible to 3.50 with a limited-slip differential, disc brakes (which are available only with power-assist), and power steering. Automatic transmissions were selected simply because, with street tires, they're the fastest way to go. Nobody can deny the importance of a tachometer in a performance car, so that part was in, and we specified styled wheels so our Econo-Racers wouldn't be confused with taxi cabs. A radio made the list for obvious reasons. That's all. Each represented our idea of a perfect performance car at a minimum price and would be judged accordingly. Oh, sure, we'd take a look at trunk space and bumper protection and rear seat hip room and all that stuff that regular cars are supposed to have, but these things would be of secondary importance. We are inclined to evaluate Econo-Racers like good whiskey—by the flavor and by the kick and who gives you the most for your money.

At this point everything seemed pretty straightforward. In our mind's eye, we could see each car in its purposeful nakedness. After all, do prize fighters wear business suits in the ring? Of course not. So, we were sure everyone would instantly tune in on these cars with perfect understanding. You can imagine our surprise when only the Road Runner and the Super Bee arrived in fighting trim. The others had bucket seats and consoles—three of them even had trick steering wheels and electric windows. The Cobra and the Cyclone CJ were wearing their 1969 Econo-Racer name tags but they also had the same gadgets and glitter that have festooned Detroit performance cars for years. And the Chevelle—a Malibu 2-door hardtop—came complete with all of the gee-whiz trim, flashing light monitors and buzzing warning devices, not to mention an absolutely flawless metallic blue paint job. It was a veteran show car Chevrolet had sprung from its duties. Each of the cars had every piece of optional equipment we had asked for, but the manufacturers didn't have the restraint to stop there. When we registered our dismay we were told we hadn't allowed enough time to build the right car. Nevertheless, since Plymouth and Dodge could do it in the six-week period we thought reasonable, we suspect some other answer is closer to the truth. We're left with the inescapable conclusion that the majority of influential executives in the Motor City can't understand that 44,599 people bought Road Runners last year because they are just plain stark. No, that straightforward explanation won't go at all.

The inevitable Detroit process of sweetening up the economy models with add-on trim has already begun.

The extra equipment on the Cobra, Cyclone CJ and Chevelle are detrimental to the results of an Econo-Racer comparison test only in that they raise the price. The added weight may marginally reduce the performance, but should in no way change the basic feel which is of prime importance in this type of car. Unless you happen to live somewhere on the Great Plains, these cars are so quick you can seldom use wide-open throttle for more than a few seconds, and even then you use it with great respect or suddenly you're in American Samoa. So most of the joy of driving one of these Econo-Racers has to

come from the potential they pump into the driver from the moment he starts the engine until he slips the key into his pocket at the end of the trip. Still, that's automotive excitement too.

You can imagine the enthusiasm with which the entire *C/D* staff responds when called upon to evaluate automotive excitement—we even let our resident Formula Vee racer take the Hemi Road Runner, which was easily the greatest thrill of his career—it was, after all, a *car;* and yes—he could indeed join us at New York National. The Speedway's amiable and efficient manager, Ed Eaton, tried not to worry when cars were going both ways at once on the drag strip or all hung out on the handling course, and in this case he had almost three days (track testing only) during which he could try not to worry.

When you have six cars and six drivers trying to compare every conceivable aspect of performance, the proceedings may look more like the Keystone Kops than scientific testing. But after two weeks, both on the track and on public roads, the staff knew which cars made the program, which didn't and why. Listed below—best first—are the Econo-Racers. And you'd better believe—this is definite.

HEMI ROAD RUNNER

The Hemi Road Runner was an easy first choice, not so much because of the Road Runner as the Hemi engine and everything that goes with it. To say the Road Runner scored heavily in the performance part of the test is Anglo Saxon understatement in the best tradition. It was the quickest in acceleration, stopped in the shortest distance and ranked second in

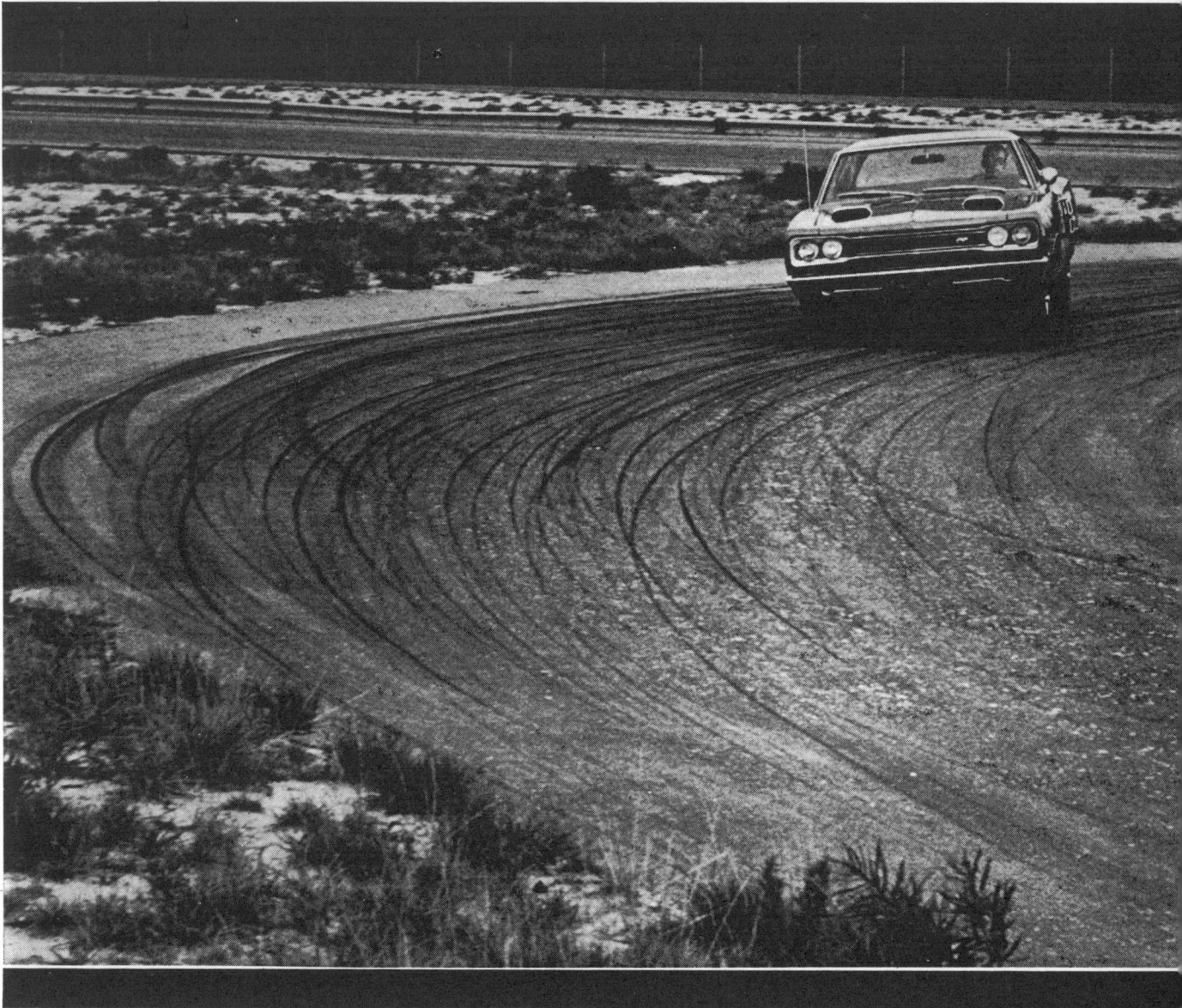

ECONO-RACER CHECK LIST						
(Cars rated numerically with 6 as maximum)	Chevelle SS396	Super Bee	Cobra	Cyclone CJ	The Judge	Road Runner
PRICE						
Price (basic econo-racer)	3409.10	3740.10	3792.78	3836.50	N/A	4239.45
Rating	6	5	4	3	2 est.	1
Price (as tested)	4048.25	3858.00	4043.23	4381.60	N/A	4362.05
Rating	4	6	5	1	3 est.	2
PERFORMANCE						
Acceleration	2	3	4	5	*	6
Braking	2	4	5	3	*	6
Handling	6	4	2	2	*	5
PERFORMANCE RATING	10	11	11	10	*	17
DRIVER CONTROLS						
Steering feel	6	4	2	2	5	4
Braking feel	1	5	4	2	3	6
Transmission shifter	1	3	4	4	6	3
Instrumentation	5	6	1	1	4	3
DRIVER CONTROLS RATING	13	18	11	.9	18	16

*Not representative

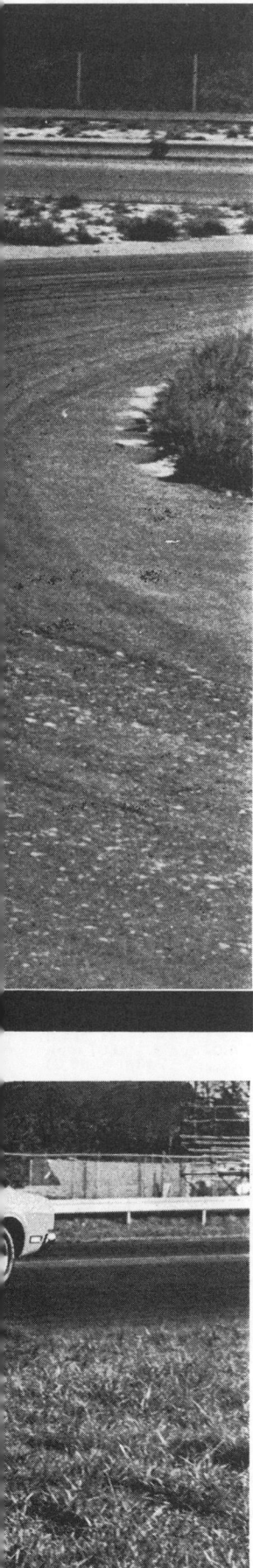

handling. That is a pretty tough record.

All the while the Hemi was proving itself to be the toughest car of the test, it was also proving to be the most exciting. Where the Chevelle, Cobra and Cyclone CJ give the impression of being hot sedans, the Road Runner comes in from the other direction—a tamed race car. And that impression isn't entirely wrong. Chrysler's 426 cu. in. hemispherical combustion chamber V-8 was never intended to quietly propel Imperials down the freeway/expressway/throughway/parkway or allow you to carry an extra lawn chair in the back of your Plymouth Fury station wagon. It was designed as a race engine, pure and simple. The whole idea was to put the hurt on Ford at Daytona because Ford was too far ahead for conventional weapons. You probably wouldn't even be able to buy one in your Road Runner if Bill France hadn't decided, with some prompting by Ford, that it was hardly fair to race those big motors if Chrysler wasn't going to sell them to the folks. Forget about the reason, the Road Runner's Hemi (although detuned a couple hundred horsepower so that it can pass the federal exhaust emission standards) is still the same basic engine used in Grand National stock cars and super stock drag machines.

What is it like on the street? Breathtaking. The Hemi Road Runner has more pure mechanical presence than any other American automobile—even more than the Z/28 Camaro which is another thinly disguised race car we've grown to love. Of course the Hemi is noisy, although its not an excessive amount of mechanical noise. After it's warmed up, the impact-extruded pistons no longer clunk around in their bores and the solid-lifter valve gear is almost totally silent. In fact in actual engine noise, the Hemi was quieter than the Cobra Jet. It's the *power* noise that sets the Hemi apart from the others. It has an impatient, surging idle that causes the whole car to quiver, particularly when the automatic transmission is in gear and being held against the brake. And there is that lump in the throttle travel. Stay on the near side of the lump and you can drive at any speed you choose up to, say, 100 mph in relative calm. Go past the lump and you open everything in the two 4-bbl. Carters. The exhaust explodes like Krakatoa and the wailing howl of surprised air being sucked into the intakes turns heads for blocks. Baby, you know you're in *the presence*.

If you are on a drag strip, as we were, you discover that standing quarter-miles can be covered in the 13.5-second range at a terminal speed of just over 105 mph. That is making it for a car which weighs in at 3938 pounds.

Of course the Road Runner's race car complexion is reinforced by its suspension. It is incredibly stiff—guaranteed to produce extreme discomfort for anyone but an enthusiast. All Hemi Road Runners are built with higher rate torsion bars and rear springs than their 383 counterparts. Obviously, it handles well. Not as good as the Chevelle because it has a strong understeering nature that requires a heavy throttle foot to get the tail out, but it does corner very predictably with very little body roll. Wherever you are, you are always reminded that the Road Runner is only a notch or two away from a true competition car just by the way your eyeballs rattle in the sockets whenever you hit a tar strip.

In a car as fast as the Hemi, you'd better have brakes equal to the task, and they were. The Road Runner stopped in a straight line from 80 mph in 245 feet (0.87 G)—shorter than any of the other cars. However, brake fade was noticeably greater than in the Ford or GM cars. We normally make three stops from 80 mph. Since it was almost impossible to obtain impending lockup on the third stop we tried a fourth, just to see what would happen. Even though the pedal did bottom out and the required pedal pressure was very high, the Road Runner stopped in less distance than the first two tries—and with no swerving. We would consider the brakes very satisfactory for street operations but fade could be a problem in very hard driving and needs improvement.

In the driver's compartment the Road Runner was—as expected—stark. That is what Econo-Racers are all about. The instruments are arranged in a horizontal line on the dash, white-on-black and very easy to read. No oil pressure gauge was present or available, which registers as a true felony considering the $813 price of the Hemi. We weren't exactly turned on by the tachometer either—it had a circular face occupying a small rectangular spot in the instrument panel, half hidden by the steering wheel rim. The Woolworth's Five and Dime appearance combined with a 5000 rpm redline (about 800 rpm below where the transmission automatically upshifts) make you wonder whether that $50.15 option is real or a decoration in bad taste.

The Road Runner's most conspicuous ornamentation change for 1969 is that the chicken decals are now in full color. No matter where you look—on the doors or the deck lid or the instrument panel or the steering wheel hub—there is that unfortunate beep-beep bird looking back at you. It's the only light touch on an otherwise totally serious car. That is if you can have a light touch with a heavy hand.

So that you will know we weren't completely distracted by the Hemi's thunder, we checked out some of the more mundane areas which add up to automotive virtue.

CONTINUED ON PAGE 34

CHEVELLE SS 396

List price as tested: $4,048.25

Options on test car: 325-hp engine with SS package including styled wheels, power disc brakes and F70 x 14 tires, $347.60; automatic trans, $221.80; 3.55 limited-slip differential, $42.15; tachometer and instrumentation, $94.80; power steering, $105.35; AM/FM radio, $133.80; H.D. suspension, $5.30; rear window defroster, $22.15; power windows, $105.35; bucket seats and console, $174.90; tinted glass, $36.90; head restraints, $16.90; light monitoring system, $26.35; auxiliary lighting, $16.35; rear speakers, $13.20; all-vinyl interior. $12.65.

ENGINE
Bore x stroke.....................4.09 x 3.76 in
Displacement.........................396 cu in
Compression ratio...............10.25 to one
Carburetion...........1 x 4-bbl. Rochester
Power (SAE)...........325 bhp @ 4800 rpm
Torque (SAE)........410 lbs/ft @ 3200 rpm

DRIVE TRAIN
Final drive ratio......................3.55 to one

DIMENSIONS AND CAPACITIES
Wheelbase.............................112.0 in
Track...............F: 59.0 in, R: 59.0 in
Length.................................196.9 in
Width....................................76.0 in
Height...................................52.8 in
Curb weight..........................3895 lbs
Weight distribution, F/R.........57.0/43.0%
Fuel capacity..........................20.0 gal
Oil capacity.............................4.0 qts
Water capacity........................23.0 qts

SUSPENSION
F: Ind., unequal length wishbones, coil springs, anti-sway bar.
R: Rigid axle, trailing arms, coil springs, anti-sway bar.

STEERING
Type........Recirculating ball, power-assisted
Turns lock-to-lock.........................4.25
Turning circle...........................39.0 ft

BRAKES
F.........11.0-in vented disc, power-assisted
R..9.5 x 2.0-in cast iron drum, power-assisted

WHEELS AND TIRES
Wheel size.........................14 x 7.0-in
Tire make and size........F 70 x 14 Goodyear Polyester
Test inflation pressures...F: 26 psi, R: 26 psi

PERFORMANCE
Zero to	Seconds
40 mph	2.9
60 mph	5.8
80 mph	10.0
100 mph	15.2

Standing ¼-mile......14.41 sec @ 97.35 mph
80–0 mph panic stop..........304 ft (0.70 G)

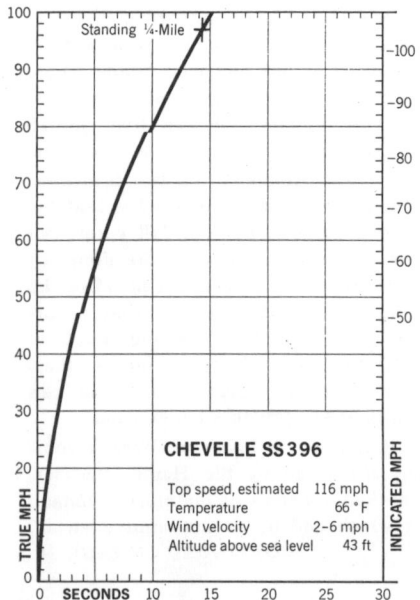

CHEVELLE SS 396

Top speed, estimated   116 mph
Temperature   66 °F
Wind velocity   2–6 mph
Altitude above sea level   43 ft

SUPER BEE

List price as tested: $3858.00

Options on test car: 3.55 limited-slip differential, $102.15; power disc brakes, $93.10; head restraints, $26.50; foam seat, $8.60; automatic trans., $40.40; remote adjust mirror, $9.65; 3-speed wipers, $5.40; undercoating, $16.60; rear quarter air scoops, $35.80; rear bumper guards, $16.00; tachometer and clock, $50.15; cold air induction, $73.30; AM radio, $63.35; power steering $97.65; styled wheels, $88.55; F70 x 14 belted tires, $26.45.

ENGINE
Bore x stroke.....................4.25 x 3.38 in
Displacement.........................383 cu in
Compression ratio...............10.0 to one
Carburetion.............1 x 4 bbl Carter AVS
Power (SAE)...........335 bhp @ 5200 rpm
Torque (SAE)........425 lbs/ft @ 3400 rpm

DRIVE TRAIN
Final drive ratio......................3.55 to one

DIMENSIONS AND CAPACITIES
Wheelbase.............................117.0 in
Track...............F: 59.5 in, R: 59.2 in
Length.................................206.6 in
Width....................................76.7 in
Height...................................54.1 in
Curb weight..........................3765 lbs
Weight distribution, F/R.........55.7/44.3%
Fuel capacity..........................19.0 gal
Oil capacity.............................4.0 qts
Water capacity........................17.0 qts

SUSPENSION
F: Ind., upper wishbones, single lower arms with struts, torsion bars, anti-sway bar
R: Rigid axle, semi-elliptic leaf springs

STEERING
Type........Recirculating ball, power assisted
Turns lock-to-lock..........................3.4
Turning circle...........................44.0 ft

BRAKES
F.........11.0-in vented disc, power-assisted
R..10.0 x 2.5-in cast iron drum, power-assisted

WHEELS AND TIRES
Wheel size.........................14 x 5.5-in
Tire make and size........F70 x 14, Goodyear Polyglas
Test inflation pressures...F: 26 psi, R: 26 psi

PERFORMANCE
Zero to	Seconds
40 mph	2.8
60 mph	5.6
80 mph	9.1
100 mph	14.1

Standing ¼-mile......14.04 sec @ 99.55 mph
80–0 mph panic stop..........250 ft (0.85 G)

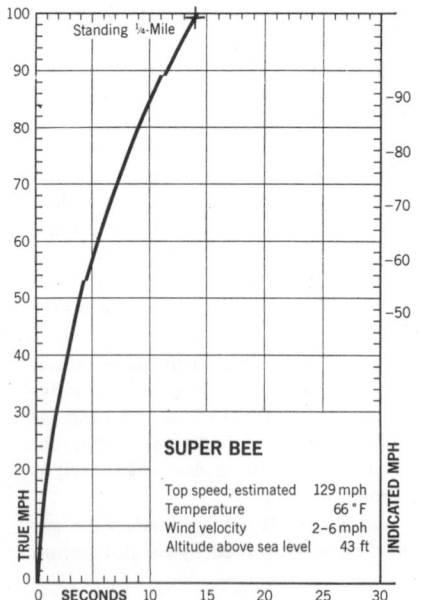

SUPER BEE

Top speed, estimated   129 mph
Temperature   66 °F
Wind velocity   2–6 mph
Altitude above sea level   43 ft

COBRA

List price as tested: $4043.23

Options on test car: Ram air engine, $133.44; bucket seats with console, $168.62; automatic transmission, $37.06; limited slip differential, $63.51; visibility group, $11.06; F70-14 belted tires, $77.73; rim-blow steering wheel, $35.70; power steering, $100.26; power disc brakes, $64.77; AM radio, $61.40; deluxe belt/warning light, $15.59; racing mirrors, $19.48; styled wheels, $17.69; tachometer, $47.92.

ENGINE
Bore x stroke.....................4.13 x 3.98 in
Displacement.........................428 cu in
Compression ratio...............10.6 to one
Carburetion.............1 x 4 bbl Holley
Power (SAE)...........335 bhp @ 5200 rpm
Torque (SAE)........440 lbs/ft @ 3400 rpm

DRIVE TRAIN
Final drive ratio......................3.50 to one

DIMENSIONS AND CAPACITIES
Wheelbase.............................116.0 in
Track...............F: 58.8 in, R: 58.5 in
Length.................................201.1 in
Width....................................74.6 in
Height...................................52.6 in
Curb weight..........................3890 lbs
Weight distribution, F/R.........57.7/42.3%
Fuel capacity..........................20.0 gal
Oil capacity.............................4.0 qts
Water capacity........................19.6 qts

SUSPENSION
F: Ind., upper wishbones, single lower arms with struts, coil springs, anti-sway bar
R: Rigid axle, semi-elliptic leaf springs

STEERING
Type........Recirculating ball, power-assisted
Turns lock-to-lock..........................3.75
Turning circle...........................41 ft

BRAKES
F.........11.3-in vented disc, power-assisted
R..10.0 x 2.0-in cast iron drum, power-assisted

WHEELS AND TIRES
Wheel size.........................14 x 6.0-in
Tire make and size........F70 x 14, Goodyear Polyglas
Test inflation pressures...F: 28 psi, R: 28 psi

PERFORMANCE
Zero to	Seconds
40 mph	2.8
60 mph	5.6
80 mph	9.1
100 mph	14.0

Standing ¼-mile......14.04 sec @ 100.61 mph
80–0 mph panic stop..........248 ft (0.86 G)

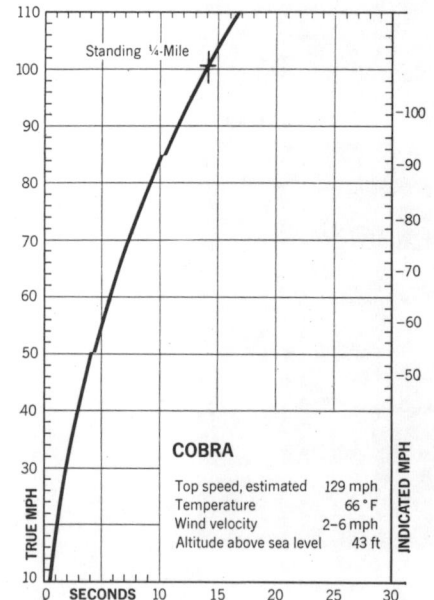

COBRA

Top speed, estimated   129 mph
Temperature   66 °F
Wind velocity   2–6 mph
Altitude above sea level   43 ft

CYCLONE CJ

List price as tested: $4381.60

Options on test car: Ram air engine, $138.60; bucket seats with console, $165.80; automatic trans, $42.00; 3.91 axle, $6.50; limited-slip differential, $63.50; light group, $19.50; rim-blow steering wheel, $35.00; power windows, $104.90; power steering, $94.60; power brakes, $64.80; AM/FM stereo radio, $185.30; rear speaker, $25.90; tinted glass, $35.00; deluxe seat belts, $15.60; racing mirror, $13.00; styled wheels, $116.60; tachometer, $48.00.

ENGINE
Bore x stroke	4.13 x 3.98 in
Displacement	428 cu in
Compression ratio	10.6 to one
Carburetion	1 x 4 bbl Holley
Power (SAE)	335 bhp @ 5200 rpm
Torque (SAE)	440 lbs/ft @ 3400 rpm

DRIVE TRAIN
Final drive ratio	3.91 to one

DIMENSIONS AND CAPACITIES
Wheelbase	116.0 in
Track	F: 58.8 in, R: 58.5 in
Length	203.2 in
Width	76.0 in
Height	53.9 in
Curb weight	3860 lbs
Weight distribution, F/R	56.7/43.3%
Fuel capacity	20.0 gal
Oil capacity	4.0 qts
Water capacity	19.6 qts

SUSPENSION
F: Ind., upper wishbones, single lower arms with struts, coil springs, anti-sway bar
R: Rigid axle, semi-elliptic leaf springs

STEERING
Type	Recirculating ball, power-assisted
Turns lock-to-lock	3.75
Turning circle	42.0 ft

BRAKES
F..........11.3 in vented disc, power-assisted
R..10.0 x 2.0-in cast iron drum, power-assisted

WHEELS AND TIRES
Wheel size	14 x 6.0-in
Tire make and size	F70 x 14, Goodyear Polyglas
Test inflation pressures	F: 28 psi, R: 28 psi

PERFORMANCE
Zero to	Seconds
40 mph	2.7
60 mph	5.5
80 mph	9.0
100 mph	13.9
Standing ¼-mile	13.94 sec @ 100.89 mph
80–0 mph panic stop	283 ft (0.76 G)

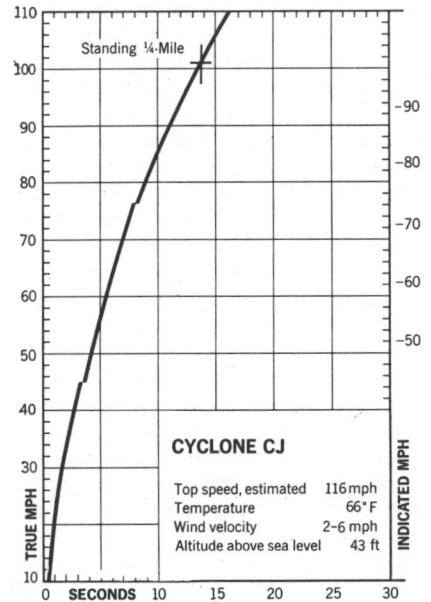

CYCLONE CJ

Top speed, estimated	116 mph
Temperature	66°F
Wind velocity	2–6 mph
Altitude above sea level	43 ft

THE JUDGE

List price as tested: N.A.

Options on test car: Power disc brakes, $64.25; automatic transmission, $227.04; power steering, $105.32; AM/FM radio, $133.76; wood rim steering wheel, $34.76; tachometer, $63.19; instrument package, $50.55; power windows, $105.32; limited-slip differential, $63.19; rear seat speaker, $15.80; remote control mirror, $10.53.

ENGINE
Bore x stroke	4.12 x 3.75 in
Displacement	400 cu in
Compression ratio	10.75 to one
Carburetion	1 x 4-bbl Rochester
Power (SAE)	366 bhp @ 5100 rpm
Torque (SAE)	445 lbs/ft @ 3600 rpm

DRIVE TRAIN
Final drive ratio	3.55 to one

DIMENSIONS AND CAPACITIES
Wheelbase	112.0 in
Track	F: 60.0 in, R: 60.0 in
Length	201.5 in
Width	75.8 in
Height	52.3 in
Curb weight	3898 lbs
Weight distribution, F/R	57.0/53.0%
Fuel capacity	21.5 gal
Oil capacity	5.0 qts
Water capacity	17.8 qts

SUSPENSION
F: Ind., unequal length wishbones, coil springs, anti-sway bar
R: Rigid axle, trailing arms, coil springs

STEERING
Type	Recirculating ball, power-assisted
Turns lock-to-lock	4.0
Turning circle	38.0 ft

BRAKES
F..........11.1 in vented disc, power-assisted
R..........9.5 x 2.0-in, cast iron drum, power-assisted

WHEELS AND TIRES
Wheel size	14 x 6.0-in
Tire make and size	G70 x 14, Goodyear Polyglas
Test inflation pressures	F: 28 psi, R: 28 psi

PERFORMANCE
Zero to	Seconds
40 mph	see text
60 mph	see text
80 mph	see text
100 mph	see text
Standing ¼-mile	see text
80–0 mph panic stop	see text

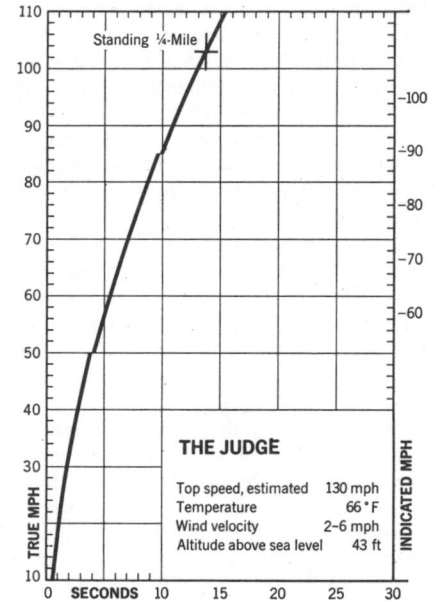

THE JUDGE

Top speed, estimated	130 mph
Temperature	66°F
Wind velocity	2–6 mph
Altitude above sea level	43 ft

ROAD RUNNER

List price as tested: $4,362.05

Options on test car: 425-hp engine, $813.45; automatic transmission, $39.30; performance axle package with automatic transmission, $64.40; decor package, $81.50; remote control mirror, $100.00; power steering, $10.45; power disc brakes, $91.65; AM radio, $61.55; rear speaker, $14.05; tachometer, $50.15; undercoating, $16.60; F70 x 15 belted tires, $90.95.

ENGINE
Bore x stroke	4.25 x 3.75 in
Displacement	426 cu in
Compression ratio	10.25 to one
Carburetion	2 x 4-bbl Carter
Power (SAE)	425 bhp @ 5000 rpm
Torque (SAE)	490 lbs/ft @ 4000 rpm

DRIVE TRAIN
Final drive ratio	3.54 to one

DIMENSIONS AND CAPACITIES
Wheelbase	116.0 in
Track	F: 59.5 in, R: 59.2 in
Length	202.7 in
Width	76.4 in
Height	54.1 in
Curb weight	3938 lbs
Weight distribution, F/R	56.4/43.6%
Fuel capacity	19.0 gal
Oil capacity	5.0 qts
Water capacity	18.0 qts

SUSPENSION
F: Ind., upper wishbones, single lower arms with struts, torsion bars, anti-sway bar.
R: Rigid axle, semi-elliptic leaf springs

STEERING
Type	Recirculating ball, power-assisted
Turns lock-to-lock	3.5
Turning circle	41.3 ft

BRAKES
F..........11.0-in vented disc, power-assisted
R..10.0 x 2.5-in cast iron drum, power-assisted

WHEELS AND TIRES
Wheel size	15 x 6.0-in
Tire make and size	F70 x 15, Goodyear Polyglas
Test inflation pressures	F: 26 psi, R: 26 psi

PERFORMANCE
Zero to	Seconds
40 mph	2.6
60 mph	5.1
80 mph	8.2
100 mph	12.3
Standing ¼-mile	13.54 sec @ 105.14 mph
80–0 mph panic stop	245 ft (0.87 G)

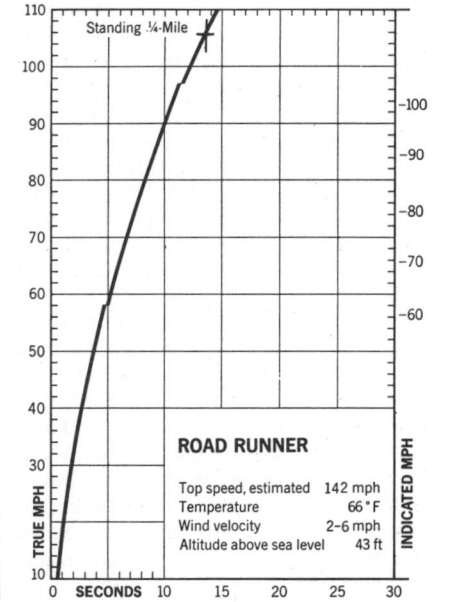

ROAD RUNNER

Top speed, estimated	142 mph
Temperature	66°F
Wind velocity	2–6 mph
Altitude above sea level	43 ft

CONTINUED FROM PAGE 31
The rear seat room in both of the Chrysler entries was substantially better than the rest of the pack, particularly in leg room, and both had more spacious trunks. Ventilation, thanks to vent windows, was another of the Plymouth and Dodge strong points as was the efficiency with which the windshield wipers went about their task.

In case you came in late, the Hemi-powered Road Runner is one hell of an Econo-Racer. It goes about its intended purpose with a sort of well prepared confidence not found in the others. It probably has zero appeal to the faint-hearted but that is the least of our worries—and it should be the least of yours. The only area in which it falls wide of the Econo-Racer goal is price. At $4,362.05, as tested, it wasn't the most expensive car of the group but it certainly would have been had they all been equipped as we suggested. With just the options we asked for, the Road Runner still would have listed at almost $4240. All we can say is that this kind of excitement doesn't come cheap, no matter what your hang-up is.

SUPER BEE

The issue was not nearly so clear in choosing a second-place car but, after polling the staff, the Super Bee was selected to fill that slot—with strong sentiment in favor of the Cobra nonetheless. The Super Bee was fourth in acceleration and third in both braking and handling, which add up to the same performance rating achieved by the Cobra. It was the exceptionally well-coordinated feel of the Dodge, combined with really outstanding instrumentation, that made the difference.

The test car was powered by the standard 335-hp 383 cu. in. V-8 breathing through the optional cold-air induction system that feeds fresh air to the carburetor through two hood scoops. Cloudbursts and storms will never see the inside of your engine because a red knob under the instrument panel (labeled "carb air") has been provided so that the driver can manually close the scoops. Of course, this little feature makes it very easy for us to see if Dodge is really giving you your money's worth in performance or if the scoops just add up to expensive decoration. Dodge does not speak with forked tongue. In a standing quarter-mile the open scoops are worth exactly one mile per hour and slightly more than one-tenth of a second in elapsed time.

Even though the Super Bee was the lightest car of the test, with a curb weight of 3765 pounds, we were a little surprised when the average of our acceleration runs was 14.04 seconds at 99.55 mph. We know that a combination of the air scoops and the extra traction of the Polyglas tires is worth about 1.5 mph in the quarter but the car still seemed faster than other Super Bees we've driven. A careful scrutinizing session turned up two questionable pieces of hardware; a dual-point distributor and a large diameter exhaust system similar to that used on the Coronet R/T. A quick check of the AMA specifications—gospel throughout the industry—indicated the parts were standard equipment. Just on a hunch, we checked further and discovered that the 383s coming off the assembly line, as we suspected, have single point distributors and smaller, 2.25-inch diameter exhaust pipes.

Knowing that, we can't consider our test car's performance to be representative of a 383 Super Bee you would buy. From our experience we would estimate a production car in good tune to run about 98.5 mph in the 14.20-second range.

In the braking tests, the Super Bee performed almost exactly like the Road Runner which is not too surprising since they both use identical braking systems. The Dodge required an additional five feet to stop from 80 mph which is well within production variation.

Since the 383-engined cars have lower rate torsion bars and rear springs than the Hemi models, it is not surprising that they also have more body roll when cornering. In fact, the Dodge had more body roll than any other car in the test. Even so, the car handles well with moderate understeer and good directional control. The relatively quick power steering is an aid in maneuvering despite its light effort.

Since both the Super Bee and the Road Runner are built on the same basic body things like trunk space, seating room and windshield wipers are identical, but the Super Bee takes a giant step forward with its instrument panel—shared with its more expensive sibling, the Charger. This panel contains a complete set of easily readable gauges mounted directly in front of the driver—all marked in a no-nonsense style. Dodge has everybody covered on this point. Not so good was the column-mounted (automatic, remember) transmission shifter—also shared with the Road Runner. It was completely average in its operation with Jello-like detents that may be satisfactory for the unenlightened millions but not for a performance advocate.

Like the Road Runner, a high degree of excitement is engendered when you are driving the Super Bee. Somehow, it just feels like a racer. The ride is taut. You are incredibly aware of the road. It is just exactly the opposite of what Detroit considers to be good manners in their bread-and-butter family sedans—but family sedans are no fun. The Super Bee is in second place because it's fun to drive.

COBRA

It's been a long time since we thought of a "Cobra" as a snake but we never expected to see the name attached to a car as big as Ford's new Fairlane-based Econo-Racer. Our test car was a fastback 2-door hardtop (there is also a formal roof hardtop available) with the standard 428 Cobra Jet (Ford is really hung up on the Cobra name) engine and optional Ram-Air package.

The Cobra grabs the third spot in the test primarily because of its strong performance in the acceleration and braking tests. The Cobra Jet is known to be a tough performer on the dragstrip so the 14.04 second performances of the test car at 100.61 mph are well within its reputation. The special white-lettered F70 x 14 Polyglas tires used on the Cobra have a unique tread compound developed for dry traction but even so, the torquey 428 could turn them with ease.

The hood scoop system, on both the Cobra and Cyclone CJ, has no manual control but, rather, is controlled by a vacuum motor that opens a trap door into the top of the air cleaner when the throttle approaches wide open. For that reason it was necessary to tape the door shut to simulate the non-Ram Air model. That little exercise paid off—we discovered the Cobra Jet has a definite appetite for fresh air because, without the scoop, it lost almost 0.2 seconds and 1.4 mph in the quarter. The Ram-Air package is expensive at $133.44, but it is very effective.

When you are trying for maximum performance—which is what these cars are all about—you become acutely aware of any shortcomings in the controls and instrumentation. The very large Cobra tachometer is mounted relatively close to the driver and aimed at his chest so that it is difficult to read. The panel contains four large, round dials but somehow everything but fuel level is left to warning lights—just what you would expect in a Falcon. The console shifter, too, was vague and Falcony in its operation. During the street driving part of the test, we noticed that the accelerator pedal assumed a low frequency up-and-down motion whenever we hit a bump. Apparently soft engine mounts are used and engine motion is translated back through the throttle linkage.

We haven't been able to fall in love with the power steering, either, which is of the high effort type—not to be confused with road feel. If we could use only one word to describe it, that word would be *numb*. If you turn the wheel two inches either direction from center, it just stays there, which demonstrates a certain degree of insensitivity. What we are trying to say is that the Cobra doesn't have controls in keeping with its performance.

But my goodness, Betsy—the Cobra *does* have good brakes. It could be stopped from 80 mph in 248 feet (0.86G) and did so three consecutive times with no serious fade and exceptional directional stability.

When it comes to handling we can only say that the Cobra performs in the current Ford pattern—strong understeer. Anyone who spins one of these cars has to be trying because it is as resistant to changing ends as anything we can remember—at the expense of the front tire sidewalls.

Both the Cobra and the Cyclone CJ have a very comfortable and silent ride—exceeded only by the Chevelle. The ride harshness is more than acceptable for this kind of car and the high roll stiffness contributes to the comfort level when you get off that straight road. We would prefer more shock absorber control to damp out the low frequency floating motion that is most noticeable at high speed.

Some of the more utilitarian aspects of the Cobra suffered because of the fastback body shape. The rear seat leg and head room are best described as marginal. In fact, leg room is almost zero when the front seat is in its rearmost position. We did find a good size cavern under the deck lid but most of it is up over the rear axle—out of reach due to the small lid opening. All of this is really academic. People turned on by Econo-Racers usually couldn't care less about space behind the driver's seat—but if they do, we would recommend the formal roof model. One problem that won't improve with the formal roof, however, is the effectiveness of the windshield wipers. On the test car they failed to clear a wide band along the driver's side-pillar—a fault we consider serious.

There were many very good qualities in the Cobra. Enough so that placing it third instead of second has started a kind of C/D civil war. Everywhere we looked we saw evidence of quality assembly. The panels fit well, the upholstery was smooth and the body was exceptionally free of rattles. Some of this was obviously aided by good design. The instrument panel, for example, was completely covered from one side to the other with a single pad so there's no chance of misalignment.

When you stand back and look at the Cobra with its competition-style hoodpins, bulging scoop and white-lettered tires you know it's a real racer. But when you drive it, it feels more like a family sedan with a big engine.

CYCLONE CJ
Differences between Mercury's Cyclone CJ and the Cobra are largely a matter of styling since both are mechanically similar. We ranked the Mercury below the Ford primarily because of its poorer braking performance—surely the result of production variation.

We found the Mercury's styling more to our liking even though both cars are nearly identical in silhouette. The Mercury seems cleaner—at least the hood scoop is. Ford, with its Better Ideas, decorated the rear of the Cobra's scoop with the turn signal indicators while Mercury was content to simply spray on some flat black paint. To us, a functional hood scoop is its own a Christmas tree to prove its worth.

The Cyclone's basic equipment list was identical to all of the other test cars with one exception—the 3.91 axle ratio. We had expected the standard 3.50 ratio but a few minutes on the expressway was convincing evidence to the contrary.

As you would calculate, the higher numerical axle ratio gave the Cyclone a slight edge in acceleration times. It was about a tenth of a second quicker in the standing start quarter; 13.94 seconds at 100.89 mph. A streetable car that will run a quarter in under 14 seconds is very quick indeed but the increase in engine noise at cruising speeds with the tall gear is not worth the performance gain.

We are also a little curious about the remarkable traction of the Cyclone's tires. Both the Cobra and Cyclone had special traction tires as standard equipment, but the Mercury would take full throttle off the line which neither the Ford nor any of the other test cars could do.

The Cyclone's greatest shortcoming came to light in the braking tests. The rear brakes suffered from premature lock-up resulting in poor directional stability and greatly increased stopping distances. Stopping from 80 mph required 283 feet (0.76G). This can be attributed to poor proportioning of the braking effort which is a chronic problem with disc/drum combinations.

Everything said about the handling and driver controls of the Cobra also pertains to the Cyclone. The Cyclone does have a slightly different instrument panel layout, however, which improves readability, particularly that of the tachometer.

The Cyclone CJ can best be described as a gentleman's muscle car. Its competition-oriented external appearance is certainly in keeping with its wide-open throttle performance but the car has been carefully developed for minimum intrusion on the occupants' senses. At $40 more than the Cobra you can have a choice of styling.

CHEVELLE SS396
If a committee of Detroit executives tested this same group of cars, the Chevelle would have been the overall winner—by miles. We ranked it fifth. There is a very fine line between endearing mechanical excellence and an automatic, remote-control automobile. Driving the Chevelle on any expressway is an uncomfortable hint of the future: sitting in an insulated capsule moving on a conveyer. Perfect for the 4-door sedan set but hard for the enthusiast to love.

The Chevelle was easily the quietest car of the test. Engine noise, including intake and exhaust, was almost undetectable with the windows up. Road noise and ride harshness were at a minimum—partly a result of the polyester cord tires on the Chevelle instead of the fiberglass belted-construction tires used on the other test cars.

We picked the Chevelle for our Econo-Racer test because we knew it belonged there. Chevrolet, bound by the GM corporate tongue-in-cheek policy concerning competition, says very little about the high performance per-dollar value of the SS396 but we know that it exists—and so do you. Since Chevrolet doesn't package an Econo-Racer in the manner of Chrysler Corporation, it was up to C/D to build one from the option list. This is a task easily done by ordering the base 325-hp SS396 package (which also includes power front disc brakes, styled 7-inch wide wheels and F70 tires) on the 300 Deluxe 2-door coupe. With the other options which we specified on all of our Econo-Racers, the Chevelle comes across the counter at $3409—more than $300 under the Super Bee. That's an ECONO-racer.

As you can glean from the check list, the Chevelle was the slowest in acceleration, the most difficult to stop and the best in handling. That is quite a spread.

The Chevelle's acceleration potential was never fully realized because the polyester tires are far too slippery for dragstrip traction (fiberglass belted tires are not currently offered from the factory). An average of the two best runs gave us 14.41 seconds at 97.35 mph, but most of the test runs were clustered in the 14.60s at 96 mph.

Those familiar with the 325-hp 396 know it's not famous for rocket sled acceleration and may be surprised that the test car went as quickly as it did. So were we, considering that a similarly powered Camaro (March, '68) could not exceed 15.0 seconds at 93.9 mph. Some investigation indicates that the Chevelle exhaust system is far more efficient than that of Camaro and that the '69 exhaust emission control system, which does not use an air injection pump, improves output. The Chevelle also had the advantage of more break-in miles than any other car in the test.

The Chevelle's performance in the braking test is barely acceptable by our standards. Premature lock-up of the rear wheels caused poor directional stability and the required stopping distance from 80 mph was a very long 304 feet (0.70G.) If the Chevelle didn't fare at all well in the acceleration and braking portions of the test, it was unbeatable in handling—and good handling is a lovely thing to have around the house. The credit goes to the new heavy duty suspension package that uses a rear sway bar to reduce understeer. We liked it a lot. The car corners flat and allows good directional control right up to the limit of adhesion. All of this is complemented by Chevrolet's very accurate power steering—its only fault is a slow overall ratio of 4.25 turns lock-to-lock. An undesirable quirk of the Chevelle's rear suspension is a tendency for the axle to hop under acceleration when the tires are just barely slipping, and during hard cornering when there is some power application. No other car had this problem.

35

Since the test car actually turned out to be a Malibu 2-door hardtop with the optional bucket seat interior, it didn't really fit the Econo-Racer mold. We did find that the seat, which has a distinct rearward rake, offered a sinfully comfortable driving position. Along with the package comes a console, however, with the numbest shifter we've ever encountered. Upshifting to second gear was out of the question. You always got third. Chevrolet plans to offer a ratcheting shifter in the motorcycle tradition later in the year, and we consider that a must.

For an additional $94.80 your Chevelle can be equipped with an optional instrumentation group which includes all of the expected gauges plus a tachometer. Even though they are all well located, they are also quite small, including the tach, and generally difficult to read because of the very fat calibration marks.

Our test Chevelle didn't do very well because it was neither econo nor racer. Don't lose heart, Chevy fans. It has the potential. We have already mentioned that the lower-priced coupe is a relative bargain—so if you throw in an extra $252.80 for the 375-hp 396 you will end up with the real thing. And we have every reason to expect the real thing—Chevy Econo-Racer wise—is a good thing indeed.

THE JUDGE

We started the Econo Racer test with six cars and ended with five. The elusive sixth car was Pontiac's entry. The people at Pontiac in charge of supplying-cars-for-six-car-comparison-tests couldn't make up their minds whether our Pontiac was a prototype or a real car and the result was we couldn't get enough accurate test information about the car to put anywhere in the standings.

The Judge's purpose in life is to add some spice to Pontiac's GTO series. It's a variation of the GTO with the 366-hp 400 cu. in. Ram Air engine as standard equipment, along with G70 black wall fiberglass belted tires and styled wheels without the customary trim rings. The Judge stands out (leaps out, really) in a crowd because of its bright orange paint and a simulated aerodynamic wing attached to the deck lid. If there is any doubt, check for "The Judge" decals on the front fenders and deck lid.

A part of our normal road test procedure is a routine technical inspection. During this phase of the test we discovered that one of the vacuum hoses that controls ignition timing had been plugged internally so that the timing was no longer retarded at idle as is normally required to meet the exhaust emissions standards. We also noted that the coolant temperature was much lower than normal for a Pontiac since the change was made to a 190°F thermostat to aid emission control. Our suspicions were further aroused when The Judge wasn't

happy even with the best fuel Sunoco has to offer.

A check of the identification numbers stamped on the block indicated the engine was actually a 1968 manual transmission Ram Air unit—which differs from the 1969 366-hp automatic transmission engine in several important areas including camshaft. "It belongs in the test," agreed Pontiac, "but it's kind of a prototype at the same time," they said. That's more-or-less mutually exclusive and *our* conclusion is that performance of The Judge would probably not be representative of a car a customer could buy.

To satisfy our curiosity about exhaust emissions we retained an independent testing laboratory (which also has government contracts for the same purpose) to test The Judge for compliance to the federal exhaust emission standards. The Judge did not pass. Federal standards allow an average of 1.5% carbon monoxide and 275 parts-per-million unburned hydrocarbons in the exhaust while the car is being driven through a predetermined cycle. Figures for The Judge were 2.65% CO and 549 ppm hydrocarbons. Pretty far off the mark.

With this evidence in mind we are convinced that Pontiac would not knowingly sell this car to a customer and, therefore, it is not suitable for a road test. A true picture of the handling or braking characteristics of The Judge was hard to get in focus because it came with seven-inch wheels—wider than the six inches which seemed to be the maximum available on The Judge at press time.

We did find several worthwhile innovations in non-mechanical areas of the Pontiac. Illumination of the hood-mounted tach has been greatly improved so that instrument is now useful at night as well as in the day time. The console-mounted automatic transmission selector is also much to our liking. When pressured to the right, the lever moves in a series of sawtooth ramps—one for each gear—so you can move only one position at a time without releasing the lever. This system is clearly the best of all the test cars.

Both the Pontiac and Chevelle 2-door hardtops are built on a short 112-inch wheelbase which gives these cars a more compact and maneuverable feeling. Rear seat leg room suffers accordingly.

The great virtue of a comparison test is that it clearly shows how each manufacturer chooses to solve the same problem. The Hemi Road Runner is an Econo-RACER while the Chevelle is more of an ECONO-Racer. The Cobra and the Cyclone CJ fall directly in the middle. The Super Bee with its 383 goes about its t with great enthusiasm but falls just sh of the middle in muscle.

Decide which one your driving record can stand. For the price of a Porsche 912 minus most of a VW, you can have your choice. ●

● With callous disregard for the innocent, Plymouth has changed everything but the name Barracuda. They aren't fastbacks anymore. No more humpy hardtops with big back windows. Plymouth has just executed a smart two-and-a-half gainer into the present—for the best of all reasons. Nobody wanted the old ones.

Even in 1965, in the first full year of its production, a mere 50,000 Barracudas trickled out of Plymouth showrooms while nearly 520,000 Mustangs, more than *10* times as many, were snapped up by eager sporty car buyers. Recent history isn't much better. The new Barracuda's assignment, and it has no choice but to accept, is to get in there and pick up Chrysler's rightful share of the business. That will be no easy task. In January the Camaro and Firebird of today will be taken out behind the Tech Center, blindfolded and given a volley. In their place will come two dazzling new fastbacks with which GM hopes to lead-pipe the Mustang into senselessness . . . and the Barracuda along with it.

If you are confused—Barracuda jettisoning its fastback only to see Firebird and Camaro picking it up—you are not alone. Plymouth's chief product planner, Joe Sturm, observing that the roomy interior and cavernous trunk were little help in selling past Barracudas, proudly announced that the 1970 version has the smallest trunk in the industry and success is expected forthwith.

Converts to the fold can choose from three models; the standard Barracuda, the luxury-oriented Gran Coupe and the high performance 'Cuda series—each in either a 2-door hardtop or a convertible. No longer is Plymouth's sporty car simply a variant of the Valiant/Dart "A-body." The new Barracuda is being built on a unique body shared only with the Dodge Challenger. Underneath is a subtly revised torsion bar front suspension very similar to that on the larger Coronet/Belvedere car line. Typical Chrysler asymmetric leaf springs are used in the rear.

At a pre-introduction day test session we discovered two 'Cudas which are guaranteed to play upon the libido of any enthusiast. Aimed directly at the Z/28 Camaro and the Boss 302 Mustang is the 'Cuda 340 which has, in addition to its lion-hearted 340 cu. in. V-8 engine, a special handling package with a rear anti-sway bar and E60-15 Polyglas tires on 7-inch wide wheels as standard equipment. For those who want the last word there is a HemiCuda with a shaker-type hood scoop and fat F60-15 tires. Weight distribution suffers with the big engined machines but then you can always fill the front tires with helium. All of the new 'Cudas are noticeably heavier than those of the past but are still a good 200 pounds lighter than a Road Runner—so look out.

From the driver's seat the difference between a sporty cockpit and one that is claustrophobic is a fine distinction and we're not sure on which side the Barracuda falls. The enormously thick door panels and a massively padded instrument panel give the illusion of a foam-filled cocoon and the steering wheel is definitely too close to the driver for our tastes. But these problems are nothing compared to the dilemma that now faces the short hood/long rear deck fanciers—they have nothing left but pick-up trucks.

BARRACUDA

By jettisoning everything but the name, Plymouth executes a two-and-a-half gainer into the present

Dimensions	1969	1970
Wheelbase	108.0 in.	108.0 in.
Track F/R	57.7/55.6 in.	60.2/60.7 in.
Length	192.8 in.	186.6 in.
Width	69.6 in.	74.7 in.
Engine		
Standard engine	225 cu. in., 145 hp.	225 cu. in., 145 hp.
Max. option	440 cu. in., 375 hp.	426 cu. in., 425 hp.
Wheels and Tires		
Standard wheel	14x4.5 in.	14x5.0 in.
Standard tire	6.95-14	E78-14
Max. optional wheel	14x5.5 in.	15x7.0 in.
Max. optional tire	E70-14	F60-15

The Rapid Transit

'Cuda

- Special high-performance 383 cu. in. 335 hp Wedge V-8, standard. ("Economy" versions not available.)
- 340 cu. in. 4-bbl., 440 cu. in. 4-bbl., 440 cu. in. 6-bbl. or 426 Hemi V-8 optional.
- High-performance camshaft, standard.
- High-performance Holley 4-bbl. carburetor, standard.
- High-flow cylinder heads and intake manifold, standard.
- Oil pan windage tray, standard.
- Heavy-duty 3-speed manual transmission, standard.
- 4-speed or high-upshift TorqueFlite automatic, optional.
- Floor-mounted shifter, standard.
- Heavy-duty suspension, standard.
- Heavy-duty 0.90" diameter front torsion bars, standard.
- Heavy-duty 4½-leaf rear springs, standard.
- Heavy-duty shock absorbers, standard.
- Heavy-duty 0.94" diameter front anti-sway bar, standard.
- Heavy-duty 0.75" diameter rear anti-sway bar, standard.
- Heavy-duty driveshaft and U-joints, standard.
- Heavy-duty 11" drum brakes, standard.
- Heavy-duty rear axle, standard.
- High-performance exhaust system with 2¼ in. exhaust pipes, twin mufflers, 2¼ in. tail pipes, standard.
- Heavy-duty, 59 amp/hr. battery, standard.
- Fiberglass-belted F70 x 14" tires, standard.
- E60, F60 x 15" tires, optional.
- Extra-wide 6 in. wheels, standard.

GTX

- High-performance 440 cu. in. 375 hp Wedge V-8, standard. ("Economy" versions not available.)
- 440 cu. in. 6-bbl. or 426 Hemi V-8, optional.
- High-performance camshaft, standard.
- High-performance Carter AVS 4-bbl. carburetor, standard.
- High-flow cylinder heads and intake manifold, standard.
- Oil pan windage tray, standard.
- Dual breaker distributor and viscous-drive fan, standard with 4-speed.
- High-upshift, competition-type TorqueFlite automatic or heavy-duty 4-speed (with mandatory extra-cost axle package), standard.
- Hurst Competition-Plus floor shift with "Pistol Grip" shift handle, standard with 4-speed.
- Extra-heavy-duty suspension, standard.
- Heavy-duty 0.92" dia. torsion bars, std.
- Heavy-duty shock absorbers, standard.
- Heavy-duty 0.94" dia. anti-sway bar, std.
- Heavy-duty 6-leaf left rear spring, std.
- Special right rear spring, 5 leaves, plus 2 half-leaves, standard.
- Heavy-duty 11 in. drum brakes, standard.
- High-performance dual exhaust system with 2½ in. exhaust pipes, twin mufflers, 2¼ in. tail pipes, standard.
- Heavy-duty driveshaft and U-joints, std.
- Heavy-duty rear axle, standard.
- Heavy-duty battery, 70 amp/hr., std.
- Extra-wide 6 in. wheels, standard.
- Fiberglass-belted F70 x 14" tires, std.
- F60 x 15" tires, optional.
- Bucket seats, standard.

Sport Fury GT

- High-performance 440 cu. in. 350 hp Wedge V-8, standard. ("Economy" versions not available.)
- 440 cu. in. 6-bbl. V-8, optional.
- High-performance Carter AVS 4-bbl. carburetor, standard.
- High-flow cylinder heads and intake manifold, standard.
- High-upshift, competition-type TorqueFlite automatic, standard.
- Heavy-duty suspension, standard.
- Heavy-duty 0.98" dia. torsion bars, standard
- Heavy-duty shock absorbers, standard.
- Heavy-duty 0.98" dia. anti-sway bar, standard.
- Heavy-duty 6-leaf rear springs, standard.
- Heavy-duty 11 in. drum brakes, standard.
- High-performance dual exhaust system with 2½ in. exhaust pipes, twin mufflers, 2¼ in. tail pipes, standard.
- Heavy-duty driveshaft and U-joints, standard.
- Heavy-duty rear axle, standard.
- Heavy-duty battery, 70 amp/hr., standard.
- Extra-wide 6 in. road wheels, standard.
- Fiberglass-belted H70 x 15" tires, standard.

System Announced

Road Runner

- Special high-performance 383 cu. in. 335 hp Wedge V-8, standard. ("Economy" versions not available.)
- 440 cu. in. 6-bbl. or 426 Hemi V-8, optional.
- High-performance camshaft, standard.
- High-performance Holley 4-bbl. carburetor, standard.
- High-flow cylinder heads and intake manifold, standard.
- Oil pan windage tray, standard.
- Heavy-duty 3-speed manual transmission, standard.
- 4-speed or high-upshift TorqueFlite automatic, optional.
- Floor-mounted shifter, standard.
- Heavy-duty suspension, standard.
- Heavy-duty 0.90″ diameter front torsion bars, standard.
- Heavy-duty 4½-leaf rear springs, std.
- Heavy-duty shock absorbers, standard.
- Heavy-duty 0.94″ diameter front anti-sway bar, standard.
- Heavy-duty driveshaft and U-joints, standard.
- Heavy-duty 11″ drum brakes, standard.
- Heavy-duty rear axle, standard.
- High-performance exhaust system with 2¼ in. exhaust pipes, twin mufflers, 2 in. tail pipes, standard.
- Heavy-duty, 59 amp/hr. battery, standard.
- Fiberglass-belted F70 x 14″ tires, standard.
- F60 x 15″ tires, optional.
- Extra-wide 6 in. wheels, standard.
- Bench seats, standard.
- Beep-Beep horn, standard.

Valiant Duster 340

- High-performance 340 cu. in. 275 hp Wedge V-8, standard.
- High-performance camshaft, standard.
- High-flow cylinder heads and intake manifold, standard.
- High-performance Carter AVS 4-bbl. carburetor, standard.
- High-flow air cleaner, standard.
- Oil pan windage tray, standard.
- Heavy-duty 3-speed manual transmission, standard.
- 4-speed or high-upshift TorqueFlite automatic, optional.
- Floor-mounted shifter, standard.
- Heavy-duty suspension, standard.
- Heavy-duty 0.87″ diameter front torsion bars, standard.
- Heavy-duty 6-leaf rear springs, standard.
- Heavy-duty shock absorbers, standard.
- Heavy-duty 0.88″ diameter front anti-sway bar, standard.
- Front disc brakes, standard.
- 10-inch rear drum brakes, standard.
- High-performance dual exhaust system with 2¼ in. exhaust pipes, twin mufflers and 2¼ in. tail pipes, standard.
- Heavy-duty driveshaft and U-joints, standard.
- Heavy-duty rear axle, standard.
- Fiberglass-belted E70 x 14″ tires, standard.
- Extra-wide 5.5 in. wheels, standard.
- Full instrumentation, standard.

Plymouth  CHRYSLER MOTORS CORPORATION

You know the kind of girl who wanders around the periphery of society; eager, willing to please, kind to her maiden aunt but somehow not quite Ali McGraw? She is forever being described by her friend as having a great personality. A crushing indictment because no sooner is it said than you know, you just *know,* that there is an implied "but." A visual "but", most likely, that has restricted most of her past trysts to drive-in movies.

Unstyled humans are one thing, unstyled cars quite another. In Detroit styling reigns supreme and Chrysler is no different than anyone else. So how do you explain the Duster? Is it simply another case of brain fade in Elwood P. Engel's office, or is it a complex plot by that company's sociological engineering department to play off truth against beauty in every Plymouth showroom. The thought even occurs that the humble Valiant is being sacrificed to make the foundering C-body (Fury, Polara and Chrysler) look good.

Perhaps we are too suspicious. Maybe the Plymouth stylists are genuinely pleased with the result of grafting their version of a Barris restyle of a Chevy II on to the back end of a 1969 Valiant. Which is about all that has happened aside from transplanting a few vitals—sporty instrument panel, 340 engine and "Formula S" suspension —from the late A-body Barracuda.

But, like the girl in the story, the Duster really does have a great personality. The base car, a stripper with a 198 cubic inch version of Plymouth's leaning Six and skinny C78-14 tires, serves as Chrysler's sole entry into the blossoming small car world. Long on competence at the expense of excitement, it's mechanically a direct carryover of past Valiants and can stand comfortably on its record. Moreover, it need not stand alone. Its sibling is the pocket Road Runner—the Duster 340. You can have it with either 3- or 4-speed manual transmissions or an automatic. Modest E70-14 fiberglass belted tires on 5.5-inch wide wheels are standard as are drum brakes. For a little extra money power steering, power disc brakes and air conditioning can also be yours. In the interior you have a choice of high-backed bucket seats with either a console or with a center armrest if the standard bench seats are not to your liking. Passenger space is noticeably smaller than previous Valiants and is, in fact, very similar to the old Barracuda except for rear leg room which is slightly less.

As this is being written Plymouth hasn't announced prices yet, but we expect them to be pretty friendly. Since the base Duster has to compete with the Maverick and Hornet, and the performance options should be no more expensive in the Duster than they are in the Barracuda, we have every reason to believe that the Duster 340 will offer more performance per dollar than any other car in Detroit—or the world for that matter. No 340 Barracuda or Dart which we've tested in the past has done less than 99 mph in the quarter and none took longer than 14.5 seconds to do it. The Duster 340 is meant to be a fun car to drive and it succeeds admirably. It feels light and agile which pumps up your courage, and the car has enough evasive capability to keep all but the most foolhardy out of trouble. Ugly, the Duster seems to be trying to say, is only skin deep.

VALIANT DUSTER

The pocket Road Runner should offer more performance per dollar than any other car from Detroit—or even the world

Dimensions	1970
Wheelbase	108.0 in.
Track F/R	57.7/55.6 in.
Length	188.4 in.
Width	71.7 in.
Engine	
Standard engine	198 cu. in., 125 hp.
Max. option	340 cu. in., 275 hp.
Wheels and Tires	
Standard wheel	14x4.5 in.
Standard tire	C78-14
Max. optional wheel	14x5.5 in.
Max. optional tire	E70-14

THE INCREDIBLE DISAPPEARING DART

A basic primer in how to steal a C/D test car for fun and profit

By Bob Brown

● "Where in hell is the car?"

The feature editor with the long hair was very clear about it, his English accent distinct through an early morning slur: He was not the man to ask. Curtly I was informed that (a) I had the keys last, (b) he was not about to be enjoined in any sort of contract that would implicate him in the disappearance of a test car, and (c) a missing car is not sufficient reason to awaken anybody at 6:30 am.

All of which was fully understandable—I would have been even more vehemently innocent over the phone. Still, there was little doubt that between us we had lost a very special Dodge Dart—one of 500 in existence.

Actually, even at this early hour, it was evident that we had not lost the car in the strict sense of the word. We knew where it had been eight hours before. We still had the keys, and neither one of us had moved it. Aha! It's been stolen. From right in front of the Grace Episcopal Church where we had parked it the night before.

Do you know how dumb you feel standing out in front of a church at 6:00 with a set of keys to a car that isn't there?—a dark metallic blue Dart with a black vinyl roof and white GTS stripes embracing its tail? But this Dart also had subtle 440 emblems nestled in the phony hood scoops and both the feature editor and I could at-

test that they were no phonies. The day before that car, equipped with a set of zero traction tires, had tiptoed its way to a 14.02-second quarter-mile at 102 mph at New York National Speedway. We had been evaluating the car to see if *C/D* should do a full road test on it, with the consensus being no—despite the fact that it gave a feeling of potential omnipotence in a straight line it was hardly what anyone would call a well-balanced car. With six turns lock-to-lock (no power steering) and unending torque, it was exactly the kind of car that you'd never want to get crossed up with in a corner. But as a street racer. . . .

Anyway, there I am in staid old Brooklyn Heights—that's where the feature editor, myself and Warren Weith live with our respective families (that's also where Rod Steiger and his ex-wife, Claire Bloom used to live until Mrs. Steiger got mugged one night on her way home)—looking for the ultimate street racer. It just wasn't possible that it had been stolen. Particularly not with the recent invasion of the Tactical Patrol Force, Mayor Lindsay's version of the Green Berets, who were holding maneuvers in the neighborhood every night. On several occasions all of us had been stopped by matched pairs of the super fuzz on "license and registration, please" spot checks. A relatively innocuous looking car parked in front of a church with an elite band of law enforcement agents bivouacked in the neighborhood, who would have the nerve to steal it?

Ha! These guys were hardly the Lavender Hill Mob and, looking back on it, it's probably a fortunate thing that neither the feature editor nor myself were in the car or else we would have gone along too.

Having a car stolen in New York City is is not what you might call a unique experience. Unique for us maybe, but according to the local blue-eyed rock station, an average of 190 cars are spirited away every day in Fun City. Which might account for the cops' cavalier dismissal of my problem, when I finally faced up to the fact and re-

From street racing wins to trophy runs at Car and Driver's test track, the stolen 440 Dart kept reappearing to embarrass us

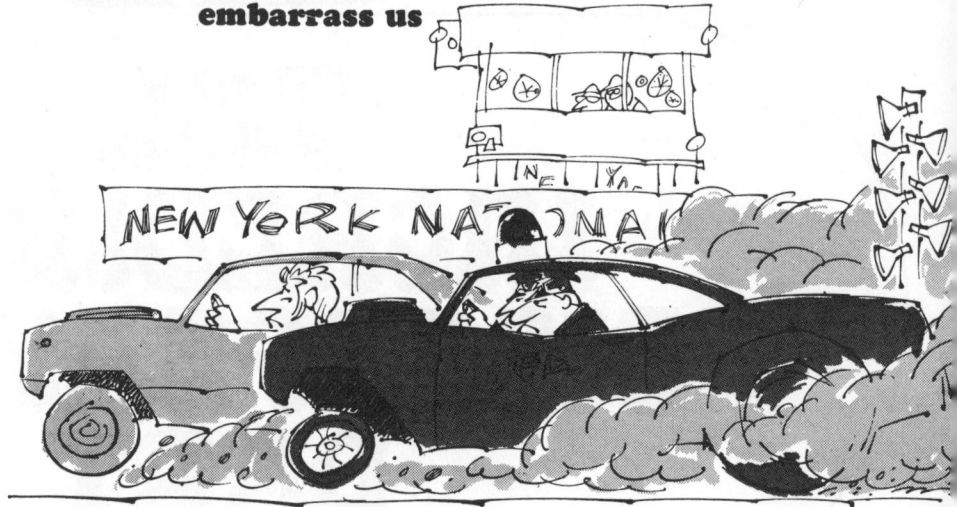

The Suffolk County Police and N. Y. National's staff tell how to spot a really hot 440 Dart

● Check dashboard identification plate with engine number stamped on the bottom of the block.
● Check inside of fender wells to see that side marker lights have not been changed.
● Note location of inside door locks—they are in the middle of the door on '69s, on the back edge in '68s.
● New cars that show up in primer are immediately suspect unless there is evidence of body damage.
● Lift upholstered door panels or rubber-molding trim to find original color of car (also check hinges).

● A 383 can be distinguished from a 440 by the configuration of the exhaust manifold and an identifying "440" or "383" stamped lightly on the left head underneath the sparkplug wire bracket. Heads on 440 are also considerably higher.
● Notice pry marks in hood trim and loose retainer clips.
● Notice pleat pattern on seats. Fully pleated in '68, partial pleats in '69.
● Cars running on public streets without mufflers or front bumpers and with lousy paint jobs, need to be looked at on general principle.

ported the missing car. It was 8:00 am Friday and the Sergeant on duty had ordained me a Class A crank within five seconds after our conversation began.

"I'd like to report a stolen car."

"Do you own the car?"

"No, it's a test car. It belongs to Dodge."

"Do you have proof of ownership?"

"No, the registration was in the glove compartment, and the car's from out-of-state."

"There's nothing I can do then."

"Wait a minute, it's one of 500 special-built cars and it's pretty valuable."

"Look, if you can't prove you own it, waddya want me to do? We get a lot of calls from cranks trying to make trouble for people they don't like, I can't send out an alarm without proof."

It went on like that for a fruitless 15 minutes more, with me getting more frustrated and the cop's coffee getting colder.

After a while I gave up—it was like arguing with the Internal Revenue Service—and called up Dodge to see if they could bring the proof of ownership over from Manhattan. They did, and *Car and Driver* became nothing more than an interested third party in the case—the only problem was that no one knew who the first party —who was now driving the car—was.

The following Monday, although the cops had been stymied, reports of the Dart began to filter back through the underground. An anonymous, but—like they say in Washington news reports—reliable source, had informed us that Friday night, less than 24 hours after the car had been stolen, it had appeared at a local street racing highway and cleaned up. The car, camouflaged in light gray primer—not unlike the old Dodge factory-sponsored Super Stocks—had put down a brace of Corvettes that had gained some local renown. The kid running the car was a regular on the street racing scene and had a reputation of being able to come on with a variety of fairly strong equipment. He'd also had the nerve, the effrontery if you will, to noise it around that this was a "factory prepared car that had been brought in from Detroit specially for *him*."

I'll say.

According to these unidentified but reliable sources the only thing different about the car, except from its paint job, was a set of decent rear tires. No dummy, this kid.

No shrinking violet, either. The next report from the underground was like being told that Raquel Welch had taken a shower in the Jets locker room and Joe Namath never even noticed.

"You the guys who's missing the 440 Dart?"

"Maybe. You know where it is?" (We've seen enough *Mission Impossibles* to know how to deal with this kind of stuff.)

"No man, but I know where it *was*. It was out at your test track on Sunday and it should have come home with a trophy."

Click.

A call to Ed Eaton, manager of New York National, confirmed that the new owner of the 440 Dart had, in fact, been mowing our grass.

By the time the car had arrived at New York National it had received some embellishments that had not been necessary for its previous triumphs on public roads. The 1969 grille had been replaced by the subtly different 1968 version (a nice touch, that), the '68 side marker light had been exchanged for '69-style reflectors, and the side trim was strictly '68 Dart. The new owner had also acquired very legal looking proof of ownership—something I hadn't been able to provide for that Sergeant two days earlier—and all the dashboard serial numbers had been changed to correspond with the new registration slip.

But like J. Edgar Hoover is always pontificating, every thief has to tell someone what he has done, and that's when the law will catch up with him. In this instance, the pseudo-owner couldn't resist making a sure thing out of an almost sure thing. At morning tech inspection he came cruising up to the line as a '68 Dodge Dart, with a 383 engine. The tech inspectors said, "No way." Although 440 Darts aren't as common as 396 Chevys, NYNS' scrutineering staff spotted the difference and gave the car a thorough checkout. The registration and trim said the car was a '68; John Olcott, chief inspector, noted the fact that the door jams were still painted a dark, almost metal-flake, blue and held out car number 251's card for checking, prior to being allowed to run at future meets. Being that the car was ostensibly legal—even if it did have a 440 —it was allowed to run, but in the "Hot Car" class (a particularly aptly named cate-

CONTINUED ON PAGE 99

The Brooklyn Branch of Midnight Auto Sales tells how to make a really hot 440 Dart

● Steal one 1969 Dodge 440 Dart GTS.
● Steal one 1968 Dodge Dart (any type) or rent one for stripping. Carefully remove dashboard-mounted identification plate, front grille, sidemarker lights, chrome fender trim, rear deck trim and taillights. Throw away the rest.
● Steal one wallet, making sure owner's driver's license is inside.
● Remove identification plate from 440 Dart and replace with 1968 plate.
● Pry "440" emblems from hood scoops and GTS insignia from hood. Replace with "383" emblems (optional).
● Remove side marker lights, carefully fill in holes and install '68 versions.
● Install chrome wheelwell trim.

● Install '68 taillights and deck trim.
● Mask car and spray with light gray primer.
● Go to motor vehicle department with forged (or stolen from dealer) bill of sale. Register the car using stolen driver's license for identification.
● Install set of M&H Racemaster slicks.
  You are now ready to go street racing; the following steps are optional:
● Install Edelbrock Hi-Riser intake manifold and 3-bbl. Holley carburetor.
● Install 440 headers (there is zero clearance, so just torch away the fender liners—it's not your car anyway, and besides you'll be saving weight).
● Crank up the torsion bars so the

hood of the car sits about five feet off the road.
● Remove front bumper assembly.
● Remove mufflers and tailpipes and throw away.
● Disconnect and discard all smog equipment.
● Paint car red and gold, being careful to cover entire car. For instance, the doors should be removed in order to get paint to inside of front fenders. Also, don't forget to paint the bottom of the doors. However, don't bother to mask any trim highlights—strive for that individualistic look.
● Fill ashtray with Raleigh cigarette butts—save coupons.

Three quick ways to catch
DODGE fever

CHARGER R/t

CORONET R/t

DART GTS

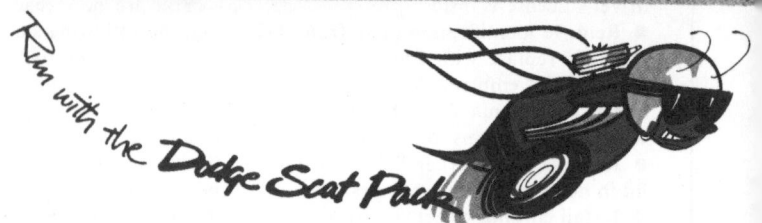

Run with the Dodge Scat Pack

THE CARS WITH THE BUMBLEBEE STRIPES

Dodge Challenger R/T Hemi

Lavish execution with little or no thought toward practical application

Major truth: Since the first Mustang rolled out of a dealer's showroom in 1964 sales of that class of car have been as high as 13% of Detroit's total yearly volume—and Dodge has not enjoyed a single dollar of that business. Second major truth: It's bad enough to be late into the market place but to be late with the wrong kind of a car can be fatal (even if only crippling it is still an offense which requires all of the product planners to fall on their swords). Now let's talk about Dodge's new Challenger—easily three years too late to be a smashing success but something Dodge is counting on to make a few bucks with nonetheless.

To understand the Challenger you first better know a little bit about Chrysler Corporation and its strategies. Chrysler doesn't do anything first. Instead, it carefully watches what everybody else in Detroit is doing and when it sees an area of abnormal market activity it leaps exactly onto that spot. Because it always leaps late —which is inevitable if it doesn't begin to prepare its entry into the market until someone else already has one—it tries to make up for being late by jumping onto said spot harder than everybody else. That is why you didn't see a real Chrysler sporty car until 1970 (and that is why Chrysler's small car will be lucky to see light of day in 1971). There is another problem, too. Sometimes when you leap late you find that by the time you hit your target everybody else has gone somewhere else. This is painfully close to being the case with the Challenger/Barracuda because it is a bald-faced replica of the Camaro/Firebird which GM is planning to completely revamp in just a few months.

To further understand the Challenger you have to go beyond corporate stratagems and straight into the Dodge division. The Dodge boys fancy themselves as the only spark of vitality in the corporation, and right now they are flying high on the Charger, a model that does nothing more than a Coronet hardtop can do, except look better, and yet has outsold Plymouth's specialty car, the Barracuda, by two-to-one for the last couple of years. According to Robert McCurry, Dodge's general manager who has to be considered as a mild outlaw in such a conservative organization as Chrysler, this is to be the plan with the Challenger. Essentially a sporty car of the type everybody else is selling, it is meant to have more interior room (Dodge attributes a good part of the Charger's success to the 5-passenger capacity) and a comprehensive list of options. McCurry admits that the Challenger is not aimed at any specific type of buyer; not at the performance enthusiasts, not at the comfort seekers who might opt for a small Thunderbird, but rather at the entire sporty car market from Camaro to Cougar and hopefully anyone on the fringe as well. The Challenger's price target is directly between the Mustang and the Cougar—and to avoid

competition from within the Dodge line the more expensive Dart models have been dropped.

That's what the Challenger is *supposed* to be. In the flesh it is a highly stylized Camaro with strongly sculptured lines, more tumble-home and a grille vaguely in the Charger tradition. There's no doubt it is a handsome car but it also has a massive feeling which is totally unwelcome in a sporty car—a massive feeling which results from a full five inches more width than a Mustang and a need to sign up with Weight Watchers. The Hemi-powered test car weighed 3890 pounds and if any normally equipped V-8 Challenger with a full gas tank weighs less than 3550 pounds we would be surprised. Dodge is quick to point out that the Challenger's 110-inch wheelbase is two inches longer than that of the Barracuda and, in fact, longer than any other sporty car ex-

cept for the 111-inch Cougar. The extra two inches are intended to provide relief for the acute shortage of rear leg room common to sporty cars. To check out this claim we parked the Challenger next to *C/D's* Blue Maxi Camaro for a little side-by-side comparison. After crawling around in both interiors it is clear that the inside of the Challenger is up to two inches wider, particularly in front seat shoulder room. But face it, width isn't *that* important in a 4-passenger car when there is already enough room for two people side-by-side. A far more important dimension is rear seat leg room and there the Challenger has, at very best, an inconsequential half-inch advantage over the Camaro. Sitting back there, you still have no choice but to spread-eagle your legs around the front seat backs when they are in their full rearward position—it's uncomfortable and damn near impossible to sustain for a trip of any duration. In addition, the Challenger has noticeably less headroom in the rear—enough less to make that seat unsuitable for anyone over six feet tall. It is true that the Challenger's front bucket seats have a longer range of adjustment which means that when the seats can

be pushed farther forward there is definitely more useful room in back than in the Camaro. One of the managers in Dodge's product planning section summed up the situation this way, "In the other sporty cars the rear seat is worthless about 95% of the time. That area in the Challenger is worthless only about 75% of the time."

You can see that the Challenger isn't a family car. The sad part is that Chrysler also passed up a splendid opportunity to make an exceptional performance car. It's simply too heavy. The idea of a "sporty" car weighing within 100 pounds of a comparably equipped Road Runner or Super Bee is ridiculous. Along with all of the weight comes a weight distribution problem—58.9% on the front wheels of the Hemi-powered test car. What has happened is that Chrysler has built itself a "performance" car that is 300 pounds heavier than a Cobra Jet Mustang and almost as nose-heavy. Nice going, you guys.

And the Challenger is so wide that it has none of the compact agility normally associated with this class of car. Before we go any further we should make it clear that the test car is perfectly satisfactory for normal maneuvers like going to church and fetching grandma but you don't buy Hemis for that kind of duty. Strong understeer is apparent in places where you might try to hurry, like expressway entrances, and really flogging on a twisting road or a tight road course is a waste of time. The car just won't cooperate. The front wheels begin to lose steering response and to keep from nosing off into the woods you have to use a fantastic amount of power—a fairly risky operation when sometimes the power brings the tail around like a swinging gate and sometimes it just pushes your nose into the woods faster. Just like everybody else in Detroit, Chrysler is afraid to build its powerful cars with anything resembling neutral steering because they are afraid that some clown will tap the throttle in a corner and spin himself into somebody's petunia patch. But we think they should worry just as much about someone finding himself moving too fast in a corner and having no steering response—the car continuing along its path regardless of which way you point the wheels—which is exactly what happens with excessive understeer.

The Hemi's road course performance was hamstrung by two distinct difficulties. First, the carburetors cut out so badly in turns that the whole operation is deprived of the power necessary to negate the understeer and you end up moving very slowly on a very erratic line. The other problem concerns the 24/28 psi tire pressure recommendation—a curious recommendation indeed for such a nose-heavy car. It turns out that this backwards bias is a palliative for tricky transient handling in the small engine Challengers, but the decal with that recommendation appears throughout the model line because whatever department is in charge of affixing the decal can't be bothered to distinguish between Hemis and Sixes.

There's no doubt the Challenger is a handsome car but it also has a massive feeling—which stems from a full five inches more width than a Mustang and a need to sign up with Weight Watchers—that is totally unwelcome in a sporty car.

We did try the Challenger with equal pressure in the tires but even that doesn't cure all of the evils. Curiously enough considering the unfavorable weight distribution, traction is not a problem. The fat F60-15 Polyglas tires and Chrysler's biased rear suspension (all 440 and Hemi Challengers have rear springs which tend to equalize loading on the rear wheels during acceleration) combine to do a good job of putting the power on the road.

The engineers who develop the ride and handling of Chrysler cars admit that the big engine Challengers (Hemis and 440s have the same suspension) were never a high priority project. Most of the effort was directed instead at the 340 and 383 4-bbl. models—which have a different suspension package that includes a rear anti-sway bar to reduce understeer—and the engineers claim that those models are every bit as agile as Z/28 Camaros and Boss 302 Mustangs. Unfortunately, the smaller engines are completely overshadowed by the two 440s—4-bbl. and 6-bbl.—and the Hemi. Moreover, the Challenger is so heavy that the smaller engines are unable to provide competitive performance so the engineers' handling efforts might better have been applied somewhere else.

There are probably a number of you out there in readerland mumbling to yourselves that anybody with a brain knows the Hemi is by far the heaviest engine Chrysler builds and if we were looking for a well-balanced car we should have picked something else. That's true, and yet the Hemi is also the only real racing engine in all of Detroit that you can dial up from your corner dealer with relative ease. You can't just tick off a Boss 429 on a Ford order form and expect to get it, and aluminum 427 Chevys certainly don't grow on trees. We try to test a Hemi every year just to stay in touch with Chrysler's big gun and to see how that hyper-active horsepower generator is fairing in the less forgiving world of exhaust emissions. Of course it makes for a fast Challenger—14.1 seconds in the quarter at 103.2 mph—but this Hemi was contrary to our past experience in that it didn't offer more pleasure than grief. It was very ill at ease in traffic with a torturous idle when held in drive against the brake and very poor low speed throttle response. Not infrequently it would backfire through the carburetor when coming off idle and, occasionally, after a backfire, die right in the middle of the street leaving us to wonder how much impertinence one should put up with just to go 103 mph in the quarter. At first we blamed the tighter 1970 emission regulations but a conversation with the manager of Chrysler's engine development laboratory dispelled that idea. The 1970 Hemis have hydraulic lifters, higher idle speeds and a solenoid valve on the primary carburetor to close the throttles completely when the ignition is shut off (to prevent after-running), but none of those things should impair driveability. We are left to conclude that this Hemi is a victim of poor quality

control—something not new to Hemis even though we have never had a bad one before. We are left to conclude that the 440 6-bbl. is a better choice for street operation because of its fatter torque curve and the Hemi should be reserved for those who want the maximum performance and are willing to spend considerable time tuning to get it.

This Challenger did point out the value of specifying the right options to go with the Hemi, however. The standard 3.23-to-one axle ratio is not enough to offset the Hemi's soft low speed performance and the cold air induction hood is essential because, without it, the test car lost 2 mph in the quarter when the underhood temperature reached its normal operating level.

This Challenger, equipped with the standard drum brakes, also pointed out the need for ordering the optional discs if you value good braking performance. The self-energizing drums are difficult to modulate and more inclined to fade. Even so, the test car's poor braking performance—294 feet (0.72-G) from 80 mph—is far more a result of poor braking distribution than of poor brakes. As seems to be normal for Chrysler products, the rears locked up well before the fronts which dramatically reduced the efficiency of the system.

As there are optional brakes and optional engines so are there a multitude of appearance options—all of which are calculated to give the Challenger that broad-based appeal which Dodge is counting upon. For example, take something as seemingly mundane as a hood: there is the standard no-frills simply-cover-the-engine hood, the bulging R/T hood (all performance models are called R/T), and the high performance hood with a big hole in it for the shaker-type scoop. Inside the car all of the R/Ts have a special instrument cluster with four round dials; one each for the tach, speedometer, clock, and the remaining one reserved for all of the small gauges. Then, for those who aren't satisfied with less than the best room in the house, there is the Special Edition trim option which can happen on either the standard Challenger or the R/T. The most straightforward part of the SE package is the seats—either cloth or leather covering. The cloth ones on the test car merit our approval even though they aren't very buckety. But the rest of the package is of dubious value. You get an overhead console with warning lights for the following offenses; door ajar, low fuel and seat belts. "Low fuel" may be helpful even though the ceiling is a strange place for that warning to appear and "seat belts," which operates on a time delay so that it stays on about 30 seconds after you close the door, may actually remind someone to buckle up. But nothing could be more worthless than "door ajar" which operates on the same time delay as "seat belts." It simply means that you have to wait that 30 seconds after you shut the door for the light to confirm that it is really closed—if you take the warning at

(Text continued on page 99
Specifications overleaf)

ACCELERATION standing ¼ mile, seconds

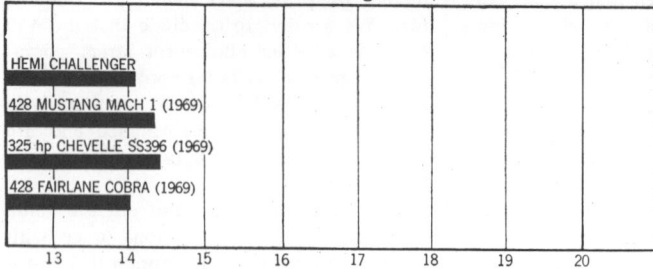

HEMI CHALLENGER

428 MUSTANG MACH 1 (1969)

325 hp CHEVELLE SS396 (1969)

428 FAIRLANE COBRA (1969)

| 13 | 14 | 15 | 16 | 17 | 18 | 19 | 20 |

BRAKING 80-0 mph panic stop, feet

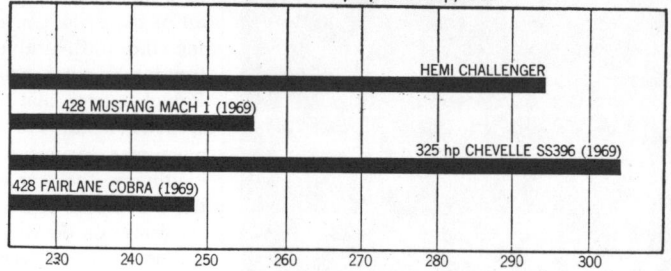

HEMI CHALLENGER

428 MUSTANG MACH 1 (1969)

325 hp CHEVELLE SS396 (1969)

428 FAIRLANE COBRA (1969)

| 230 | 240 | 250 | 260 | 270 | 280 | 290 | 300 |

FUEL ECONOMY RANGE mpg

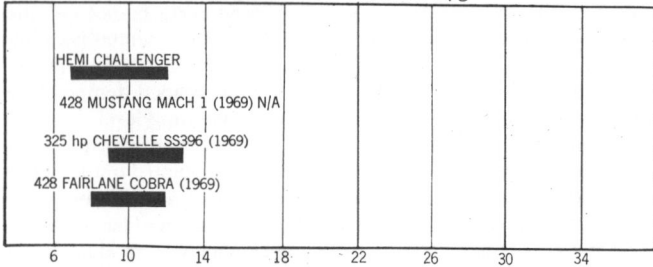

HEMI CHALLENGER

428 MUSTANG MACH 1 (1969) N/A

325 hp CHEVELLE SS396 (1969)

428 FAIRLANE COBRA (1969)

| 6 | 10 | 14 | 18 | 22 | 26 | 30 | 34 |

PRICE AS TESTED dollars x 1000

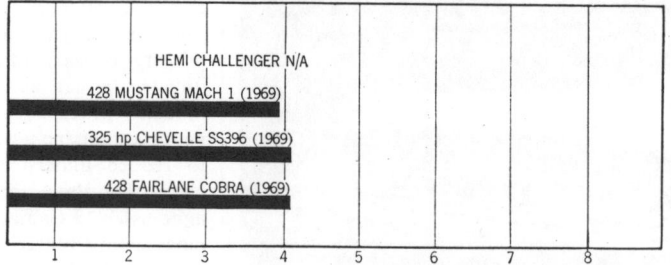

HEMI CHALLENGER N/A

428 MUSTANG MACH 1 (1969)

325 hp CHEVELLE SS396 (1969)

428 FAIRLANE COBRA (1969)

| 1 | 2 | 3 | 4 | 5 | 6 | 7 | 8 |

DODGE CHALLENGER R/T

Manufacturer: Dodge Division
Chrysler Corporation
P.O. Box 1259
Detroit, Michigan 48231

Vehicle type: Front engine, rear-wheel-drive, 4-passenger coupe

Price as tested: $ N.A.
(Manufacturer's suggested retail price, including all options listed below, Federal excise tax, dealer preparation and delivery charges, does not include state and local taxes, license or freight charges)

Options on test car: 425-hp Hemi engine, styled wheels, F60-15 tires, automatic transmission, limited-slip differential, power steering, power brakes, Special Edition trim package

ENGINE
Type: V-8, water-cooled, cast iron block and heads, 5 main bearings
Bore x stroke..4.25 x 3.75 in, 108.0 x 95.2mm
Displacement...............426 cu in, 6990cc
Compression ratio.................10.3 to one
Carburetion............2 x 4-bbl Carter AFB
Valve gear........Pushrod operated overhead valves, hydraulic lifters
Power (SAE)............425 bhp @ 5000 rpm
Torque (SAE)..........490 lbs-ft @ 4000 rpm
Specific power output........1.00 bhp/cu in, 60.9 bhp/liter
Max recommended engine speed...6500 rpm

DRIVE TRAIN
Transmission.............3-speed, automatic
Max. torque converter.............2.1 to one
Final drive ratio.................3.23 to one

Gear	Ratio	Mph/1000 rpm	Max. test speed
I	2.45	9.6	58 mph (6000 rpm)
II	1.45	16.2	97 mph (6000 rpm)
III	1.00	23.6	111 mph (4700 rpm)

DIMENSIONS AND CAPACITIES
Wheelbase.............................110.0 in
Track, F/R....................59.7/60.7 in
Length..............................191.3 in
Width.................................76.4 in
Height................................51.4 in
Ground clearance.....................N.A. in
Curb weight........................3890 lbs
Weight distribution, F/R....58.9/41.1%
Battery capacity.........12 volts, 70 amp/hr
Alternator capacity................444 watts
Fuel capacity.......................18.0 gal
Oil capacity..........................5.0 qts
Water capacity.......................16.0 qts

SUSPENSION
F: Ind., unequal length control arms, torsion bars, anti-sway bar
R: Rigid axle, semi-elliptic leaf springs

STEERING
Type........Recirculating ball, power assisted
Turns lock-to-lock.......................3.5
Turning circle curb-to-curb............42.0 ft

BRAKES
F:..11.0 x 3.0-in cast iron drum, power assisted
R:..11.0 x 2.5-in cast iron drum, power assisted

WHEELS AND TIRES
Wheel size.........................15 x 7.0-in
Wheel type..............Stamped steel, 5-bolt
Tire make and size..........Goodyear F60-15
Tire type.............Polyglas, tubeless
Test inflation pressures, F/R.......24/28 psi
Tire load rating.....1500 lbs per tire @ 32 psi

PERFORMANCE

Zero to	Seconds
30 mph	2.3
40 mph	3.3
50 mph	4.3
60 mph	5.8
70 mph	7.3
80 mph	8.0
90 mph	10.9
100 mph	13.4

Standing ¼-mile......14.1 sec @ 103.2 mph
Top speed (estimated)...............146 mph
80-0 mph...............294 ft (0.72G)
Fuel mileage.......7–12 mpg on premium fuel
Cruising range..................126–216 mi

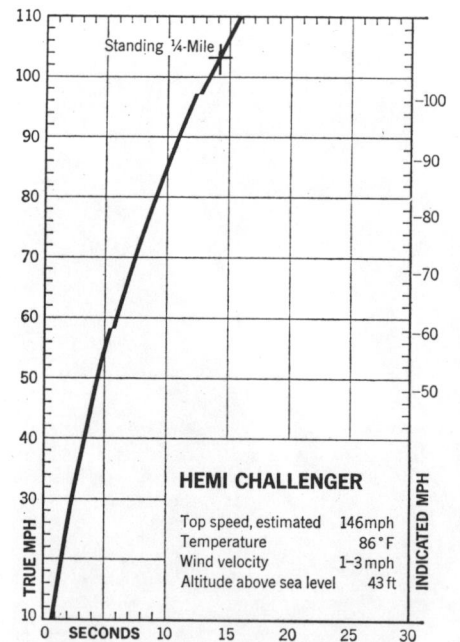

HEMI CHALLENGER

Standing ¼-Mile

Top speed, estimated	146mph
Temperature	86°F
Wind velocity	1–3 mph
Altitude above sea level	43 ft

TRUE MPH

INDICATED MPH

SECONDS

AAR CUDA

*Everything makes sense if you forget all about Dan Gurney
and think of it in terms of the Burbank Blue Bombers*

When the original Trans-Am rules were written, it was assumed that the automobile manufacturers would be racing the cars they made for sale to the public. Now, with the pressure from competition being what it is, we find that the whole thing has been reversed: That they are making available to the buying public the cars they race. At least, they are the same cars to such extent as is necessary to comply with the rules, which say that you must have hood scoops and spoilers on a minimum number of cars for the customer before you can use those items on the race track. Hence, the Pontiac Firebird Trans-Am, the Donohue Javelin, and, as you see here, the Plymouth/AAR 'Cuda.

Almost certainly, these gussied-up lovelies would not exist but for the racing thing, and in the case of the Firebird Trans-Am we may all feel grateful about what racing hath wrought.

Unfortunately, the racing-generated AAR 'Cuda—which we have just finished testing—strikes us as a mixed blessing, but we can't

be sure just how mixed it is because of the cobbled, tatty condition of the "first-off-the-line" press unit provided us for testing. On this particular car, the fiberglass engine-lid *cum* air-scoop was warped enough to create a gap between itself and the fender of a width nearly sufficient to permit checking the oil without ever pulling the NASCAR hood-pins. And then there was the driver's-side window, which fairly consistently jammed about an inch short of being closed, and a "racing" clutch (which found its way into our test car in some mysterious manner) that was so hair-trigger and prone to convulsive shudders when getting away from a stop that it would have been unacceptable even for racing.

Now then, apart from these defects making it difficult for us to build up much enthusiasm, they are probably not significant—unless they prove to be typical of subsequent AAR 'Cudas off the assembly line, which seems unlikely. What *will* be built into all AAR 'Cudas, we must assume, is a kind of rough, hot rod flavor. The car

feels like it might have come about because the Burbank Blue Bombers decided to build a "street rod" as a club project using a Plymouth 340 cu. in. V-8 'Cuda.

And if you look at the AAR 'Cuda as a ready-made street rod, what you see begins to make sense. Like the trick paint, with the dash-to-ditto stripes down the sides, and the twin exhaust pipes—capped with chromed megaphones sticking out from under the bodywork just ahead of the rear wheels. And bigger tires fitted on the rear wheels than up front (G60-15 and E60-15 Goodyear Polyglass GTs, respectively) and a nonfunctional but highly zoomy-looking louvered strip that runs from wheelwell to wheelwell, under the doors. And finally, it has those magical, Lamont Cranston "Elastomeric" bumpers.

As you might expect, and as is appropriate, the AAR 'Cuda comes with a special suspension package, which consists of heavier sway bars, front and rear, and stiffer rear springs, and special shocks. Our test car had the optional "Sure Grip" differential, too,

The new AAR 'Cuda is every inch a "street rod," from its offset-rim wheels to the chrome-plated pipes, and right through such things as dash-slash stripes, hood-scoop, NASCAR hood pins, peekaboo bumpers and other such sine qua non *of sporting life on wheels*

and it did all the things limited-slips are supposed to without any clanks or thuds.

Today's styles being what they are, many a nothing engine huddles under a fancy, air-scooped hood. Thus, it was with a mild flush of pride rather than our usual embarrassment that we allowed various attendants to check the AAR 'Cuda's dipstick. There is actually racy hardware to be seen under the lid: Three 2-throat carburetors, which are fairly completely shrouded by a big, tub-shaped air cleaner—this last in turn being surrounded by a collar that forms a seal against the hood-scoop duct. Nothing else that is at all remarkable is to be seen on the engine's exterior, but we are told that the AAR 'Cuda's engine has extra material cast into its block so that 4-bolt mainbearing caps can be installed for racing. Also, that the pushrods have all been moved slightly to provide room for wider ports. The porting work isn't done; Plymouth has just provided the room.

With or without the porting, the AAR 'Cuda is a strong runner. The engine gets some help from the 3.55-to-one axle ratio, but any 3600-pound car that will run the quarter-mile in the low 14-second range, and register a trap speed a fraction from 100 mph is just naturally strong. The Burbank Blue Bombers can be proud of that engine.

Whoever it may concern can also feel pleased with the AAR 'Cuda's brakes. It isn't every day that we find a car that can be yanked down from 80 mph in 220 feet. In fact, you can do it twice in a row without giving the brakes time to cool between stops; the third time, though, you will probably find that the rear brakes (drums) have gone all funny and are beginning to lock.

We might have finished the test thinking that the AAR 'Cuda handled well, except that it occured to us to drive the car in the manner (Trans-Am) for which it was theoretically intended. And right there is where we found that while the Burbank Blue Bombers had everything well arranged to wow them down at the Burger King, they hadn't quite gotten it all together for rapid travel around a road course. For instance, it might have been better to put the fat tires on the front wheels—considering the 56/44% weight bias—because the AAR 'Cuda doesn't want to answer the helm when you start trying hard.

Eventually, we worked out a driving technique that involved holding braking right into a turn (which borrowed some bite from the rear to help the front) and then getting off the brake and gassing it hard to hold the tail after it yawed-out from the braking. Onlookers who said the AAR 'Cuda appeared to get around tidily didn't see the furious activity inside the car.

This fun-and-games session was terminated when the pistol-grip shift lever pulled right out of its socket on a fourth-to-third downshift. Not a Big Deal, considering that it could be plugged right back in (minus the securing bolt, which had vibrated loose and dropped away.) But it *was* annoying, and it was more or less typical of the entire AAR 'Cuda, which is all made up of basically good hardware and forms a basically good package— unhappily rather shabby in detail and assembly. If the Burbank Blue Bombers can just get after those details, they might have themselves a really good street-rod •

Specifications overleaf

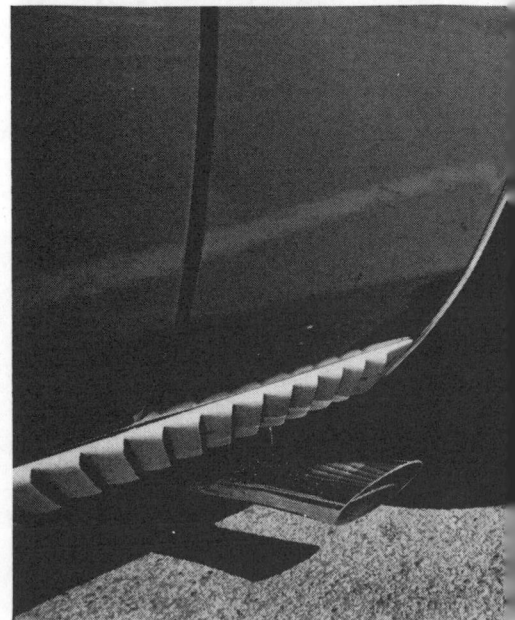

ACCELERATION standing ¼ mile, seconds

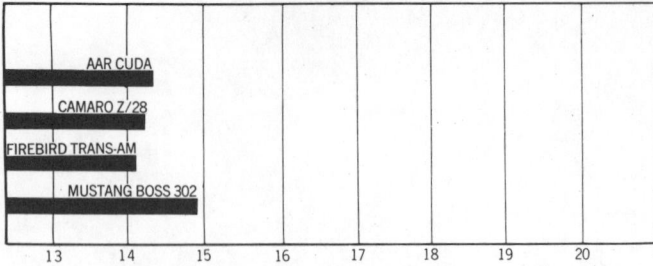

AAR CUDA	
CAMARO Z/28	
FIREBIRD TRANS-AM	
MUSTANG BOSS 302	

13 14 15 16 17 18 19 20

BRAKING 80-0 mph panic stop, feet

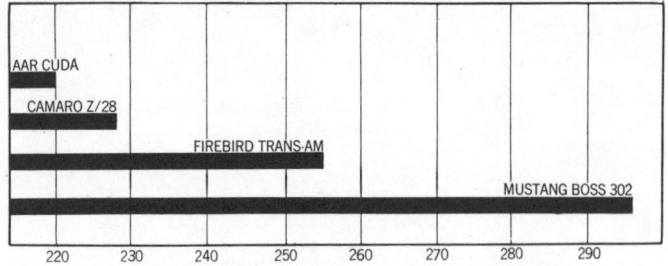

AAR CUDA	
CAMARO Z/28	
FIREBIRD TRANS-AM	
MUSTANG BOSS 302	

220 230 240 250 260 270 280 290

FUEL ECONOMY RANGE mpg

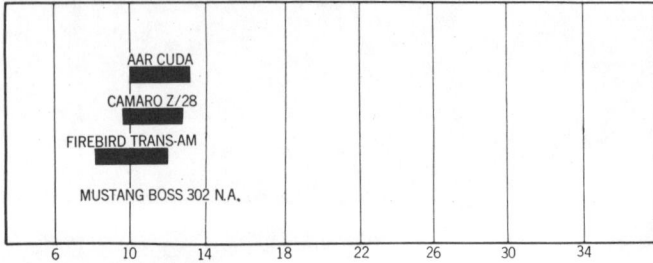

AAR CUDA	
CAMARO Z/28	
FIREBIRD TRANS-AM	
MUSTANG BOSS 302 N.A.	

6 10 14 18 22 26 30 34

PRICE AS TESTED dollars x 1000

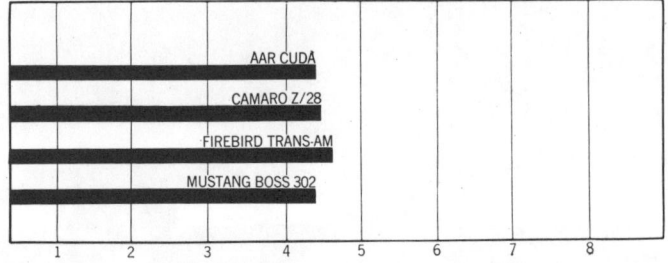

AAR CUDA	
CAMARO Z/28	
FIREBIRD TRANS-AM	
MUSTANG BOSS 302	

1 2 3 4 5 6 7 8

AAR CUDA

Manufacturer: Chrysler-Plymouth Division
Chrysler Corporation
Detroit, Michigan 48231

Vehicle type: Front engine, rear-wheel-drive, 4-passenger coupe

Price as tested: $4340.10
(Manufacturer's suggested retail price, including all options listed below, Federal excise tax, dealer preparation and delivery charges, does not include state and local taxes, license or freight charges)

Options on test car: Base AAR Cuda, $3966.00; Elastromeric bumpers and racing mirrors, $94.00; instrument package, $90.30; tinted windshield, $20.40; undercoating, $16.60; radio, $61.55; power steering, $90.35

ENGINE
Type: V-8, water-cooled, cast iron block and heads, 5 main bearings
Bore x stroke..4.04 x 3.31 in, 102.5 x 84.0 mm
Displacement...............340 cu in, 5580 cc
Compression ratio...............10.5 to one
Carburetion.................3 x 2-bbl Holley
Valve gear........Pushrod operated overhead valves, hydraulic lifters
Power (SAE)...........290 bhp @ 5000 rpm
Torque (SAE).........345 lb/ft @ 3400 rpm
Specific power output........0.85 bhp/cu in, 52.0 bhp/liter
Max recommended engine speed...6500 rpm

DRIVE TRAIN
Transmission.............4-speed, all-synchro
Final drive ratio................3.55 to one

Gear	Ratio	Mph/1000 rpm	Max. test speed
I	2.47	8.6	49 mph (5700 rpm)
II	1.91	11.2	64 mph (5700 rpm)
III	1.39	15.3	87 mph (5700 rpm)
IV	1.00	21.3	110 mph (4700 rpm)

DIMENSIONS AND CAPACITIES
Wheelbase.......................108.0 in
Track, F/R...................59.7/60.7 in
Length.........................186.7 in
Width..........................74.9 in
Height.........................51.9 in
Curb weight.....................3585 lbs
Weight distribution, F/R........56.1/43.9%
Battery capacity.........12 volts, 46 amp/hr
Alternator capacity...............444 watts
Fuel capacity...................19.0 gal
Oil capacity....................4.0 qts
Water capacity..................16.0 qts

SUSPENSION
F: Ind., unequal length control arms, torsion bars, anti-sway bar
R: Rigid axle, semi-elliptic leaf springs, anti-sway bar

STEERING
Type.........Recirculating ball, power assist
Turns lock-to-lock.................2.7
Turning circle curb-to-curb...........41.3 ft

BRAKES
F:...........10.7-in vented disc, power assist
R:..10.0 x 2.5-in cast iron drum, power assist

WHEELS AND TIRES
Wheel size........................15 x 7.0-in
Wheel type......stamped, styled steel, 5-bolt
Tire make and size, F/R:...........Goodyear E60-15/G60-15
Tire type........fiberglass belted, tubeless
Test inflation pressures, F/R........26/28 psi
Tire load rating, F/R:....400/1620 lbs per tire @ 32 psi

PERFORMANCE
Zero to	Seconds
30 mph	2.1
40 mph	3.1
50 mph	4.4
60 mph	5.8
70 mph	7.5
80 mph	9.4
90 mph	11.9
100 mph	14.4

Standing ¼-mile.........14.3 sec @ 99.5 mph
Top speed (estimated)...............128 mph
80-0 mph..................220 ft (0.96 G)
Fuel mileage.....10-13 mpg on premium fuel
Cruising range...................190-247 mi

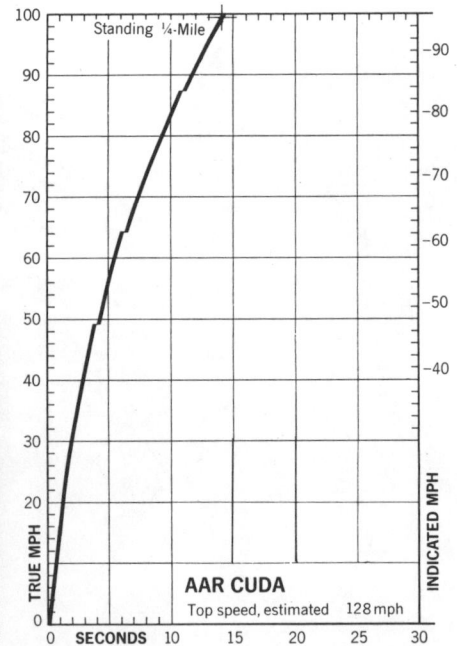

Standing ¼-Mile

AAR CUDA
Top speed, estimated 128 mph

Sam Posey and the C/D staff
Compare Detroit's 1970 Performance Cars

SS454 CHEVELLE·DUSTER 340
MUSTANG BOSS 302

To The Ultimate of the '60s
SHELBY AC COBRA

Through the windshield the horizon is tilted. Neck muscles strain against G-forces to support the weight of a crash helmet. Senses are bombarded with sounds —the painful scream of tires against asphalt, the belligerent roar of a 289 Ford— and smells; good British leather and traces of gasoline vapor. We are halfway through the Hook, Lime Rock's unforgiving hairpin that is conquered with two carefully chosen apexes or not at all. The black Cobra snorts and bellows against an unseen force as Sam Posey works on the huge wooden steering wheel, correcting minute slides before they become malignant. He shouts over the auditory assault, "No doubt about it, this has the feel of a real racing car— very, very serious."

His description couldn't have been more accurate. The Shelby Cobra was as menacing as its name from the very first. With malice aforethought it attacked and annihilated the Corvettes in SCCA's A/production, and after that taste of blood a coupe-bodied version went on to win its class at Le Mans in 1964. So successful was it as a racer that it was the first car to break Ferrari's hold on the World Manufacturers Championship in the years after that title became based on competition among production automobiles. It is a single purpose car—a powerful, high-winding V-8 in a stark, lightweight English AC chassis— for men who equate truth with speed and agility, and ask for nothing more. Production ceased in 1966 but the Cobra's performance still stands as a high water mark for all to see. It is the yardstick by which all other performance cars must be measured.

Today a yardstick (and a long one at that) is essential if we are to comprehend the improvements Detroit is engineering into its performance cars. The need became obvious this past summer as we previewed the 1970 models. Small cars are being outfitted with big engines—medium-size cars have engines that are enormous. Wheels and tires are now as wide as what you would have found on pure racing cars a few years ago, and truly sophisticated handling packages (many with rear anti-sway bars) are standard equipment. The point was forcefully pounded home at the GM proving grounds when we discovered that a Buick GS455 (of all things), loaded down to 4300 pounds with every conceivable comfort option, would still drive circles around an Opel GT, a "sports car," on the handling course. Detroit is building some very athletic automobiles, not just in acceleration but in handling and braking as well. Urged on by our natural curiosity about the sporting side of these devices we set out to ascertain the state of the art in Detroit.

Thanks to model proliferation, testing every one of Detroit's super cars is out of the question—it would take about five years for the task. Instead, we would take a sample, one car from each of the three distinct performance car categories, and

see how they measured up to the Cobra yardstick. Which cars? Well, there had to be an intermediate sedan because that is what Detroit's super cars have been since the beginning. Chevrolet is fixing to sell a 450-horsepower SS454 Chevelle—the highest advertised horsepower rating in all of Detroit—and that is reason enough that it should be in the test. Walter Mackenzie, a gray-haired veteran of Chevrolet's diplomatic corps, was up for the idea as soon as we phoned him. He remembered the Cobra ("You mean that low, skinny, lightweight thing?") and what it had done to the Corvettes and he wanted just one more chance. Production of the 450-hp Chevelle wasn't scheduled until January—but there were engines and there were cars—it was just a matter of putting the two together. Not to worry—there would be an SS454 Chevelle for the test.

Of course, there had to be a sporty car. These scrappy coupes have hyped up the Trans-Am Series popularity to the point where it threatens to eclipse the Can-Am. Deciding on a representative from this class was more difficult. Eventually, all the big engine versions were dismissed in favor of the 5-liter, Trans-Am-inspired models because they specialize in carefully tailored overall performance rather than merely dazzling acceleration. We finally settled on the Boss 302 Mustang for the most straightforward of all reasons—we just like to drive it. We've been enchanted by its capabilities since we drove the first prototype in Dearborn (*C/D,* June '69) and Brock Yates has proven that a mildly modified Boss can be competitive in SCCA regional racing (*C/D,* January '69) while still remaining streetable. After all of this favorable experience we wanted to see how an absolutely stock Boss ranked on Cobra yardstick.

That left one category to be filled—a category that we feel is the start of a trend. For a long time we've been questioning Detroit's logic in concentrating its performance efforts on the heavy intermediate-size cars when there were lighter

models around which could do the same job but with smaller engines and, ultimately, less expense to the customer. Plymouth's junior Road Runner, the Duster 340, is a giant step in this sensible direction. By including a Duster in the test we could get an early reading on the validity of the concept and perhaps even encourage its growth. But in Detroit our motives were not so transparent. Plymouth felt picked upon. Remembering past *C/D* comparison tests designed to ferret out the most capable car in a given class, Plymouth figured it had been singled out for the booby prize. "What are you guys trying to do? How can a Duster compete against a 454 Chevelle?" The Cobra was obviously beyond comprehension. "Let us bring a Hemi Cuda. That'll show those bastids." But we finally convinced Plymouth that this wasn't the apples-to-pumpkins comparison test that it appeared to be. In fact, it wasn't a comparison test in the conventional sense at all. Rather, it was to be the definitive statement on the whole range of Detroit performance cars, using as reference what most enthusiasts consider to be the world's fastest production car, the Shelby Cobra.

And, of course, we had to have a Cobra. Because it was the 289 that established the Cobra's all conquering reputation we chose that model. The 427 is faster, to be certain, but in reality it only made the Cobra legend burn a bit more brightly. Besides, classifying the big-engined brute as a production car is something of a dubious practice since only about 200 of them were built.

Cobras are where you find them. Walter Perkins, a bright young engineer with a bumper crop of red hot corpuscles, had a well-oiled 1965 model—bright, shiny and unmodified—that he figured was more than a match for any Chevelle, 454 or otherwise. We would find out. So would Sam Posey, our consulting arbitrator, who can be counted upon to hand down a decision in effusive pear-shaped tones. Posey is perfect for the job. That he is an intrepid

Front lock-up on the Chevelle makes for a straight, if smokey, stop while rear lock-up aims the Mustang at the guard rail.

competition driver is merely a proven fact, but his ability to drive to the ragged edge in anything with wheels *and* coolly describe its behavior in detail at the same time is a source of wonderment. And no one knows the way around Lime Rock better than he does. Any lingering doubts about that should have been erased by his two professional-series victories there in this past season alone; one in a Shelby-prepared Trans-Am Mustang and the other in his Formula A McLaren-Chevrolet. With this kind of background our 4-car road test couldn't help but be revealing.

A varied group converged at Lime Rock on the appointed day—a handful of escapees from the *C/D* office; Posey and his stopwatch expert, John Whitman; Bill Howell, an engineering wizard from Chevrolet who can always be found stalking around in the pits at Trans-Ams making sure that Chevrolet isn't racing; Don

Wahrman from Ford, one of Jacque Passino's disciples; and a couple of Detroit-owned PR men whose job is always to influence the outcome if possible. Plymouth had planned to send an engineering-type but the one chosen fell off a motorcycle at the last minute and couldn't make it. Perkins and Mrs. Perkins arrived with the Cobra and everything was set.

The cars had arranged themselves as to straight-line performance the day before at New York National. Perkins had kept the Cobra reputation alive by charging his machine through the quarter at 101.58 mph in 13.73 seconds—a scant 0.08 seconds ahead of the Chevelle—proving that there is no substitute for weight distribution. The Chevelle was decidedly more powerful, pushing its 3885-pound bulk through the traps at 103.80 mph, but with 57.1% of its weight on the front wheels it just couldn't quite get a good enough

grip on the asphalt to move out ahead of the Cobra. The big 454 did prove itself however. It is a fairly straightforward derivative of the 435-hp Corvette 427 with a 0.24-inch longer stroke and a single 780 cubic-feet-per-minute Holley 4-bbl. instead of the Corvette's three 2-bbls. Because its solid-lifter valve train is very stable at high engine speeds, Howell felt that 6500 rpm wasn't an unreasonable redline—even though the Chevelle seemed to go just as quickly when shifted at 6000.

Just behind the Cobra and Chevelle in acceleration was the Duster. At 3368 pounds it was the lightest of the Detroit cars—though still 1046 pounds heavier than the Cobra. It also had the best weight distribution of all the Detroit iron with exactly 55% on the front. Its quarter-mile performance of 14.39 seconds at 97.2 was hampered by a balky shift mechanism but, even so, the Duster speaks well for the compact super car concept.

The Mustang turned out to be a disappointment. It was only a bit heavier than the Duster, 3415 pounds with a full tank, but it was significantly less powerful, something we hadn't expected from an engine that was developed specifically for racing. When our best efforts were no better than 14.93 seconds at 93.45 mph we asked Wahrman to try, just to see if the factory knew something about driving Boss 302s that we didn't. In the best drag racer, gas-pedal-flat-to-the-floor tradition, he made two runs but neither bettered the Mustang's standings. The real point to be made here is that small displacement, high specific output engines suffer mightily in passing the exhaust emission and exhaust noise standards. Now that the SCCA allows production engines to be destroked down to the 5-liter maximum for the Trans-Am, the high performance 302s will soon disappear as a production option. In fact, the Boss 302 is the only one left right now.

That the acceleration portion of the test was out of the way meant that we had the whole day to evaluate handling and breaking at Lime Rock with Posey. Braking distances and cornering speeds would be measured, and to understand the behavior of each car as it approached the limit, one of the staff would ride along on all but the fastest laps to record Posey's observations. In the lead-off spot was the Chevelle.

We could have predicted Posey's first comment, which came within 100 feet after pulling onto the track.

"Oh, look at that little louver. Whenever I accelerate a little trapdoor on the hood opens."

It is a great piece of entertainment. With the "Cowl Induction" option, Chevrolet's version of a hood scoop, a little backwards-facing hatch at the rear of the hood opens whenever manifold vacuum drops below a predetermined value. In goes cold air and up goes horsepower or something like that. But Posey's next observation was far more serious.

"The rear view mirror is placed exactly where I want to look for a right turn. I have to scrunch down if I want to see."

This has been a problem in many Detroit cars since the federal safety standards requiring larger rear view mirrors went into effect. Now you have a blind spot in front instead of behind, which is a most unsatisfactory trade-out. And there are more comments about the interior.

"The driving position is really quite good but I can't brace my knees against the side panel—it is too far away. I just have to hold on to the steering wheel."

The observations continued in a calm, analytic flow, but there was absolutely nothing calm about what he was doing with the Chevelle. Three-digit numbers on the speedometer, airborne over the brow of the hill, 6000 rpm on the tach—the straights were now brief bursts of

SHELBY AC COBRA

Price as tested: $6167.00

Options on test car: dress-up group, $172.00 (price does not include chrome wire wheels or hardtop).

ENGINE
Bore x stroke....................4.00 x 2.87 in
Displacement...........................289 cu in
Compression ratio................10.5 to one
Carburetion.................1 x 4-bbl Autolite
Power (SAE)..............271 hp @ 6000 rpm
Torque (SAE)..........312 lbs-ft @ 3400 rpm

DRIVE TRAIN
Final drive ratio....................3.77 to one

DIMENSIONS AND CAPACITIES
Wheelbase.................................90.0 in
Track...................F: 51.5 in, R: 52.5 in
Length.....................................151.5 in
Width..61.0 in
Height.......................................49.0 in
Curb weight............................2322 lbs
Weight distribution, F/R..........48.5/51.5%

SUSPENSION
F: Ind., lower wishbones, upper transverse leaf spring
R: Ind., lower wishbones, upper transverse leaf spring

STEERING
Type...........................Rack and pinion
Turns lock-to-lock..........................2.75
Turning circle............................34.0 ft

BRAKES
F:.................................11.6-in disc
R:.................................10.8-in disc

WHEELS AND TIRES
Wheel size........................15 x 6.0-in
Tire make and size.........Goodyear F70-15, polyester
Test inflation pressure....F: 30 psi, R: 30 psi

PERFORMANCE

Zero to	Seconds
40 mph	2.7
60 mph	5.2
80 mph	8.5
100 mph	13.4
Standing ¼-mile	13.73 sec @ 101.58 mph
80-0 mph panic stop	256 ft (0.84 G)

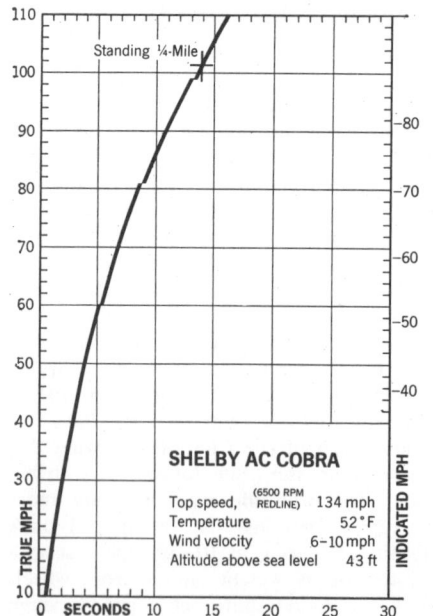

SHELBY AC COBRA

Top speed, (6500 RPM REDLINE)	134 mph
Temperature	52 °F
Wind velocity	6-10 mph
Altitude above sea level	43 ft

MUSTANG BOSS 302

Price as tested: $4318.45

Options on test car: fastback coupe with Boss package (includes: 290-hp engine, bucket seats, 4-speed transmission, front disc brakes, racing mirrors, collapsible spare, quick-ratio steering, competition suspension, front spoiler, carpets, gauges, fiberglass belted tires), $3720.00; rear spoiler, $20.00; limited-slip differential, $43.00; 3.91 rear axle, $13.00; convenience check group, $32.00; sport slats, $65.00; AM/FM stereo radio, $214.00; decor group, $78.00; tinted glass, $32.00; deluxe belts, $15.00; HD battery, $13.00; tachometer $54.00.

ENGINE
Bore x stroke....................4.00 x 3.00 in
Displacement...........................302 cu in
Compression ratio................10.6 to one
Carburetion.................1 x 4-bbl Holley
Power (SAE)..............290 hp @ 5800 rpm
Torque (SAE)..........290 lbs-ft @ 4300 rpm

DRIVE TRAIN
Final drive ratio....................3.91 to one

DIMENSIONS AND CAPACITIES
Wheelbase.................................108.0 in
Track...................F: 59.5 in, R: 59.5 in
Length.....................................187.4 in
Width..71.7 in
Height.......................................50.2 in
Curb weight............................3415 lbs
Weight distribution, F/R..........55.9/44.1%

SUSPENSION
F: Ind., unequal-length control arms, coil springs, anti-sway bar
R: Rigid axle, semi-elliptic leaf springs, anti-sway bar

STEERING
Type...........................Recirculating ball
Turns lock-to-lock............................3.6
Turning circle..............................38 ft

BRAKES
F:.................11.3 in vented disc, power assist
R:..10.0 x 2.0-in cast iron drum, power assist

WHEELS AND TIRES
Wheel size........................15 x 7.0-in
Tire make and size.........Goodyear F60-15, Polyglass
Test inflation pressure....F: 28 psi, R: 28 psi

PERFORMANCE

Zero to	Seconds
40 mph	3.3
60 mph	6.5
80 mph	11.1
100 mph	17.0
Standing ¼-mile	14.93 sec @ 93.45 mph
80-0 mph panic stop	296 ft (0.72 G)

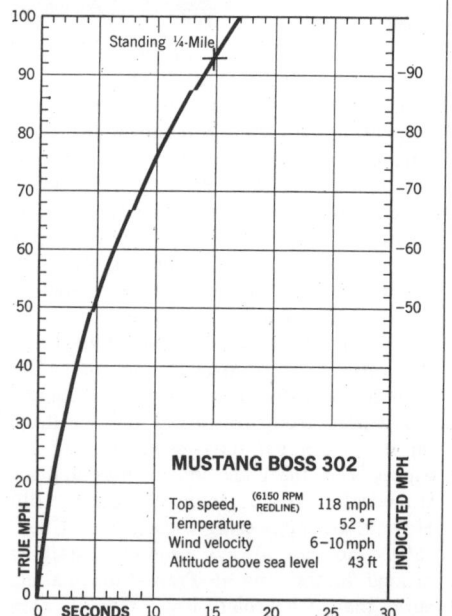

MUSTANG BOSS 302

Top speed, (6150 RPM REDLINE)	118 mph
Temperature	52 °F
Wind velocity	6-10 mph
Altitude above sea level	43 ft

CHEVELLE SS454

Price as tested: $4470.05

Options on test car: Chevelle coupe, $2809.00; SS package $445.55; 450-hp engine, $263.30; automatic transmission, $290.40; power steering, $105.35; bucket seats, $121.15; deluxe belts, $12.15; floor mats, $11.60; door edge guards, $4.25; vinyl roof, $94.80; console, $53.75; visor vanity mirror, $3.20; cushioned rim steering wheel, $34.80; AM/FM radio, $133.80; rear speaker, $13.20; bumper guards, $15.80, clock, $15.80; limited-slip differential, $42.15.

ENGINE
Bore x stroke	4.25 x 4.00 in
Displacement	454 cu in
Compression ratio	11.0 to one
Carburetion	1 x 4-bbl Holley, 780 cfm
Power (SAE)	450 hp @ 5200 rpm
Torque (SAE)	500 lbs-ft @ 3600 rpm

DRIVE TRAIN
Final drive ratio	3.70 to one

DIMENSIONS AND CAPACITIES
Wheelbase	112.0 in
Track	F: 60.0 in, R: 59.8 in
Length	197.2 in
Width	75.4 in
Height	56.2 in
Curb weight	3885 lbs
Weight distribution, F/R	57.1/42.9%

SUSPENSION
F: Ind., unequal-length control arms, coil springs, anti-sway bar
R: Rigid axle, trailing arms, coil springs, anti-sway bar

STEERING
Type	Recirculating ball, power assist
Turns lock-to-lock	2.9
Turning circle	42.0 ft

BRAKES
F: 11.0-in vented disc, power assist
R: 9.5 x 2.2-in cast iron drum, power assist

WHEELS AND TIRES
Wheel size	14 x 7.0-in
Tire make and size	Goodyear F70-14, polyester
Test inflation pressure	F: 35 psi, R: 35 psi

PERFORMANCE
Zero to	Seconds
40 mph	2.9
60 mph	5.4
80 mph	8.7
100 mph	13.0
Standing ¼-mile	13.81 sec @ 103.80 mph
80-0 mph panic stop	272 ft (0.79 G)

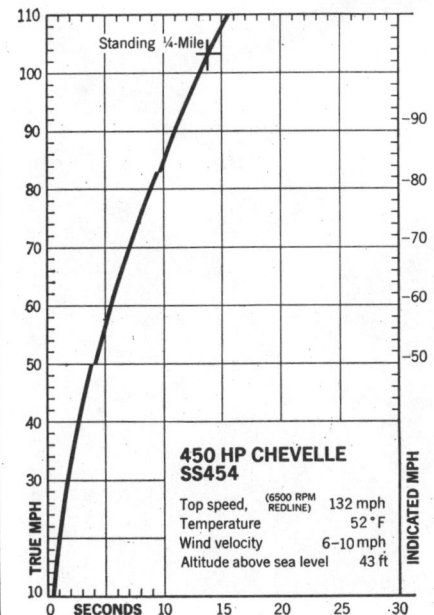

450 HP CHEVELLE SS454

Top speed	(6500 RPM REDLINE)	132 mph
Temperature		52°F
Wind velocity		6-10 mph
Altitude above sea level		43 ft

VALIANT DUSTER 340

Price as tested: $3455.70

Options on test car: Duster 340, $2547.00; bucket seats, $112.60; light package, $29.60; basic group, $82.60; decor group, $23.90; deluxe seat belts, $13.75; 4-speed transmission, $187.90; limited-slip differential, $42.35; special paint, $14.05; 50-amp alternator, $11.00; 59-amp battery, $12.95; tinted windshield, $20.40; day-night mirror, $7.10; dual horns, $5.15; pedal dress up, $5.45; undercoat, $16.60; door edge molding, $4.65; custom sill, $13.15; wheel lip molding, $7.60; belt molding, $13.60; bumper guards, $23.80; tach, $50.15; power steering, $85.15; vinyl roof, $83.95; vinyl side molding, $14.80; E70 tires, $26.45.

ENGINE
Bore x stroke	4.04 x 3.31 in
Displacement	340 cu in
Compression ratio	10.5 to one
Carburetion	1 x 4-bbl Carter AVS
Power (SAE)	275 hp @ 5000 rpm
Torque (SAE)	340 lbs-ft @ 3200 rpm

DRIVE TRAIN
Final drive ratio	3.91 to one

DIMENSIONS AND CAPACITIES
Wheelbase	108.0 in
Track	F: 57.7 in, R: 55.6 in
Length	188.4 in
Width	71.6 in
Height	52.6 in
Curb weight	3368 lbs
Weight distribution, F/R	55.0/45.0%

SUSPENSION
F: Ind., unequal-length control arms, torsion bars, anti-sway bar
R: Rigid axle, semi-elliptic leaf springs

STEERING
Type	Recirculating ball, power assist
Turns lock-to-lock	3.6
Turning circle	41.0 ft

BRAKES
F: 10.8-in vented disc, power assist
R: 10.0 x 1.8-in cast iron drum, power assist

WHEELS AND TIRES
Wheel size	14 x 5.5-in
Tire make and size	Goodyear E70-14
Test inflation pressure	F: 35 psi, R: 35psi

PERFORMANCE
Zero to	Seconds
40 mph	3.0
60 mph	5.9
80 mph	9.9
100 mph	15.1
Standing ¼-mile	14.39 sec @ 97.2 mph
80-0 mph panic stop	287 ft (0.74 G)

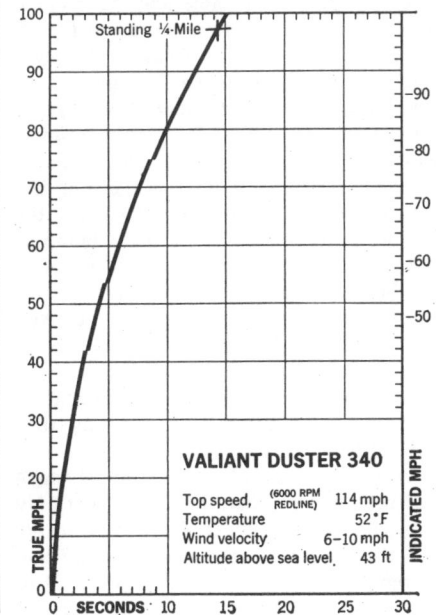

VALIANT DUSTER 340

Top speed	(6000 RPM REDLINE)	114 mph
Temperature		52°F
Wind velocity		6-10 mph
Altitude above sea level		43 ft

---

wide-open throttle and the curves abrupt changes of heading.

"The brakes are good for only about two laps and then they begin to fade. While they're working they are predictable, though. The biggest problem is the abrupt downshifts in the automatic transmission which breaks the tires loose and throws the rear end out. To get good control I have to shift manually at some point where I can stand a little twitch."

When it came to getting around corners the Chevelle proved to be quite agile in Posey's hands.

"The engineers who did this thing understand their problem—all that weight up front—and I think they've coped very well. The track is rough and the bumps are not throwing it off badly. It understeers but the understeer kind of cancels out the bumps. When the front tires are at the limit the rears aren't working so hard, just enough so they get some power to the ground and contend with the bumps too. Now, if we were teetering through these corners in an oversteer posture the car would be very sensitive to them."

From the lap times it was obvious that he was getting along well with the Chevelle. Already he was down to 1:10:4, which is a very good time for a street car. How would the other super car, the Duster, do? It was time to find out.

"For a gearshift here, hell, it looks like a stick for pole vaulting. And the funny little round knob. I don't know why they tried to make it look like wood. It is one of the most conspicuously fake things I've ever set my eyes on. Look at the little tach. It's *tiny*. I do like looking out over the orange hood though—gives me just a hint of being a McLaren driver. I'm a little apprehensive about all of this noise. We are going to have to shout."

After the smooth, quiet Chevelle the Duster was a vivid contrast. It rattled and buzzed at anything approaching speed and just generally broadcasted the same vibrance that made the Model A Ford seem so sophisticated in its day. As he started to work on faster lap times Posey wasn't optimistic.

"The power steering has nowhere near the road feel of the Chevelle and the car is not reacting well to the Gs. The suspension doesn't feel like the final solution. I don't detect the subtle hand of Colin Chapman in the geometry. What's happening is that as the body rolls in the turns it uses up all of the suspension travel and comes right in solid against the rubber bumpers. At that instant the weight transfer is complete on that wheel and the tire takes a terrible beating."

And, all the while the poor confused little Duster is being hurled around the track in a fashion it never dreamed possible. Through the Hook and into the Esses, tail out, tires howling and the lionhearted 340 moaning spasmodically as Sam played the throttle for just the right amount of torque.

	Cobra	Chevelle	Mustang	Duster
Average speed through HOOK	67.5 mph	66.0 mph	64.6 mph	63.9 mph
Average speed through ESSES	63.8 mph	61.4 mph	61.1 mph	60.2 mph

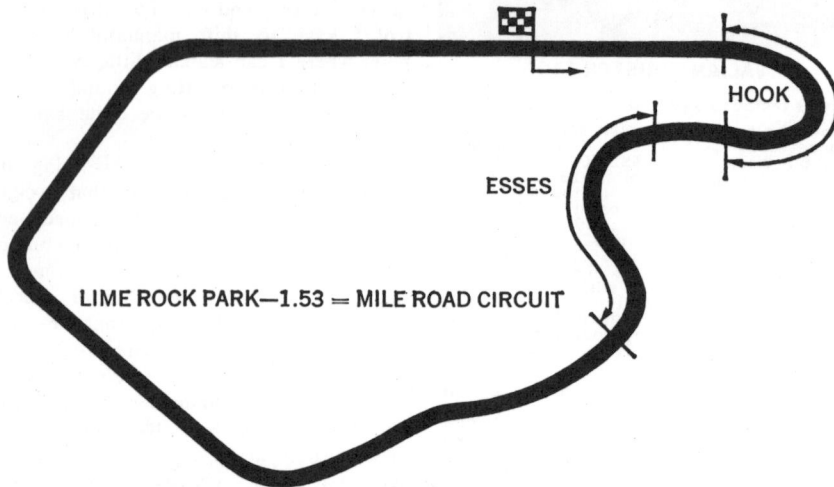

LIME ROCK PARK—1.53 = MILE ROAD CIRCUIT

HOOK

ESSES

"It is both understeering and oversteering simultaneously, which is to say that it's sliding right off the road. The carburetor isn't helping either. It cuts out at the most inopportune times. Also, I'm having a lot of trouble with the shift, particularly into third."

The shifter problem is unfortunate. Chrysler buys the Hurst linkage, but because of confusion on the part of the executives as to which is most important, a solid, dependable shift or total absence of noise, the engineers are forced to rubber isolate the shifting mechanism to the point where its usefulness in changing gears is merely coincidental. And the tall lever contributes its share to the confusion by making the throw unreasonably long. Even though the Duster was having its problems Sam wasn't ready to give up.

"Notice that the tires are leaving black marks in the turns which suggests that they need more pressure."

With a best lap of 1:13:95 the Duster didn't appear to be much of a threat to the Cobra. Still, with more air in the tires it figured to improve. As the pressures were being raised from 30 to 35 psi we went on to the Mustang.

"The instruments may be at the end of the Holland Tunnel down there. They are big enough but still difficult to read because of the complex markings. The driving position is a bit peculiar. The steering wheel is plenty close but the floor is too far away to brace my left foot satisfactorily. A telescoping steering column would be a good idea. This car has far more lateral support than the others and it feels very solid and secure."

We had been impressed by the same sensation when driving the Mustang on the road. It is quiet and exudes quality, very much like an expensive European GT

car. The stiff suspension and high shock absorber control give it a very purposeful feel, and because the body doesn't quiver or rattle when you hit a bump the overall impression is most satisfying.

"With the manual steering it feels very heavy up front, particularly after the Duster which, although it didn't generate high lateral forces, was very easy to toss around. The steering effort is extremely high—certainly higher than any race car."

Within a few laps the Mustang's virtues and vices, which tend to be extreme, were laid out for inspection.

"The brakes are fabulous. I can go in way deeper before I have to brake with this car than I could with the other cars. And the pedal feel is excellent. Here, I can control the braking with pressure on the pedal where in the other cars the pressure stays about the same and the braking seems to depend on how far down I push the pedal. That is very tricky to do accurately, especially when you are going fast. But boy, does it understeer. Look, you'd think I was going into the pretzel business with my arms. I've got the wheel really cranked over and it just isn't getting the job done. The only way I can get the tail out is to trick it by hitting a bump at just the right time or setting it up with the brakes. Funny, I expect more of this car in handling than it's giving me. And it's busting my hands. Every time we hit a bump in the turns the wheel kicks back so hard that I can hardly hold on to it with my arms crossed up the way they have to be."

With a best lap of 1:12:35 the Mustang had been quicker than the Duster, but only with considerable effort. Once back in the pits the hardships of manual steering and extreme understeer were obvious for all to see. Sam's hands, in the crotch between

the thumb and first finger, were bruised and swollen from being battered by the steering wheel spokes. The front tires hadn't escaped either. The outer tread rib was badly shredded—so bad, in fact, that it looked like the tread might start to peel. This brings up an interesting point about wide tires like the Mustang's F60-15s. Chevrolet is reluctant to use them, particularly on cars like the Chevelle, because the front suspension camber pattern is such that it lifts the inside of the tread patch in hard cornering to the point where the front tires are operating at a disadvantage relative to the rears—which exaggerates understeer. Curiously, the Chevelle wasn't wearing bias-belted tires (which are standard equipment this year) but rather last year's Goodyear bias-ply, polyester cord Wide Tread GTs. As a point of interest, the Cobra and the Chevelle both had exactly the same type of tires.

With the preliminaries out of the way it was time to explore the limits of Detroit performance. The Chevelle was charging around the track, its ears laid back and its hood louver snapped open to battle position. In compliance with California noise laws the exhaust has been restricted to a benevolent rumble, but the air rushing into the carburetor to feed those 454 cubic inches sounded like it was trying to take half the landscape with it. The Chevelle is a big car, enormous on Lime Rock, a tight, twisty, 1.53-mile circuit normally inhabited by Formula Vees and other assorted fruit-cup racers, but it didn't matter. Across the start-finish line at 110 mph, hard on the brakes for the Hook, wheels cocked in for the turn and clipping the infield grass at the apex—it seemed right at home. And it was doing very well, too. With a best lap of 1:08:00 it was the fastest non-race car that Jim Haynes, the track manager, could remember. The cornering speeds were good too—

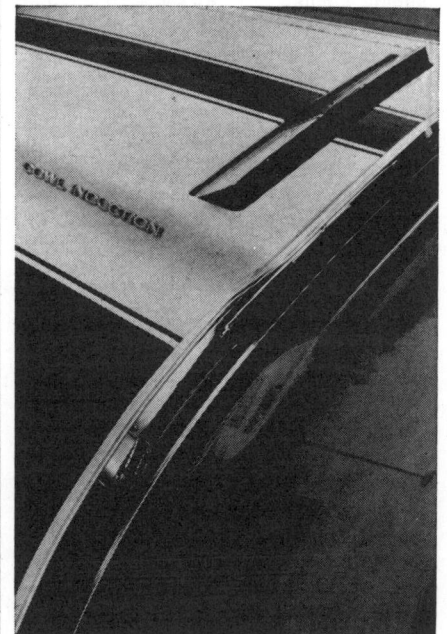

The "louver," more fun than functional.

COBRA VS. THE 1970'S

66.0 mph through the Hook and 61.4 mph through the Esses, a section with a left/right transition that is difficult for softly sprung passenger cars.

The Duster, now with 35 psi in its tires, began to show a new personality. At the end of the test Posey had revised his earlier opinion.

"Somehow, as the laps went by, this turned out to be the car that was a ball to drive. The steering is very, very light. Tremendous drift angles are possible, as are huge oversteers through the Esses with armloads of opposite lock. The car assumed nutty postures all the way around the course. It seemed to sort of get up on its tiptoes with the body rocking back and forth in a spectacular way and go really fast once I got used to it."

Of course, it still wasn't nearly as quick as the Chevelle, lapping at 1:11:7 and averaging 63.9 mph through the Hook and 60.2 through the Esses. But it was fun —a commodity that Posey didn't find much of in the Mustang.

"With the wide tires and stripes and louvers it looked so exciting in the pits. Perhaps because of my Trans-Am victory here in May with the Shelby car I had such high expectations for this one, but they just dwindled away as the laps went by. All I got out of it was sore hands. I'd rather just stand here and look at it."

At the beginning of the test we expected the Boss 302 to give the Cobra real chase, but with its 1:11:2 lap times it was only slightly quicker than the Duster. Of interest, however, was that its excellent transient handling made it only 0.3 mph slower through the Esses than the Chevelle.

With the Chevelle having established itself as the toughest of the Detroit representatives, the question now was how would it fare against the formidable Cobra. That confrontation could be put off no longer. Posey was already buckling himself into the cockpit.

"The most incredible feeling of immediacy exists in this car. Everything is up close to you. None of the remoteness found in the other cars. There was a feeling, in the others, that you had to penetrate the styling concepts to figure out which controls did what. Everything here is very obvious."

The Cobra is a shockingly single purpose car. No frills, no extra sound deadener, only the implements (tube frame, 4-wheel disc brakes, fully independent suspension) required for rapid transit. The flat instrument panel has simple, round, white-on-black gauges—one to monitor every factor you might need to check, including oil temperature. The external body sheetmetal extends right into the cockpit to form the top of the instrument panel and the windshield clamps down on the cowl, in traditional British sports car fashion, just inches in front of your nose. If there

is any doubt, at a skeletal 2322 pounds stuffed with a 271-hp Ford V-8, the Cobra is the archetypal high performance car.

"Oh, listen to the exhaust. If we were rating these cars on the basis of sound, this one would be the winner. The clutch is a heavy mutha. So is the steering, but it's very direct—much less lock required than in the other cars. And the suspension is very, very stiff. You feel *every* bump. Ah, see how nicely the tail comes out. This car has the feel of a racing car. The others didn't."

Because of its undisguised race car personality Posey adjusted to the Cobra in only a few laps. Partly because of its rearward weight bias—51.5% on the rear wheels—and partly because of its suspension rates, the Cobra was the only one of the cars that oversteered, and he used it to good advantage. In corners the Cobra adopted a curious posture. Because of its equal length arms, the independent suspension cambers the wheels in the same direction as body roll—which is exactly the wrong way. This, combined with the wide swinging tail, would have been humorous, except that the Cobra was ferociously eating up the circuit. Although the brakes began to fade after several laps the Cobra still made its point. With a best lap of 1:06:95 it was quicker than the Chevelle by slightly more than a full second. And, despite its suspension histrionics, the cornering speeds were faster too—by 2.5 mph in the Hook and 2.4 mph in the Esses.

Although lap times are a reliable indicator of a car's balance between handling and useful power, it doesn't tell the whole story about brakes, primarily because you never come to a complete stop on a road course. Fade and controllability of the braking process are measured but stopping ability is not. For that reason, the braking test had some interesting conclusions. The Cobra stopped quickest, requiring 256 feet (0.84G) from 80 mph. It was also the most controllable. The Chevelle was next at 272 feet (0.79G). Although it stopped in a straight line the braking was heavily biased toward the front wheels which meant that, to realize the full potential of the rears, the fronts had to be fully locked up, which will (and did) badly flat-spot the front tires. The Duster stopped in 287 feet (0.74G) with the rears tending to lock slightly before the fronts. The Mustang suffered from extreme rear wheel lock up—something that didn't show up significantly in the road course part of the test because a racing driver always avoids that situation if possible. Rear wheel lock up is a highly unstable situation which causes a car to skid sideways—which happened to the Mustang on one of its stops. Its best stop was 296 feet (0.72G)—an unseeming contrast to its stellar performance on the road course.

A point that Posey feels very strongly about, and so do we, is that controls, like brakes, should be sensitive to effort rather than travel. This problem shows up fre-

quently with the strong power assists that are necessary in Detroit's heavy cars. The Mustang's brakes are very good in this respect while the Chevelle's leave much room for improvement. And somewhat the same problem exists with power steering. The Duster's steering is so highly assisted that you sense the direction of the front wheels, not by feel, but by the position of the steering wheel.

After two solid days of testing we can see that improvement is required before Detroit can knock the Cobra off its "world's fastest car" pedestal—but not nearly as much as you may have thought. Those tweedy-capped purists who have been accusing Detroit's performance cars of being ill-handling hogs capable of little more than straight-line travel have had their legs kicked out from under them by the Chevelle. Naturally, the Chevelle was quicker in the straights, but it also made the fastest cornering speeds—significantly faster than the Boss 302, in fact, which has a reputation for good handling. After the test Posey commented on the Chevelle. "It's typically GM—wouldn't have offended anybody. It's quiet and well behaved—almost innocuous . . . I can't even remember what the dashboard looked like. But it has striking performance that you'd never suspect in traffic."

The Duster, although not the fastest, is certainly the most amusing. It's whimsical and has a kind of disposable air about it. Breaking it would not be a catastrophe—you just won't get your deposit back. For the price it delivers a full measure of performance but it has been badly compromised by confused priorities (the shift linkage) and inept stylists. Not only are the stylists responsible for many unnecessarily cheap looking details in the interior (fake wood knob, for example), but by their decree the Duster has been lowered on its suspension. This little trick for snuggling the Duster down against the ground has left the suspension jounce travel in an impoverished condition, detrimental to both ride and handling. Still, the Duster is a good start toward a compact super car—the basic mechanical parts definitely do the job—and with some work could be every bit as satisfying as the Chevelle.

Most of the Boss 302's problems could be cured by power steering (which is available) and less understeer. After driving the prototype Boss in Dearborn last spring we thought Ford had finally cured the understeer problem but, apparently, we were wrong. With its strong styling and quality feel the Mustang is an appealing road car, but that is quite apart from the implication of "Boss."

For now Perkins can continue along carefree paths, snuffing Corvettes in gymkhanas and autocrosses, confident in the knowledge that his aluminum-bodied Anglo-American hand grenade has got Detroit pretty well covered. But he is definitely not as anxious for the 1971 Chevelle as we are. ●

• They're going to be eating their livers, those other car company guys, when they see the new Road Runner. It has a look born of purpose and muscles where the others have flab. While the government-fearing opposition has been putting antimacassars on their street racers, Chrysler has been standing on the gas, and the car kids are going to be driving Road Runners just because last year's hot set-up now looks 10 years old.

What we're telling you is that the Road Runner and the other Plymouth intermediates are all new. Well, they aren't *all* new but the part that you see is. Underneath they're pretty much the same as what Plymouth has been serving up for the last handful of years—with strategic improvements, of course. All of the standard engines will have lower compression ratios so that they can live on 91 octane fuel. New sound deadening devices are scheduled to kill off some of the din associated with Plymouth's unit body, and company officials have promised to ream out those guys down in the plant who are in charge of quality control. All of this will hopefully bump Pontiac out of third place once and for all and, right now, that's Plymouth's biggest project.

Some years ago, in anticipation of this struggle, Plymouth summoned its elite corps of product planners from their long winter's naps for some sort of invincible marketing plan. The planners responded with an idea that has come to fruit in the 1971 intermediates—now called Satellites rather than Belvederes—the scheme is curious enough to merit discussion.

The cornerstone of the plan is the observation that a large volume of customers will part with an extra lump of cash for a uniquely styled 2-door hardtop. The Monte Carlo is based on the Chevelle; the Charger springs forth from the Coronet; the Grand Prix is little more than a stretched and re-skinned Tempest— yet the folks are willing to pay upwards of $150 more for the *special* hardtop, just for its styling. So Plymouth reasoned that if the customers want the unique coupe that much, why not drop the standard hardtop altogether and just offer the special one? And to make it more attractive, sell the new coupe at the price they would have charged for the standard model. Everybody will think they are getting something for nothing and the assembly will have to run double speed.

The result of all this circuitous logic is two separate lines of Plymouth intermediates—Satellites (4-doors) and Sebrings (2-door hardtops). The sedans have 117-inch wheelbases; the hardtops are 115 inches. And each has a unique skin, right down to the bumpers so that each looks entirely different.

Plymouth readily admits that two suits of sheetmetal cost more than one and since they will be selling the new hardtops for about the same increment over the sedans as they did before, there will be a squeeze on the per-car profit. "Have to make it up by selling more cars," they say. On hearing that, it is pretty hard to keep a straight face. How does that old car salesman's line go? "Lose a little bit on each one but make it up in volume."

Assuming that it is possible, there are still a few questions. Will the customers recognize this as a *special* hardtop when there is no standard one to compare it to? Since the scheme obviously relies on establishing the 4-doors as the "basic" models, it was decided to make their styling very conservative. The stylists outdid themselves—its possible the hardtops look so good in comparison, that *no* one will want the sedans.

Whether or not the whole thing works, good has come from the idea. The Road Runner and its Sebring companions have a lap on everybody in styling.

Dimensions	1970	1971
Wheelbase	116.0 in.	115.0 in.
Track, F/R	59.7/59.2 in.	60.1/62.0 in.
Length	204.0 in.	203.2 in.
Width	76.4 in.	79.1 in.
Engine		
Standard engine	383 cu. in., 335 hp. V-8	383 cu. in., 300 hp. V-8
Compression ratio	9.5 to one	8.7 to one
Max. option	426 cu. in., 425 hp. V-8	426 cu. in., 425 hp. V-8
Compression ratio	10.2 to one	10.2 to one
Tires		
Standard	F70-14	F70-14
Max. option	F60-15	G60-15

PLYMOUTH ROAD RUNNER

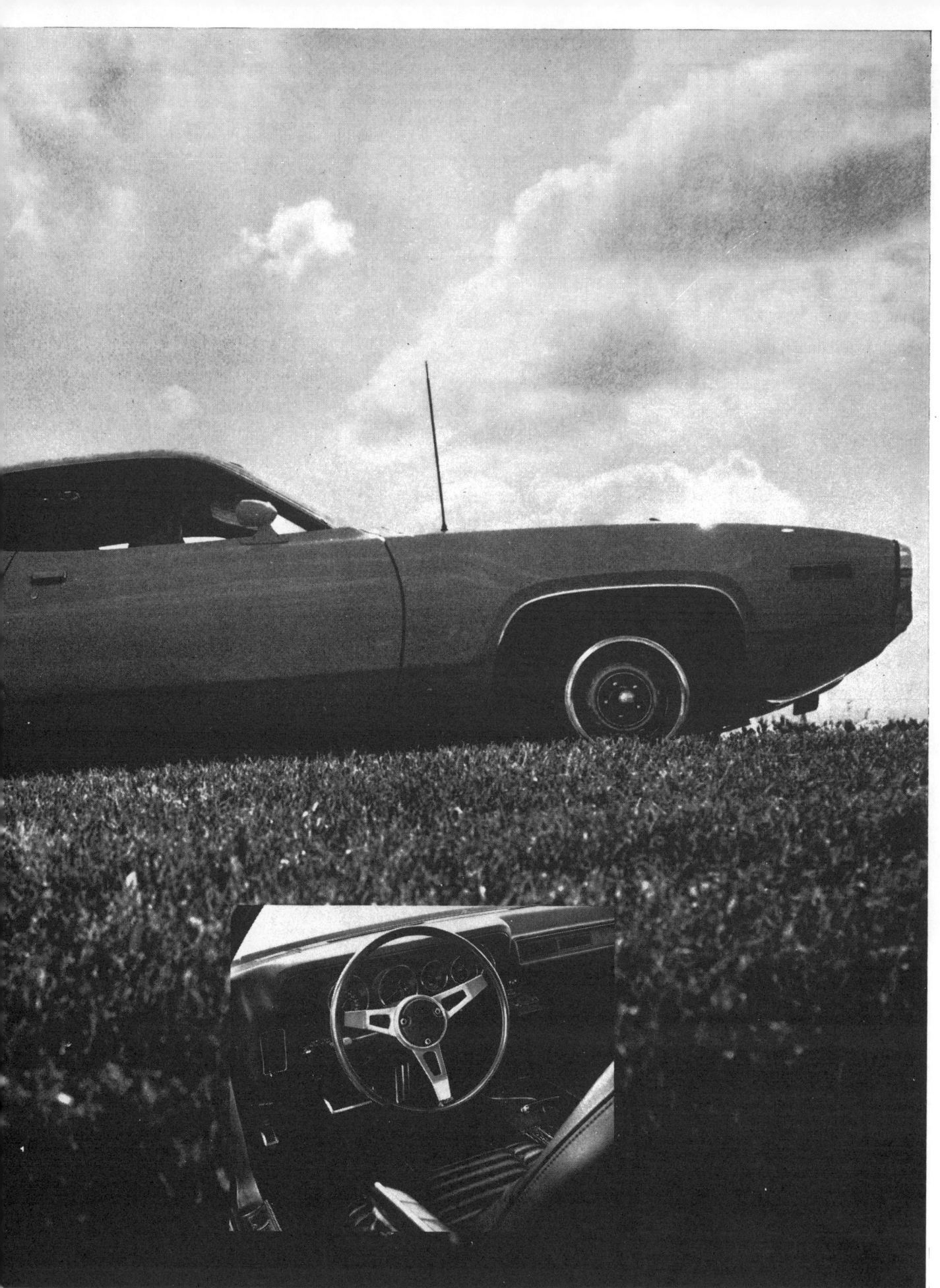

PREVIEW: PLYMOUTH CRICKET

Functional, sturdy and utterly conventional

PHOTOGRAPHY: PETE BIRO

ENGINE SPECIFICATIONS
Type—4 in-line, ohv
Bore and stroke—3.39 x 2.53 in.
Displacement—91.4 cu in, 1488cc
Compression ratio—8.0 to one
Carburetion—1x1-bbl Zenith/Stromberg
150 CDS
Power—70 bhp @ 5000 rpm
Torque—83 lbs/ft @ 3000 rpm

CHASSIS SPECIFICATIONS
Wheelbase—98.0 in.
Track, front—51.0 in.
Track, rear—51.0 in.
Length—162.0 in.
Width—62.5 in.
Height—54.6 in.
Curb weight—1966 lbs.
Fuel capacity—10.8 gal.
Axle ratio—3.9 to one
Tires—6.30 x 13
Brakes, front—9.5 in. disc, power assist
Brakes, rear—8.0 in. drum, power assist
DECEMBER 1970

64

● Plymouth, like Dodge, is part of the Chrysler family, and like Dodge has just announced its new "sub-compact" automobile. In fact, Plymouth's introduction (to the press) of their Cricket came only one day after Dodge's unveiling of the Colt, and the festivities were held at Orange County Raceway —less than an hour's drive from Ontario. And the delegation of Mitsubishi executives attending the Colt intro' showed up for the unleashing of the Plymouth Cricket. So much for the similarities; the rest of the story is entirely different.

For one thing, where Dodge shouts-out the Colt's Japanese origins, Plymouth's PR types mumble something about the Cricket being produced by "Chrysler UK" and divert your attention to the nifty promotional slogans they have dreamed up to sell their small car (sample: "Here comes the Cricket. Chirp! Chirp!"). But enough of that; the fact is that Plymouth's Cricket is really a Hillman Avenger made by Rootes, which is Chrysler's English subsidiary, and apparently there is a production capacity for the Cricket/Avenger substantially in excess of British demand, as the car will be available at Plymouth dealerships throughout the country very shortly.

Perhaps because Rootes had such limited success with the rear-engined Imp, the Cricket—an all-new design—is utterly conventional, with a 4-cylinder pushrod engine up front driving a live rear axle *via* a 4-speed all-synchro transmission and tubular driveshaft. The only departure from Detroit-style convention is in the suspension system, which features MacPherson struts up front and coils instead of leaf springs at the rear axle. Axle location is provided by a system of trailing rods and diagonal links, and this arrangement provides both a better ride and better handling than is usually obtained by bolting the axle to a pair of leaf springs.

You'll take your Cricket, if you buy one, as a 4-door sedan, as that's the only body style being made. Chrysler's engineers feel that the only way to get a decent 4-door package is to design with only that in mind and not worry about 2-door or coupe or station wagon versions. They may be right, for the Cricket does offer quite a good seating package within the overall dimensions of what is definitely a small car. We're still not convinced that the 4-door configuration is the answer in small sedan terms, but the Cricket does have four doors of decent size and will carry four adults in reasonable comfort if those up front do not get piggy about leg room. And it will carry a lot of luggage under the hatch in that rather bulbous tail.

As was the case with the Colt, driving impressions were to a great extent shaped by the fact that all of the driving had to be done on a race track, away from the real world of traffic. And on a track, the Cricket comes across fairly well. You get just bags of understeer in turns, but the little jasper tries hard to go where it is being aimed and it doesn't lean nearly as much as most of its contemporaries. It's very drivable.

A lot of effort has gone into making the Cricket a practical car (simplicity in all of its parts, with few lubrication points and a lifetime supply of oil in the transmission and axle; bolt-on fenders, etc.) and one that is safe—with front and rear structure designed to collapse progressively under impact, to protect the occupants. They've worked hard to make it light, too, and it is, with a curb weight under 2000 pounds, which helps keep the price down and the performance up. It needs all the help it can get, here, with a 91.4 cu. in. engine producing only 70 hp. It does manage acceptable performance, in small-car terms, with the 4-speed manual transmission, but has less urge when fitted with the optional 3-speed automatic. Obviously, too, you'll notice the difference with each added passenger.

The Cricket's brakes are good (better than the Colt's) and it has a really fine-shifting transmission. There isn't anything obviously amiss about the general fit and finish, but somehow it comes through as functional and sturdy —but slightly crude. Indeed, that's our lingering impression of the entire car. The engine seems willing, and it does haul the car around in a manner that is, if not brisk, then at least rates as acceptable—but when you take it up around its 5000-rpm power peak there is a sound of great mechanical business filtering back through the firewall. Similarly, the fact that the seats are comfortable is a little less impressive after you notice that the vinyl that covers them (and the door panels, etc.,) looks like kitchen-floor linoleum and the rubber mats on the floor suggest that maybe they've been peeling the hides from giant Sumatran toads. Lord knows we've seen similar splendor in many a made-in-America automobile, but the buy-in-America customer tends to get critical when he's looking at an import with an eye toward making a purchase, and Chrysler UK could do the Plymouth dealer in Keokuk a big favor by upgrading the vinyl and splurging on a bit of genuine carpeting for the car's floor. People who buy "funny little foreign cars" worry about what their friends and neighbors are saying. They'll pay for those touches that pass for quality—and they won't touch a car that doesn't have them.

PLYMOUTH GTX

*In an era when the term
"Super Car" is being whispered rather
than shouted through the
halls of Detroit,
Plymouth bucks
the trend by proudly announcing
the birth of its
all-new GTX*

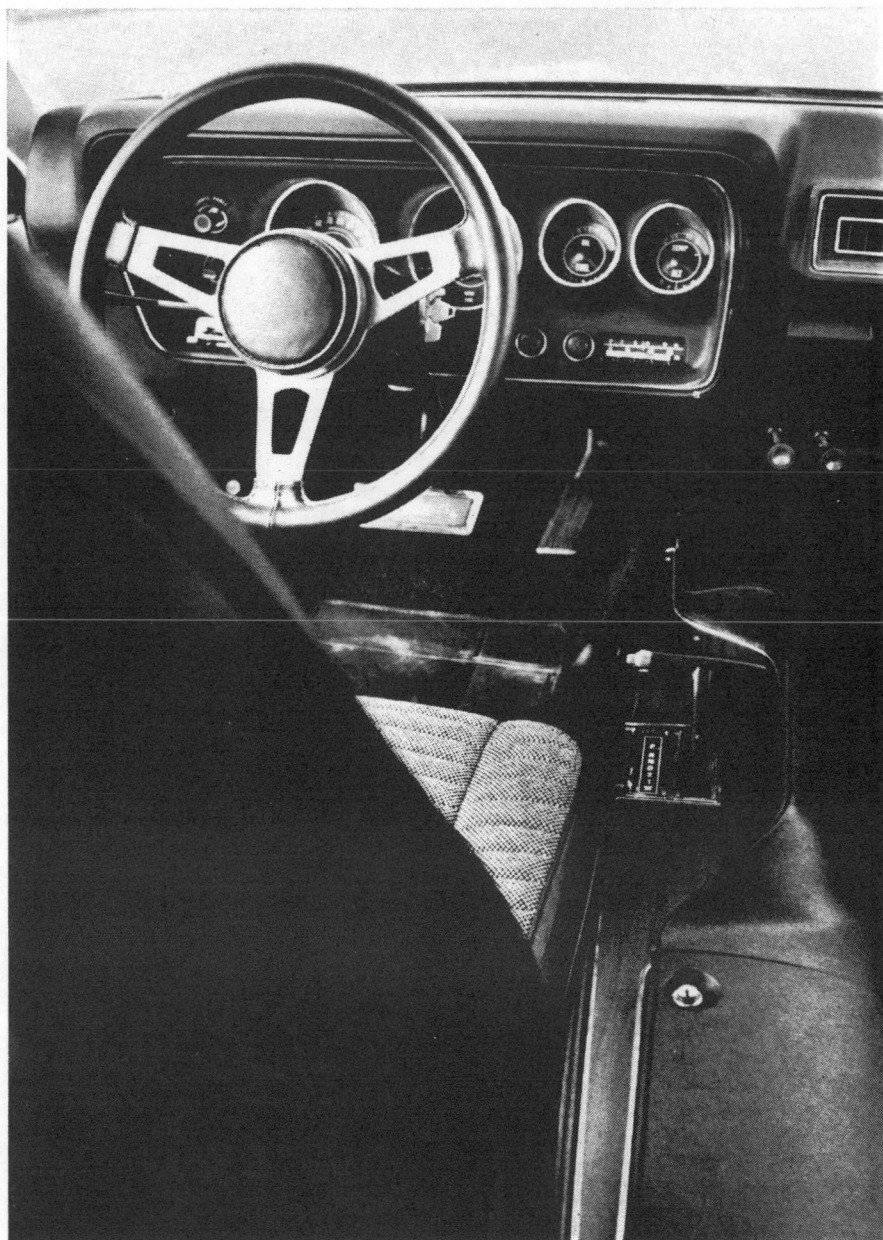

As it crouches in its parking space under a coat of Curious Yellow paint and a white vinyl top, the 1971 Plymouth GTX seems neither malignant nor odious. Its tires, incredibly fat, black Goodyears, with raised white letters on the sidewalls, and its stripes, issuing forth from nostrils on each side of the hood and streaming down the front fenders, suggest "sport" in much the same visual language as stainless steel tennis rackets, exotic metal skis or even those "competition-striped" sneakers. But the difference is that the Plymouth GTX is a "performance car"—it has a 440 cubic-inch, *high* compression engine—and that is enough to provoke a measure of public wrath. Many—disciples of Ralph Nader, Sierra Club-inspired conservationists, and urban planners—are proclaiming the death of performance cars. And the insurance companies, with their "horsepower surcharges," are doing their best to nail shut the coffin.

All of this has not gone unnoticed within the insulated walls of Detroit. The car manufacturers are apprehensive and, with the exception of Chrysler, have noticeably pulled in their horns. Super Cars are still being built but they are not being aggressively merchandised like they were before —their place in the limelight is being taken by low-powered compacts.

Obviously, the climate is different for performance cars. Certainly changed from just a year ago. But does that mean that Detroit is being pressed toward a new frontier or that we have merely crested another wave in a repeating cycle of customer vacillation? History offers pregnant parallels. Turn back the pages of *Car and Driver,* back to 1957 when it was still called *Sports Cars Illustrated,* and read what one perceptive journalist had to say in a road test of an automobile advertised as, "The Mighty Chrysler 300C. America's Most Powerful Car—375HP."

"*. . . there's no doubt that the horse-*

power cycle is coming to the end of its course. State and federal governments are fed up with it and reaching for legal weapons to kill it. Detroit's current stock cars are so hot that it's questionable whether most operators are quick enough and competent enough to control them. Costs of purchase, operation and maintenance have become excessive. Most sane minds in Detroit, and there really are many, know that the time for housecleaning is overdue. It's a case of killing the goose that lays the loot-filled eggs before the goose kills you. And in an environment suddenly dedicated to "slow down and live," it's hard to see much of a future for projectiles like the 300C. . . . In fact, it's more than likely that the 300C is the last of its line, that there will be no 300D. This report on the most "super" of all Detroit super-stock models, on the Tyrannosaurus Rex of the automobile dinosaurs, is more than an ordinary road test. It's a look at a machine that stands as the culmination of an era that's ending."*

That author was clearly premature in signing the coroner's report. The Chrysler 300 lived to see the letter L suffixed to its name and was succeeded by squadron after squadron of Detroit Super Cars whose capacity for rushing over the face of the earth made the old 300 seem like more of a family sedan. Let's go back to that forgotten road test again, back to the performance data on the specifications panel. "America's Most Powerful Car," the one thought to be beyond the capabilities of more than a few drivers, recorded a standing quarter-mile time of 16.9 seconds at 84 mph.

Early in September of 1970, in an air conditioned office overlooking the entrance to Chrysler's Jefferson Assembly Plant, public relations man Jim Stickford and Gordon Cherry, Plymouth's Manager of Planning and Administration, were disappointed and apologetic when we told them that the new GTX we had just finished testing could do no better than 14.9 seconds at 95.4 mph at Detroit Dragway. Never mind that it was two full seconds and 11 mph faster than the legendary Chrysler 300—the GTX turned out to be a pretty lethargic Super Car by today's standards. "It was a very early production car," Cherry explained, "and you never can tell what parts those guys down on the line will use on the first few dozen cars." They knew that it didn't have a limited-slip differential, which was no help on the drag strip, and the new GTX, at 4022 pounds, was somewhat heavier than past models. Still, they also knew it should have been faster.

But even though the GTX's acceleration was less than first-rate, by today's standards, it is still very much a Super Car. The insurance companies say so and Plymouth is not denying it. Cherry allows as how performance cars have recently fallen on hard times but he doesn't believe that the market for them has permanently

dried up. "With the Road Runner and the GTX we were selling almost 100,000 performance cars per year. That has dropped off to about half now." He believes that increased unemployment and tight money (which makes it more difficult for youthful buyers to obtain financing) plus the recently increased insurance costs are responsible for the sluggish sales. With characteristic car manufacturer's optimism, he points out that an upswing in the economy will eliminate all of the problems—except for insurance cost—and that he expects to see sales pick up later in the year.

But even if sales don't pick up, Plymouth will continue to offer models like the Road Runner and the GTX. "Maybe if the volume dropped below 10,000 cars per year we'd cancel them out, but then only if we were pretty sure those 10,000 customers would change into some other Plymouth model. If it looked like they would swing over to a competitor, of course we'd continue them. You can't give away sales."

Right now, Plymouth and Dodge have a stronger commitment to performance cars than anyone else in Detroit. With the exception of American Motors, Chrysler is the only car maker who has not announced an intention to lower the compression ratios of all engines to the point where they will operate on 91 octane fuel. "Not an easy decision," according to Cherry. "First off, we didn't have time to do it across the board so we concentrated where it would do the most good—the standard engines (which account for about 93% of Chrysler's sales). And there are some very strong reasons for not lowering the compression of performance engines—it hurts the power too much for one—so we decided to continue to offer the high compression engines as an option as long as customers want them."

The "option" part isn't strictly true in that the 440 4-bbl which is standard in the GTX has a 9.7-to-one ratio and does require premium fuel. The Road Runner 383, which is by far the biggest seller, has been lowered to 8.7 however, and it will run on regular. The 440 6-bbl and the 426 Hemi, optional on the Road Runner and GTX, have not been changed.

While insurance companies concentrate primarily on the engine, there definitely is more than that to a performance car according to Cherry. Plymouth holds to the theory that the youthful buyers of this class of car usually go deeply in debt to buy it, consider it to be a strong social expression of their individual personalities and, therefore, want it to be easily recognizable. Hence such add-ons as styled wheels, scooped hoods and tape stripes. Unfortunately, the more years tape stripes are in use the harder it is for the stylists to find a scheme that is both new and pleasing. But Plymouth hasn't stopped trying. You can draw your own conclusions about the GTX's front fender stripes and the Road Runner's segmented arrangement

that angles down each rear roof pillar onto the rear quarter. Without them, however, the new Plymouth hardtop is a genuinely handsome car—one of those rare combinations of smoothly integrated curves that all of Detroit seems to be unable to generate more often than once every four or five years.

Actually, styling may be sufficient recommendation for the GTX. As a car, it suffers only a few minor hardships from being in the "performance" category. Ride quality is probably its greatest deviation from normal-car character. The GTX has, as standard equipment, the stiffest suspension rates of any Plymouth intermediate, stiffer even than the station wagons, and the high spring-rates, combined with the wide Polyglas tires, add up to a relatively harsh ride—decidedly more so than in an equivalent Chevelle SS or Pontiac GTO. And there is also more road noise than in the competition. In trade for the hard ride and extra road noise you get a car that doesn't really handle any better than the run-of-the-mill Super Cars but, to the traditionalist, feels like it will. For most drivers, that is enough.

While, considering the current state of the art, one might be tempted to say that the suspension was deficient, there is little room for complaint about the powertrain. Engine idle is slightly rough but not any rougher than Super Cars were five years ago when there were no emission control systems to make things difficult. In fact, it seems that every phase of the engine's operation is well disciplined. Certainly the exhaust sound is. Nothing there to make you think of a gut-level performance car. It is quiet at all times and at full throttle is almost drowned out by the moan from the air intake, which in itself is not all that loud. The level of the engine's intrusiveness is in every way keeping with the car's performance level—moderate.

One thing that works particularly well is the console-mounted gear selector for the 3-speed automatic. Plymouth calls it a Slap Stick which is an attempt to convey to you that it is a device which specialized in one-gear-at-a-time manual upshifts. When you are in low, just give the lever a whack and it shifts to second—another whack and it is in drive—all without the worry of moving one notch too far into neutral. Other manufacturers have shifters born of similar intentions but none of them work with the precision of this one.

With an eye toward easing the driver's task, Plymouth has worked on more than just the shifter—it has revised the whole driving position. Where the steering wheel was always too close to the driver and too high before, not unlike Captain America's ape-hangers, it is very well located now. In addition, there is an optional, smaller diameter (14 inches) wheel with a thick, padded rim that is enough to make you

Text continued on page **100**
Specifications overleaf

ACCELERATION standing ¼ mile, seconds

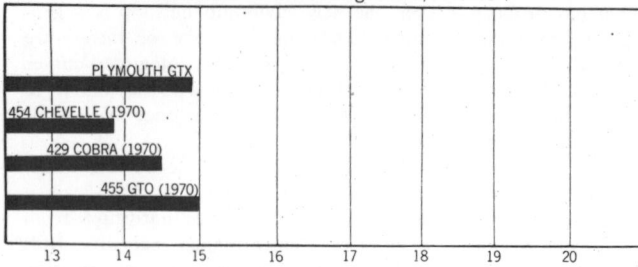

	13	14	15	16	17	18	19	20
PLYMOUTH GTX								
454 CHEVELLE (1970)								
429 COBRA (1970)								
455 GTO (1970)								

BRAKING 80-0 mph panic stop, feet

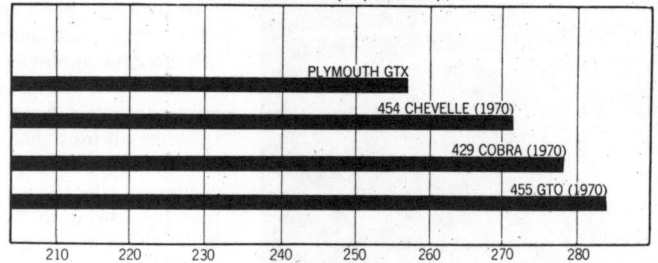

	210	220	230	240	250	260	270	280
PLYMOUTH GTX								
454 CHEVELLE (1970)								
429 COBRA (1970)								
455 GTO (1970)								

FUEL ECONOMY RANGE mpg

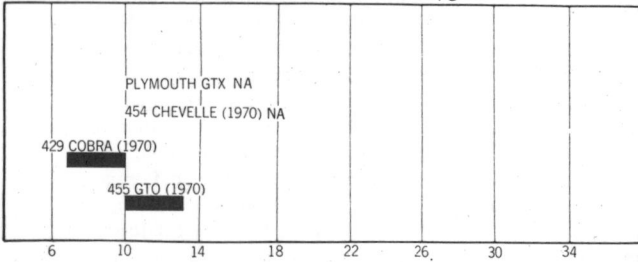

	6	10	14	18	22	26	30	34
PLYMOUTH GTX NA								
454 CHEVELLE (1970) NA								
429 COBRA (1970)								
455 GTO (1970)								

PRICE AS TESTED dollars x 1000

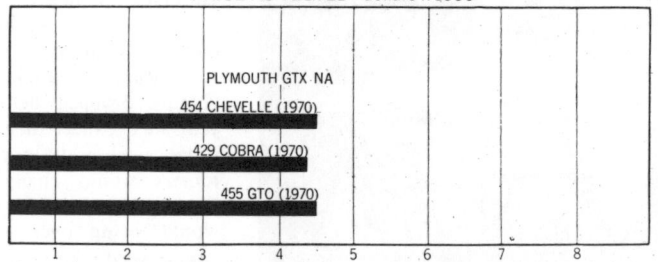

	1	2	3	4	5	6	7	8
PLYMOUTH GTX NA								
454 CHEVELLE (1970)								
429 COBRA (1970)								
455 GTO (1970)								

PLYMOUTH GTX

Manufacturer: Plymouth Division
Chrysler Corporation
Detroit, Michigan 48231

Vehicle type: Front engine, rear-wheel-drive, 5-passenger 2-door hardtop

Price as tested: $ N.A.
(Manufacturer's suggested retail price, including all options listed below, Federal excise tax, dealer preparation and delivery charges, does not include state and local taxes, license or freight charges)

Options on test car: Power steering, power disc brakes, automatic transmission, vinyl roof, special steering wheel, tachometer, console, styled wheels, G60-15 tires, luggage rack

ENGINE
Type: V-8, water-cooled, cast iron block and heads, 5 main bearings
Bore x stroke.4.31 x 3.75 in, 109.2 x 95.2 mm
Displacement.................440 cu in, 7200 cc
Compression ratio...................9.7 to one
Carburetion...............1 x 4-bbl Carter
Valve gear.Pushrod operated overhead valves, hydraulic lifters
Power (SAE)............370 bhp @ 4600 rpm
Torque (SAE)..........280 lbs/ft @ 3200 rpm

Specific power output........0.84 bhp/cu in, 51.5 bhp/liter
Max recommended engine speed...5500 rpm

DRIVE TRAIN
Transmission..............3-speed, Automatic
Max. torque converter.............2.02 to one
Final drive ratio.................3.23 to one

Gear	Ratio	Mph/1000 rpm	Max. test speed
I	2.45	9.6	53 mph (5500 rpm)
II	1.45	16.2	89 mph (5500 rpm)
III	1.00	23.5	110 mph (4700 rpm)

DIMENSIONS AND CAPACITIES
Wheelbase.........................115.0 in
Track, F/R......................60.1/62.0 in
Length............................203.2 in
Width..............................79.1 in
Height.............................53.0 in
Curb weight.......................4022 lbs
Weight distribution, F/R........54.0/46.0%
Battery capacity..........12 volts, 70 amp/hr
Alternator capacity................444 watts
Fuel capacity.....................21.0 gal
Oil capacity.......................4.0 qts
Water capacity....................15.5 qts

SUSPENSION
F: Ind., unequal length control arms, torsion bars, anti-sway bar
R: Rigid axle, semi-elliptic leaf springs

STEERING
Type..........Recirculating ball, power assist
Turns lock-to-lock.....................3.5
Turning circle curb-to-curb............40.6 ft

BRAKES
F:.........10.7-in. vented disc, power assist
R:.. 10.0 x 2.5-in. cast iron drum, power assist

WHEELS AND TIRES
Wheel size.........................15 x 7.0-in
Wheel type......Styled, stamped steel, 5-bolt
Tire make and size.........Goodyear G60-15
Tire type..........Fiberglass belted, tubeless
Test inflation pressures, F/R........28/28 psi
Tire load rating.....1620 lbs per tire @ 32 psi

PERFORMANCE
Zero to	Seconds
30 mph	2.3
40 mph	3.4
50 mph	4.8
60 mph	6.5
70 mph	8.5
80 mph	10.8
90 mph	13.5
100 mph	16.2

Standing ¼-mile.........14.9 sec @ 95.4 mph
Top speed (at redline)...............130 mph
80-0 mph.....................257 ft (0.83 G)
Fuel mileage.......N.A. mpg on premium fuel

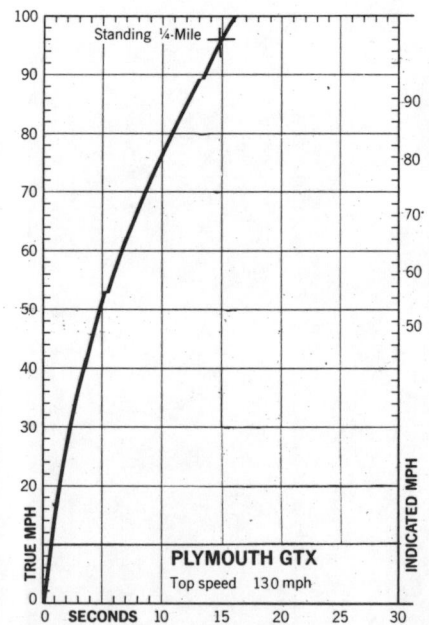

PLYMOUTH GTX
Top speed 130 mph

DODGE CHARGER SE

By far and away it's 1971's best styled new car

"Heigh ho, Lance. This is Rob. You know, *Rob*, I met you over at Samantha's during the Tactile Encounter session. I had on the purple Yves Saint Laurent jump suit and was sitting between that tacky copy of Oldenburg's "soft hamburger" and the dynamite Ernst Troler original. Right . . . right, we were rapping about the relevancy of Dusty and Marty Balsam's pivotal encounter in *Big Little* when she turned on the whale thing, right.

"Yea, well what I was calling about, really, was to see if you'd like to fall by my digs sometime this weekend. I just picked up on a dynamite, *really* dynamite new sculpture that I figure you'll be into, too, as soon as you see it.

"Right, *right on*, Tom Owen is going to go out of his gourd on this one.

"It's called 'Charger' and it's—are you ready for this?—it's made by Dodge.

"Hello? . . . Lance? . . ."

That's the way it goes nowadays, Rob old buddy. Had you said that *Playboy's* sculptor laureate, Frank Gallo created the Charger from ground-up polyurethane coffee cups, Lance would have been rattling your blue anodized aluminum doorknob instead of leaving you standing there in front of your Lucidity clear plastic phone with his curt *ciao* still searing across your eardrum.

A Dodge Charger? A piece of sculpture? What the hell kind of individual artistic statement can that be when

50,000 people a year make the same statement? Besides, you've got to admit that an *objet d'art* created by a guy with a name like Gallo, or Toler, or Quasar (who everybody knows works in a vital environment like Ibiza or Johnson's Pasture, or St. Tropez) has a bit more of a cachet than anything Bill Brownlie can slap together out of modeler's clay in gay, romantic Hamtramck, Michigan.

But that does not alter the fact that Brownlie and his
(Text continued on page 73; Specifications overleaf)

The new Dodge Charger SE proves that a marketing compromise need not result in a styling disaster

NATURAL OPOSSUM COAT PROVIDED BY GEORGES KAPLAN FURS

ACCELERATION standing ¼ mile, seconds

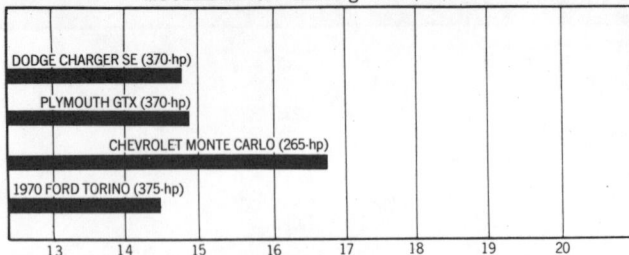

DODGE CHARGER SE (370-hp)
PLYMOUTH GTX (370-hp)
CHEVROLET MONTE CARLO (265-hp)
1970 FORD TORINO (375-hp)

13 14 15 16 17 18 19 20

BRAKING 80-0 mph panic stop, feet

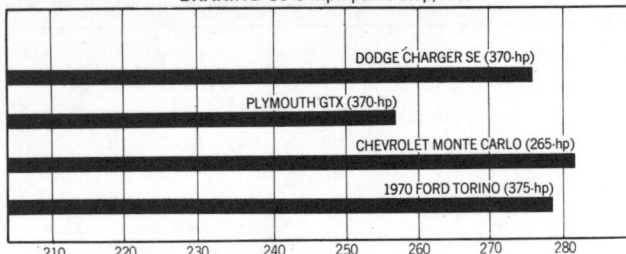

DODGE CHARGER SE (370-hp)
PLYMOUTH GTX (370-hp)
CHEVROLET MONTE CARLO (265-hp)
1970 FORD TORINO (375-hp)

210 220 230 240 250 260 270 280

FUEL ECONOMY RANGE mpg

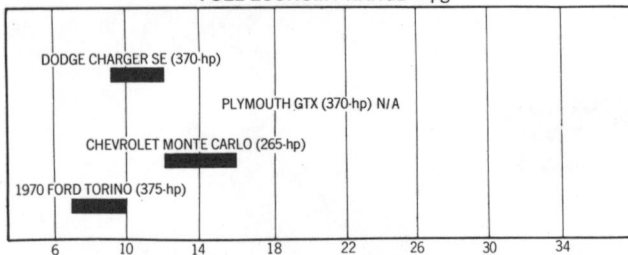

DODGE CHARGER SE (370-hp)
PLYMOUTH GTX (370-hp) N/A
CHEVROLET MONTE CARLO (265-hp)
1970 FORD TORINO (375-hp)

6 10 14 18 22 26 30 34

PRICE AS TESTED dollars x 1000

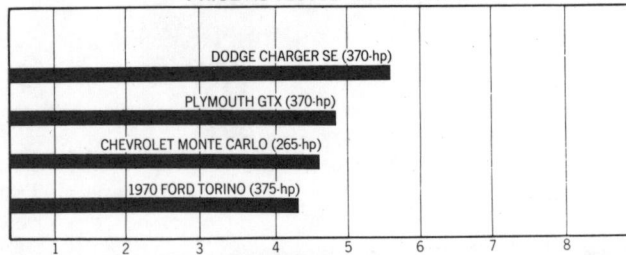

DODGE CHARGER SE (370-hp)
PLYMOUTH GTX (370-hp)
CHEVROLET MONTE CARLO (265-hp)
1970 FORD TORINO (375-hp)

1 2 3 4 5 6 7 8

Dodge Charger SE

Manufacturer: Dodge Division
Chrysler Corporation
Detroit, Michigan

Vehicle type: Front engine, rear-wheel-drive,
5-passenger 2-door Hard top

Price as tested: $5670.75

(Manufacturer's suggested retail price, including all options listed below, Federal excise tax, dealer preparation and delivery charges, does not include state and local taxes, license or freight charges)

Options on test car: Base car, $3422.00; leather bucket seats, $52.50; front disc brakes, $24.45; power brakes, $45.15; console, $57.65; 6-way adjustable seat, $35.00; automatic transmission, $237.50; limited-slip differential, $45.35; 440 4-bbl. V-8, $281.25; tinted windows, $43.40; right outside mirror, $11.75; remote control driver's outside mirror, $16.25; rear window defogger, $31.45; air conditioning, $388.00; headlight washer, $29.30; variable speed windshield wipers, $5.85; undercoating, $22.60; fender mounted turn signals, $11.60; time-delay headlights, $25.05; front and rear bumper guards, $33.70; engine block heater, $15.55; exhaust tips, $21.90; automatic speed control, $60.90; power windows, $121.75; AM/FM radio and stereo tape recorder, $366.40; microphone, $11.70; power steering, $116.25; special steering wheel, $30.50; wire wheel covers, $42.90; G70x14 tires, $63.10

ENGINE

Type: V-8, water-cooled, cast iron block and heads, 5 main bearings

Bore x stroke . . . . 4.31 x 3.75 in, 109.2 x 95.2 mm
Displacement . . . . 440 cu in, 7200 cc
Compression ratio . . . . 9.7 to one

Carburetion . . . . 1 x 4-bbl.
Valve gear . . . . Pushrod operated overhead valves
Power (SAE) . . . . . 370 bhp @4600 rpm Net (305 @4600)
Torque (SAE) . . 480 lbs/ft @ 3200 rpm Net (400 @ 3200)
Specific power output . . . . 0.84 bhp/cu in, 51.5 bhp/liter
Max recommended engine speed . . . . 5500 rpm

DRIVE TRAIN

Transmission . . . . 3-speed, auto-synchro
Max. torque converter . . . . 2.02 to one
Final drive ratio . . . . 3.23 to one

Gear	Ratio	Mph/1000rpm	Max. test speed
I	2.45	9.9	54 mph (5500 rpm)
II	1.45	16.6	91 mph (5500 rpm)
III	1.00	24.1	110 mph (4570 rpm)

DIMENSIONS AND CAPACITIES

Wheelbase . . . . 115.0 in
Track, F/R . . . . 59.7/62.0 in
Length . . . . 205.4 in
Width . . . . 79.1 in
Height . . . . 52.2 in
Ground clearance . . . . 4.7 in
Curb weight . . . . 4092 lbs
Weight distribution, F/R 58.5/41.5%
Battery capacity . . . . 12 volts, 70 amp/hr
Alternator capacity . . . . 444 watts
Fuel capacity . . . . 21.0 gal
Oil capacity . . . . 6.0 qts
Water capacity . . . . 15.5 qts

SUSPENSION

F: Independent unequal length control arm, torsion bars, anti-sway bar
R: Rigid axle, semi-elliptic leaf springs, anti-sway bar

STEERING

Type . . . . Recirculating ball, power assist
Turns lock-to-lock 3.5
Turning circle curb-to-curb . . . . 44.5 ft

BRAKES

F: . . . . 10.7 vented disc, power assist
R: . . . . 11.0 x 2.5-in. cast iron drum, power assist

WHEELS AND TIRES

Wheel size . . . . 14 x 6.0-in
Wheel type . . . . Stamped steel, 5-Bolt
Tire make and size . . . . Goodyear 670 x 14, Polyglas
Tire type . . . . Tubeless, Belted
Test inflation pressures, F/R . . . . 26/26 psi
Tire load rating . . . . 1620 lbs per tire @ 32 psi

PERFORMANCE

Zero to	Seconds
30 mph	2.3
40 mph	3.4
50 mph	4.8
60 mph	6.5
70 mph	8.5
80 mph	10.8
90 mph	13.5
100 mph	16.2

Standing ¼ -mile . . . . 14.8 sec @ 95.7 mph
Top speed (at redline) . . . . 133 mph
80-0 mph . . . . 276 ft (0.78 G)
Fuel mileage . . . . 9-12 mph on premium fuel
Cruising range . . . . 189-252 mi

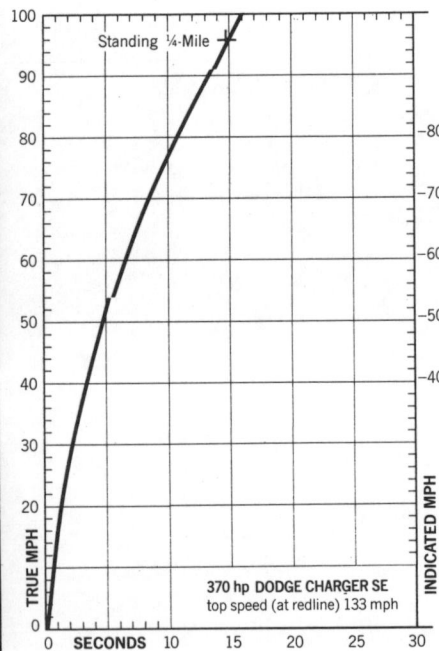

Standing ¼-Mile

370 hp DODGE CHARGER SE
top speed (at redline) 133 mph

TRUE MPH / SECONDS / INDICATED MPH

CONTINUED FROM PAGE 70

associates at Dodge have come up with the best-styled new car for 1971. Or that Dodge, not Georg Jensen, is selling it. Dodge? The company that gave the world such exquisite creations as the original Charger—a tribute to the ever-popular Rambler Marlin; the station wagon that has a rear silhouette like a drain culvert, and has pursued the evolution of the neo-DeSoto design school with the fervor that only graduates of such an academy could muster. But even before the '71 Charger there have been signs that someone in Dodge Division was doing more than mimicking whatever trend the GM Styling Center was into. The second generation Charger was the first significant departure. It was so far out of the Detroit styling mainstream that it remained unique throughout its three-year model run despite its public acceptance—which, in light of Detroit's copycat styling syndrome means it was radical. And, it turns out that Brownlie was also responsible for that car with its high, wide hipline and small tunnelroof greenhouse.

Subsequently, a corporate reorganization had Brownlie working for both Dodge and Plymouth and one can see the embryonic lines of this year's Charger taking shape with the 1970 Plymouth Barracuda and Dodge Challenger. And actually that experience probably proved most valuable as, for the first time this year, the Charger series of Dodge's intermediate line-up has lost its exclusivity. When you buy a 2-door Dodge intermediate it's automatically a Charger. No more separate sheetmetal as in the past when the Coronet was available as a 2-door and a 4-door in addition to the sportier-imaged Charger hardtops. What this new policy meant was that the stylists had to come out with a car that retained some of its sporting flair but was not wild enough to turn off middle-aged, middle of the road, middle Americans. In other words a compromise between a Charger/Pontiac Grand Prix/Chevrolet Monte Carlo-type car and a plain-jane business coupe or 2-door sedan. Incredibly, given these parameters, Dodge has pulled it off, and done so with élan. Meanwhile Dodge's sister division, Plymouth, attempting the same marketing gambit with its Sebring model (which uses the same basic under-the-skin hardware) ended up with a compromise that looks just that.

The Charger comes off as anything but a styling compromise. Not only is it apparent to people viewing the car from the outside but the driver is aware that he is controlling something far from normal as well.

From the driver's seat you find the front part of the Charger sloping down and away, giving the impression that there's a set of Honest Charley extended spring hangers jacking up the rear. The raked impression is also reinforced by the upward sweep of the sheetmetal at the roof's rear corners. It may make for great exterior styling but it does little for rear corner vision, leaving large blind spots that only the Charger's extreme tunnelroof predecessor outdid in recent memory. And although proper positioning of the inside rear view mirror has alleviated most of the visibility problem in normal driving conditions both driver and passenger-side outside mirrors should be considered mandatory options on the Charger.

One of the more enjoyable aspects of the third-generation Charger is its feeling of compactness. The wheelbase has been reduced by 2 inches and overall length by 3 inches, but in one of those curious juxtapositions of fact over feeling, a dimension which has actually grown, makes the car feel smaller. This is the width: the '71 Charger is over 2 inches wider than its im-

By Brownlie out of Hamtramck, Dodge's Special Edition Charger is, on styling alone a desirable car, and a wave of the option list will make it do handsomely, too.

mediate predecessor but you feel more secure. The older Charger with its narrow greenhouse and bulging side sheetmetal, made you feel that you were sitting in the middle of the car and you were never quite certain how much side clearance was required. The new styling, although physically wider, eliminates this feeling and also provides more hip and shoulder room for the driver and passengers.

The driving position has also been improved by repositioning of the steering-wheel. Previous Charger styling required that the driver sit low in the car, however the steering wheel was mounted relatively high in relation to the driver's arms. The result was an automotive equivalent of a Chopper seating position—an ape-hanger steering wheel if you will. Our Charger also came equipped with an optional small fat, leather covered steering wheel. We can certainly live without the breathless appellation—Dodge is calling it the "Tuff" steering wheel—but it represents a vast improvement over the standard version by offering the driver a firm, non-slip grip. However, just because you can buy a steering wheel that looks like it came out of a Formula One car, don't get carried away and start thinking of the Charger SE as a sports car.

Our test car was loaded down with nearly every option known to exist which caused this "intermediate" to weigh over two tons and resulted in a front to rear weight bias of 58.5/41.5%. Consequently it should come as little surprise that the Charger SE was victim of massive understeer. For normal expressway driving this presents no problem as the car will track beautifully, and is predictable to the extent of being boring. And for this type of driving the optional 370-hp 440 cu. in. engine performed effortlessly and was surprisingly responsive. But on New York National Speedway's extremely tight handling course the Charger was anything but graceful. It would plunge into turns with its front wheels on full lock but the rest of the car maintaining a stubborn desire to continue on its previous course. The wide G70 tires screamed in their painful attempt to change the car's direction—both front *and* rears as the fronts would be doing most of the work in altering course while the rears would be trying just the opposite—and for their effort they were also getting their outside tread shaved off because of a combination of body lean and insufficient wheelwell clearance.

Normally, this type of problem can be overcome by inducing power oversteer but with our test Charger this was hardly the solution because of the suddenness with which the secondaries would come in. One second your foot would be progressively applying more power via the primary barrels of the 4-bbl. carburetor, the next the floodgates were thrown wide-open and all hell broke loose. Most often the result was a spin—its suddenness and severity depending on what degree the tires were able to maintain traction through this surge. The reason for this problem probably lies in the fact that Dodge's engine development department is still having problems in adapting certain engines to smog-control equipment. This would seem to be reinforced by the fact that the recent 440 engines we've tested, particularly with automatic transmissions, have a tendency to "stumble" coming off idle, and will occasionally backflash through the carburetor under hard acceleration from low rpm.

And although our Charger SE came equipped with massive 10.7-in. vented front disc brakes and 11.0-in. drum rears, there was little to inspire confidence. The brake pedal had a spongy feel, which may have resulted from some flex in the system, making it hard to modulate, and during both the braking and handling portions of our test procedure we experienced brake fade and overheating. In fairness it should be mentioned that our test car had less than 1000 miles on it and the brakes may not have been broken in at that point. A similarly equipped Plymouth GTX we tested (*C/D*, November) did not have this problem.

While the Charger did not perform up to expectations in the extreme conditions we created during the track evaluation testing portion of our road test procedure, it came into its own in the over-the-road evaluations where it proved to be predictably competent and comfortable.

In this latter respect, the car had damn well better be comfortable! Take a good look at the specifications page—you'll discover that the Charger SE which sailed into our garage had a two-page window sticker telling why it should cost $5670.75. Attsa some expensive automotive sculpture you got there, art lover. For that money you'd figure that Brownlie or Dodge's General Manager Bob McCurry ought to sign each model of this Special Edition (that's what SE stands for, not super expensive). Things get a little more reasonable when you consider that you can get a 318 cu.in. V-8 Charger for a base price of $3422—if your life style will permit a depradation of things like a high-performance 440 cu.in. V-8, speed control power windows, paint strips, automatic headlight washers, wire wheel covers, leather upholstery that has been sprayed with color-coordinating paint to make it undetectable from genuine vinyl, or a vinyl "canopy" roof that has been embossed to look like real leather. The point is that all this trash is available and, in fact, dealer's love to have you check it off on the order form—some of them are even nice enough to check it off for you—because that's where the highest percentage of profit comes in. Which accounts for an "order to build" form that provides spaces for 220 different entries. *Car and Driver* has long been an advocate of special ordering any car you buy in preference to taking whatever is lying on the dealer's floor at the moment (no matter how friendly a price he'll let it go for), but when $3500 cars can easily come in with $2200 of whipped cream on top it's time to issue a warning. You damn well better cast a judicious eye over the order form and know exactly what you want and what you can afford beforehand because a slip of the pen is liable to win you a convertible top with a sunroof sewn in it. No questions asked, no excuses accepted.

For instance with the Charger SE, the base 318 V-8 just isn't going to provide the type of performance that any enthusiast will want. But going to a 440 in a car of this type comes close to cubic inch overkill, in between lies two versions of the 383—although inexplicably no 340 is presently available—which offer a proper level of performance and economy both in terms of fuel mileage and purchase price, and, with most companies, insurance classification.

In particular with this Charger it's difficult not to fill up every box in sight with a check mark. After all, if you want to make an individual artistic statement you can create it yourself through the option list. If 50,000 or 100,000 or 1,000,000 Chargers are built the combinations and permutations of possible options almost guarantees that yours will be unique. It's just a matter of how unique you can afford to be—and $2200 worth is a bit steep.

The Charger SE, on its styling alone is a desirable car. It has a completed look that has been sorely missing from many Detroit cars since the advent of making everything except the chassis and seats extra cost options. This even extends to the interior wherein the options look like they were custom designed for a particular model and not just universal parts that can be bolted into anything from a Demon to a Polara.

That this isn't a false impression is brought hope by the fact that the car feels and sounds solid. The theorem that "The greater the number of options, the greater the number of things to rattle and go thump in the night" just doesn't work with this car. Despite its taut ride quality, and a considerable amount of road harshness transmitted through the tires, the Charger SE was one of the quietest cars we've recently tested. The only rattles came from the cassette tape recorder which, coincidentally, was the only item that didn't look like it had been specifically designed for this car (being clumsily perched on the front console—an open invitation to theft). With a little self-will and discretion in the face of a sales form that makes the menu in the Russian Tea Room look barren—and unimaginative—you can come out with a spectacular looking American-style grand touring car for around $4000. Which is no bad price to pay for a combination of practicality and individuality these days. •

• Plymouth is raising the ante in the economy sedan ranks. It has been importing the Hillman Avenger (made by the Chrysler British subsidiary) into this country as the Plymouth Cricket, and selling it as a competitor to Chevy's Vega and Ford's Pinto. For some reason, its origins are being soft pedaled, making you think that in some vague way the car might have been hammered out in an anonymous small town in Michigan. Anyone who has driven one will not be deceived, for it is emphatically a *British* economy sedan.

This has some distinct advantages, not the least of which is a hotter version of the standard car. In England this is sold as a separate model called the Avenger GT, but since the primary difference is a second Stromberg carburetor for the engine, in America it will pass as merely a performance option for the base Cricket.

Plymouth Cricket

The added performance of the Twin Carb engine is scant compensation if it sounds like a 2-8-2 Mikado

---

This second carburetor raises the power rating up from the 55 hp of the standard version to 70 hp. Aside from the additional carburetor and attendant plumbing, the engine follows standard economy sedan tenets unchanged. It is a workmanlike cast iron Four of 1500cc, with overhead valves and mechanical lifters, and it is set into an equally conventional chassis. Built on a 98-inch wheelbase, the one-piece body and frame unit is suspended by MacPherson struts and coil springs with an anti-sway bar at the front, but gets by with a rigid axle, coil springs, and four trailing links at the back.

This classic suspension is not one of the car's better features. Primarily, it is ride quality that suffers. Over even the smallest pavement expansion joints, the front of the car comes crashing down, making a drop of two inches feel more like two feet. And the rear end does its part by cracking you at the base of the spine as it follows over the height. In normal driving, the Cricket understeers. Even at low speeds it is very definitely a follower, not a leader. And the quicker you go, the more it will rely on its front tires to do the work. If one is in the mood, the rear end can be broken away, and then it becomes a matter of steering with the throttle, and hoping the rear axle linkage will cooperate by keeping both tires on the road instead of lifting the inside rear. Our resident expert on Olde English Sporting Motorcars claims that the Cricket handles much like one of its sporting predecessors—the Sunbeam Alpine. In more contemporary terms, it is only average for an economy sedan—both sports cars and sedans have progressed that much in the intervening decade.

The addition of an extra carburetor also can be thought of as one step up from a strict economy car rather than an overt move to sportiness—much the same relationship, although different in execution, as a Pinto 1600 and a Pinto 2000. The additional carburetor makes the Cricket difficult to start and almost impossible to keep idling until up to its usual operating temperature. Drivability also suffers due to the effects of engine surge which makes smooth part-throttle driving a real test. And all the while, there is a Force 8 gale of noise all around. Interior sound level is 80.5 dbA at 70 mph, and a furious 88 dbA under acceleration. Part of the problem on our test car can be blamed on its air conditioning unit. In mounting the optional AC unit, the balance was shifted somewhat forward because of the extra weight hanging off the front of the engine. No compensating change in engine mount location or mount material was made however, and the changed center of gravity resulted in annoying harmonic imbalance—*loud* and annoying. From the outside, the Cricket with its Twin Carb engine sounds like a 2-8-2 Mikado laboring up hill, and on the inside, although reduced in volume and not hitting you at the same intensity, the noise is just as bothersome.

For all this audible effort, the Twin Carb Cricket accelerates through the quarter-mile in 19.2 seconds, which is, once again, in the middle group for economy sedans: faster than the Pinto 1600, slower than the Toyota Carina. But the Cricket feels quicker. A low first gear allows you to launch like a Junior Pro Stock, and second promises at least as much. Then, on the two-three shift, the tap is turned off. The long third gear is excellent for making it quickly through heavy traffic—not for acceleration runs. It is here, and in fourth, that the other small sedans will catch up again.

A good part of the Cricket's more-than-minimal feel for an enthusiast can be attributed to its quick-shifting transmission. It has to be one of the best around, with throws that are precise, light, and asking to be used. In fact, the driver controls as a group form a strong point on the Cricket. The transmission linkage, the clutch, the brake pedal and steering wheel all require only light effort, and are appropriately precise. The brakes (disc front, drum rear) proportion the stopping effort well, and maintaining directional stability is no problem in the Cricket. The stopping distances are also better than one might usually expect for this type of car, averaging only 180 ft. from 70 mph to 0 mph, with complete confidence.

An important part of any sedan, which by its very nature is intended as reasonable transportation for four, is the quality and convenience of the interior accommodations. In this area the Cricket proves very competitive, beginning with the fact that it is only available as a 4-door—a fact that many marketing savants point to as one of the prime factors in the Toyota Corona's original success in this market. And unlike many of its competitors, the Cricket's dashboard contains instrumentation that reveals a bit more than an after-the-fact disaster report. Included are a ribbon-type speedometer and four postage stamp-size gauges to monitor major mechanical functions. Except for night driving when they are feebly illuminated, all are readable, in spite of their small size. The important hand controls for lights, wipers and windshield washers, are incorporated into two large, purposeful-looking knobs set straddling the steering column at its base. We prefer column stalks that do not require reaching around the steering wheel to operate, but the Cricket's system is still far better than dashboard mounted knobs, and is very accessible. Also convenient are the large bins provided at the forward edge of each front door for storing the detritus of living. In addition, there is a tiny locking glove box to hold the owner's manual.

The Cricket's seating position is first rate, high and comfortable, with a nice reach to the wheel, the pedals and the shift

Specifications overleaf; Text continued on page **100**

75

ACCELERATION standing ¼ mile, seconds

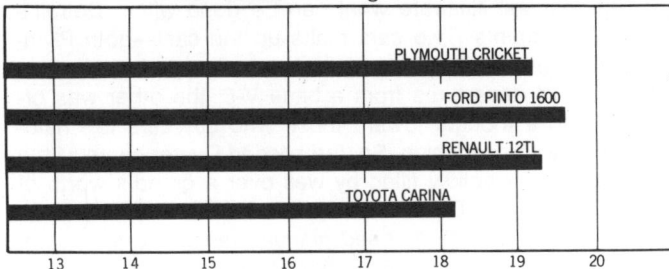

PLYMOUTH CRICKET	
FORD PINTO 1600	
RENAULT 12TL	
TOYOTA CARINA	

Scale: 13 14 15 16 17 18 19 20

BRAKING 70-0 mph panic stop, feet

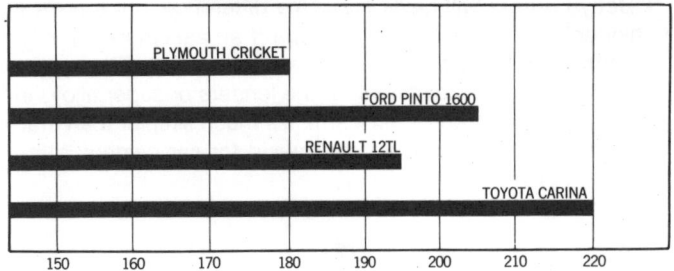

PLYMOUTH CRICKET	
FORD PINTO 1600	
RENAULT 12TL	
TOYOTA CARINA	

Scale: 150 160 170 180 190 200 210 220

FUEL ECONOMY RANGE mpg

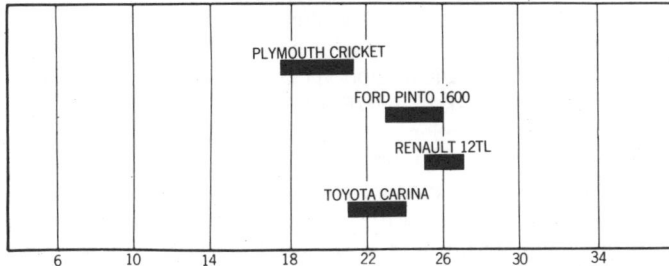

PLYMOUTH CRICKET	
FORD PINTO 1600	
RENAULT 12TL	
TOYOTA CARINA	

Scale: 6 10 14 18 22 26 30 34

PRICE AS TESTED dollars x 1000

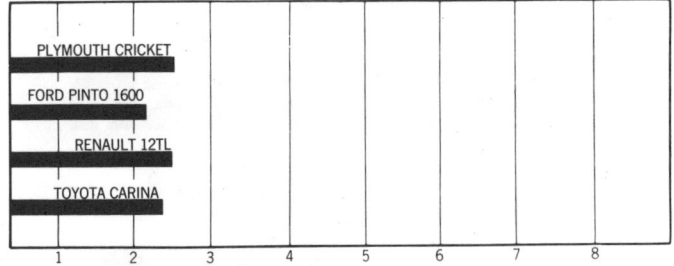

PLYMOUTH CRICKET	
FORD PINTO 1600	
RENAULT 12TL	
TOYOTA CARINA	

Scale: 1 2 3 4 5 6 7 8

Plymouth Cricket

Importer: Chrysler Motors Corporation
P. O. Box 857
Detroit, Michigan

Vehicle type: Front engine, rear-wheel-drive, 4-passenger 4-door sedan

Price as tested: $2526.75
(Manufacturer's suggested retail price, including all options listed below, dealer preparation and delivery charges, does not include state and local taxes, license or freight charges)

Options on test car: Base Plymouth Cricket, $2017.00; Air conditioning, $339.00; AM radio, $59.50; Decor group, $83.40; Whitewall tires, $27.85

ENGINE
Type: 4-in-line, water-cooled, cast iron block and head, 5 main bearings
Bore x stroke . . . . .3.39 x 2.53 in, 84.7 x 63.2 mm
Displacement. . . . . .91.4 cu in, 1500 cc
Compression ratio . . . . .8.5 to one
Carburetion .2 x 1-bbl Stromberg
Valve gear . . . . .Pushrod operated overhead valves, mechanical lifters
Power (SAE net) . . . . .70 bhp @ 5400 rpm
Torque (SAE net) . . . . .75 lb-ft @ 3750 rpm
Specific power output . . . . . . .0.77 bhp/cu in, 46.7 bhp/liter

DRIVE TRAIN
Transmission . . . . .4-speed, all-synchro
Final drive ratio . . . . .3.88 to one

Gear	Ratio	Mph/1000 rpm	Max. test speed
I	3.59	4.4	24 mph (5500 rpm)
II	2.20	7.1	39 mph (5500 rpm)
III	1.40	11.2	62 mph (5500 rpm)
IV	1.00	15.7	85 mph (5400 rpm)

DIMENSIONS AND CAPACITIES
Wheelbase . . . . .98.0 in
Track, F/R . . . . .50.8/51.1 in
Length . . . . .161.8 in
Width . . . . .62.5 in
Height . . . . .56.0 in
Ground clearance. . . . . .5.0 in
Curb weight. . . . . .2055 lbs
Weight distribution, F/R. 56.2/43.8%
Battery capacity . . . . .12 volts, 55 amp-hr
Alternator capacity . . . . .476 watts
Fuel capacity . . . . .10.8 gal
Oil capacity . . . . .5.0 qts
Water capacity . . . . .7.8 qts

SUSPENSION
F: Ind., MacPherson strut, coil springs, anti-sway bar
R: Rigid axle, four trailing links, coil springs

STEERING
Type . . . . .Rack and pinion
Turns lock-to-lock 3.7
Turning circle curb-to-curb . . . . .31.8 ft

BRAKES
F: . . . . .9.5-in disc, power assist
R: . . . . .8.0 x 1.5-in drum, power assist

WHEELS AND TIRES
Wheel size . . . . .4.5 x 13-in
Wheel type . . . . .Stamped steel, 4-bolt
Tire make and size . . . .Goodyear Custom G800, 155SR-13
Tire type . . . . .Radial ply, tubeless
Test inflation pressures, F/R . . . . .24/24 psi
Tire load rating. . . . . .950 lbs per tire @ 32 psi

PERFORMANCE
Zero to	Seconds
30 mph	3.6
40 mph	6.1
50 mph	9.2
60 mph	13.4
70 mph	19.7
80 mph	29.5

Standing ¼-mile . . . . .19.2 sec @ 69.2 mph
Top speed (observed) . . . . .85 mph
70-0 mph . . . . .180 ft (0.91 G)
Fuel mileage . . . . .17.5 - 21.5 mpg on 91-octane fuel
Cruising range . . . . .190 - 230 mi

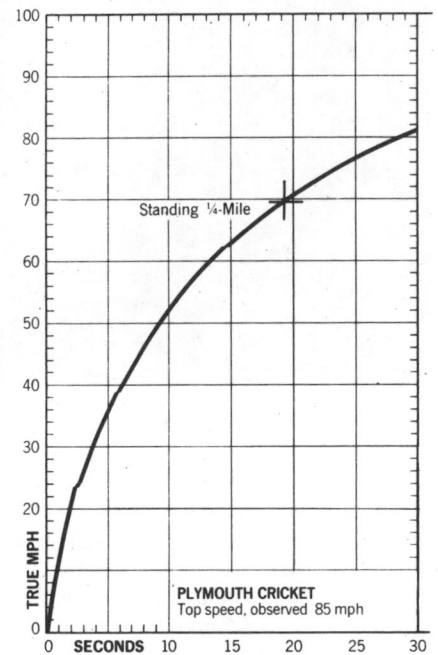

PLYMOUTH CRICKET
Top speed, observed 85 mph

Standing ¼-Mile

TRUE MPH / SECONDS

• Betty Furness will never know the difference, but there's a "hidden" value in every car to pop off an assembly line programmed by Detroit. But it's not what you think. Those who would guess a thicker gauge for the fenders or super alloys in the crankshafts aren't even warm. It's much simpler than that. Detroit's contribution to a better world for car owners is the lengthy options sheet.

Plymouth Duster 318 vs 340

An example of what can happen to a single model through some sleight of hand with an option list

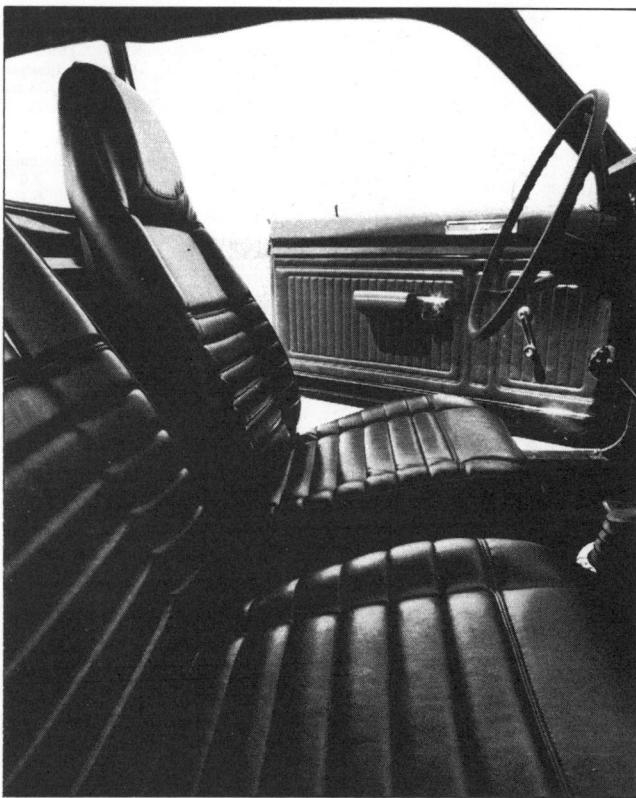

This magic piece of paper has long fostered a situation in which everyone wins. For the knowledgeable car buyer, it's like a grocery store. Every option is on the shelf, all properly engineered and ready for business—but only items the shopper selects will cost him money. The dealer benefits from a greater wholesale discount for optional equipment, so he has every incentive to help you with the check marks. The manufacturer can't go wrong either because he can effectively tender a multitude of models, all based on a single shell.

This test will illustrate what can be done within Detroit's broad constraints. Two cars make up the cast—both Plymouth Dusters. One of them is a low-budget stripper with a minimum of departures from a base V-8; the other was ordered with a thought toward those who buy cars like hamburgers—with everything. So, the second Duster came with a window sticker solidly filled by well over a grand's worth of options. The first Duster is stark—low cost simplicity—with the 318 2-barrel V-8, 3-speed manual transmission . . . not even a radio to seduce its critics. The second is the most expensive Duster model, the 340, which includes a heavy duty prefix before many chassis items, in conjunction with the most responsive engine Chrysler has to offer. Added to that are a Torqueflite transmission, air conditioning, power steering, power disc brakes, AM/FM radio and a host of convenience and decor options to blast the Duster's low-buck conception right into the $4200 range.

These two cars represent the extremes of a car line that Chrysler is most happy with. The Duster was hewn out of the straight-laced Valiant and arrived in 1970 with a more contemporary coupe body and swing-out rear windows. Economy was the central theme and the new package received a glowing reception from those with a firm grip on their wallets. Even today, all Dusters respectfully display the Valiant insignia and, in no small part because of that, the Valiant has become the best selling single nameplate within the Chrysler Corporation. If you add in the Dodge counterparts with Dart and Demon labels, you're talking about a combined total responsible for 34% of Chrysler's entire sales volume.

In spite of the fact that Chrysler's compact car assembly plants must run overtime to meet the demand, the Duster is not the perfect car that the sales volume suggests. For one thing, the steering column is much too high and close to the chest, pressing the driver into a Praying Mantis position. The stylists' attempts to smooth the boxy Valiant lines with a fastback roofline have destroyed the old sedan's rear seat head room and, with bucket seats, you have nothing more than a four passenger interior. But the base V-8 Duster sport coupe at $2407 is a logical alternative to an import, when you consider it takes $2399 to get serious about a VW Fastback, $2435 for a Toyota Corona, $2529 for an Opel 1900 Sport Coupe and $2528 for a 2-liter Capri. Such a low base is hard to argue with, and Plymouth has found it most effective in sending their showroom traffic out the door with time payments.

But the price leader is simply an invitation to select the real car. Once you've made that first check mark promising to buy the shell—the empty Duster—you've gained a free run of the options sheet and access to a computer's memory bank full of equipment codes. That's the beauty of it all when you do business the Detroit way.

All those with a Silas Marner complex will soon notice that there exists an even cheaper Duster than we've acknowledged. It's the 6-cylinder version, the lowest price car Chrysler builds in the U.S. at $2287. But that model is best left to those who would rather hoard money than enjoy their cars. The slant six will offer meager fuel economy advantages for those patient enough to endure its gentle acceleration and omnipresent noise. The $120 difference between the 198 cu. in. Six and 318 cu. in. V-8 not only buys 50 additional net horsepower, but also more capacity in the alternator, clutch, transmission, rear axle and brakes. The skinny 6.45-14 tires of the six are upgraded to 6.95-14s and the V-8 cars also get stiffer front torsion bars. Without a doubt it's the most important $120 you could spend on a Duster and you'll get every

nickel back when you sell the car.

With that base 318 V-8, the torque peak lies at a low 1600 rpm. It is the very model of a low speed engine and revs above 4500 rpm will level off in terminal emphysema due to the 2-barrel carburetor and single exhaust system. Such a Duster will clear the quarter mile in 16.4 seconds at 85.5 mph, and while that will put you yards ahead of any Super Coupe, the Duster 318 belongs in the parking lot when there is any real competition going on.

Those really serious about straight line acceleration will consider the optional 340 engine and nothing else. That check mark will up the ante by $321 over the 318, but once again, more than the engine is included. Above and beyond the equipment standard with the Duster 318 you'll get a heavy duty suspension with stiffer torsion bars and rear springs, as well as a front anti-sway bar and firmer shock absorbers. Dual exhausts and a viscous-drive fan are also part of the scheme with the more powerful engine and Goodyear bias-belted

E70-14 tires on 5.5-inch wheel rims (wider by 1.0 inch) will help in delivering all that good stuff to the ground. A smooth floor shifter is also standard for the 3-speed all-synchro transmission if you select the 340 package.

The test Duster 340's performance was hampered by its load of options, the most significant of which was the 115 lb. penalty of the air conditioner. The time slips read 15.6 seconds at 89.5 mph, but selecting the 4-speed transmission and 3.55 Suregrip differential, and deleting the A/C would yield a clearly faster car. Thirteen second Dusters are a thing of the past however, since the 340 has been emasculated with an 8.5 to one compression ratio as well as cylinder heads and exhaust manifolds borrowed from Chrysler's low performance 360 engine. Since fuel economy goes hand in hand with high compression, you can expect mileage to descend into the dismal range of 10 to 12 mpg. with the 340 option, making the

318 option look like a veritable miser by comparison.

Unfortunately, very few realize that the power has gone away . . . including the Insurance Services Office which has branded the Duster 340 an Intermediate Performance Car. Their recommendations specify higher insurance premiums based purely on what they consider the higher risk nature of the car. This means a 30% penalty over a Duster 318 for Bodily Injury and Property Damage, a 62% penalty for Comprehensive coverage and a 53% penalty for Collision insurance. If you add factors like a poor violation record and "youthful" drivers, your insurance agent will be ecstatic while running out about three yards of single spaced adding machine tape to accommodate all the surcharges.

And now for the good news: Many of the performance pieces can be ordered without the 340 engine—if you fear the wrath of the insurance magistrates. The heavy duty suspension is almost free at $13, and the 5.5-inch wheels come automatically with the E70-14 bias-belted tires for $56. On the skidpad, that combination was worth .66G lateral acceleration in the Duster 340 as compared with .62G with the skinny-tired, softly sprung Duster 318. The real advantage is more dramatic, however. The 318 test car sets up a list angle while cornering that would disorient a stunt pilot, while the 340 corners in a relatively flat, controlled attitude that is distinctly more comfortable to the occupants. With the wide tires and heavy duty suspension you get rapid responses from a machine that promises to deliver all it has. There is no such willingness with the 318's standard suspension. A limp response follows every control movement and if the demands are too rapid or too severe, the system simply goes on strike, delaying all requests from the driver.

The ride in the 340 Duster was slightly harsher, primarily due to the stiffer tires, but that should in no way prejudice your thoughts against the heavy duty suspension—it's an essential. If you choose Chrysler's all-synchro 3-speed transmission behind any engine other than the 340, you have to pay an extra $24 for the floor shifter, but it provides such a positive link to the gear box that you'll never lust for a Hurst replacement. The linkage is rattle-free and stout enough for Deacon Jones. Unfortunately, the product planners have failed to offer the 4-speed transmission without the 340 engine, but they

With the standard suspension: an unnerving list angle

> Detroit builds the shell—it's
> up to you to build the kind of car that
> suits you from their options sheet

With the S13 option: more composure in cornering

will allow you to select their Torqueflite automatic for $185.

With any combination there are some essentials you'll need to bolster the car's all around performance. Power disc brakes ($62) are a must to eliminate the erratic and unpredictable nature of the Duster's all drum system. The standard brakes invariably insisted on locking one wheel before the others and some tire grinding was essential before all the wheels would seriously contribute to halting the car. Stopping distances were shorter with the disc-braked Duster, but they were hampered by early locking rear wheels. It's the lesser of two evils however, because the system was always completely predictable, with brake pedal effort and travel greatly reduced by the use of a vacuum booster.

Of the two Dusters, only the 340 had the optional power steering ($92), and without this assist a Duster approaches the steering responsiveness of an ocean liner. That was the unfortunate case with the 318, as 5.7 turns of the wheel were required from lock-to-lock as compared to 3.3 turns with the power assist. Without a doubt the manual steering must be rated L for Languid audiences.

That group will likely contain a majority of the 6-cylinder Duster buyers. Even they cannot afford to bypass larger tires because the standard 6.45-14 tires' only virtue, aside from being rim protectors, is that the spare doesn't take up much room in the trunk. The 6.95-14 bias-ply tires are the first step up at $12. Even better are the D78-14 bias-belted tires at $50 ($37 for the Duster 318). They should be the most cost effective of all if you consider their better wearing characteristics. The ride may be slightly harsher, but you can expect sizable cornering and braking advantages as well as a greater margin of safety with heavy loads. The top of the line is the E70-14 option at $68 for 6-cylinder models and $56 for the Duster 318. However, there will be a substantial contribution to ride harshness and road noise from these tires and they will most likely not wear any better than the D78s. Raised white letters or white sidewalls are yours for $26 to $37.

For adverse driving conditions a Suregrip differential ($41) will be equally as important as tires. This device will route power through both rear wheels and will keep the car moving even though one side has little traction.

Once the chassis is under control with the correct options, it takes only a few more check marks to insure a livable interior. The Duster's standard bench seat is fine for Drive-ins, but as soon as any motion is involved, the bucket seat option ($120) demonstrates its merit. The advantage is better location and support of the driver. And while the Duster bucket is no competition seat, any restraint is better than none . . . which is what the bench offers. The buckets are also individually adjustable fore and aft and their tall vinyl-covered backs impart a purposeful aura to the whole interior. The "Tuff" steering wheel will continue that action theme with a rim much smaller in diameter than the standard wheel. It's the latest attempt at simulating 20-grand Italian hand-built elegance in a dimestore car. Your hands touch what seems to be a supple padded-leather rim, complete with hand stitching, lightened spokes and a large black hub. It's all yours through the magic of smooth-skin vinyl molding for only $28.

Still, many will object to the stark frugality that dominates the Duster's interior. Carpeting comes with the bucket seat option or you can get it in the Interior Decor group for $36. That package will put woodgrain on your instrument panel and doors, as well as arm rests with ash trays in the back seat. The Interior Convenience group ($18 with the 340; $22 without) contains a lock for the glove box door, a cigar lighter,

Text continued on page 83; Specifications overleaf

ACCELERATION standing ¼ mile, seconds

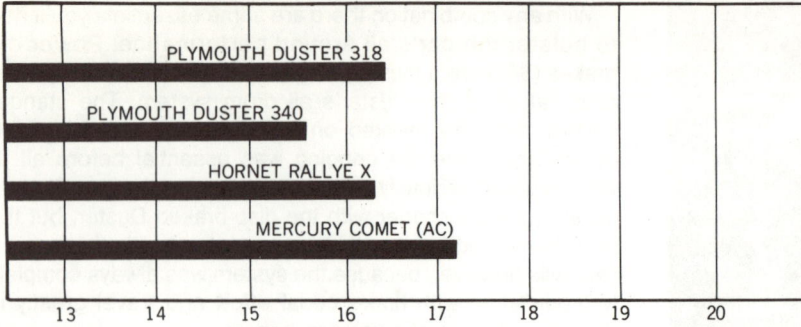

PLYMOUTH DUSTER 318	
PLYMOUTH DUSTER 340	
HORNET RALLYE X	
MERCURY COMET (AC)	

13 14 15 16 17 18 19 20

FUEL ECONOMY RANGE mpg

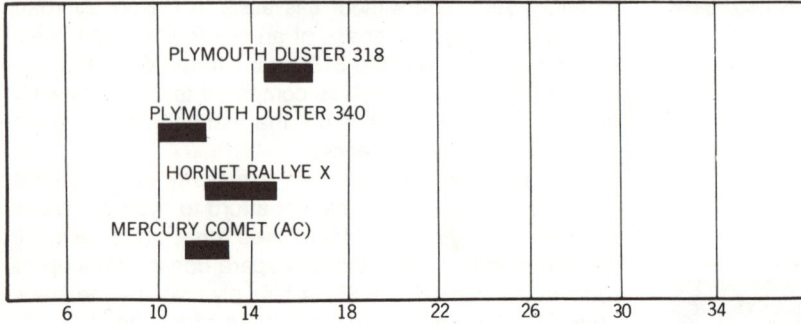

PLYMOUTH DUSTER 318	
PLYMOUTH DUSTER 340	
HORNET RALLYE X	
MERCURY COMET (AC)	

6 10 14 18 22 26 30 34

BRAKING 70-0 mph panic stop, feet

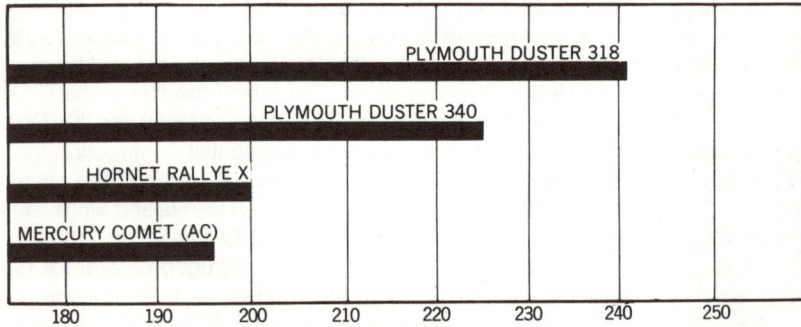

PLYMOUTH DUSTER 318	
PLYMOUTH DUSTER 340	
HORNET RALLYE X	
MERCURY COMET (AC)	

180 190 200 210 220 230 240 250

PRICE AS TESTED dollars x 1000

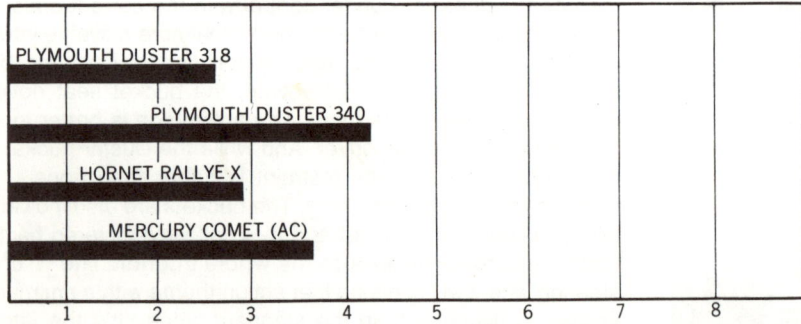

PLYMOUTH DUSTER 318	
PLYMOUTH DUSTER 340	
HORNET RALLYE X	
MERCURY COMET (AC)	

1 2 3 4 5 6 7 8

INTERIOR SOUND LEVEL, dbA

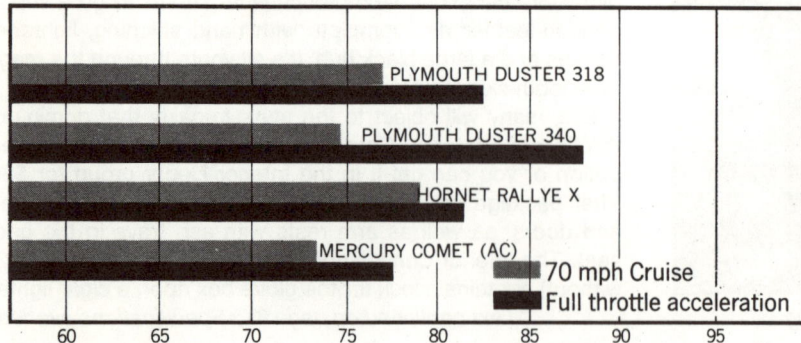

PLYMOUTH DUSTER 318	
PLYMOUTH DUSTER 340	
HORNET RALLYE X	
MERCURY COMET (AC)	

■ 70 mph Cruise
■ Full throttle acceleration

60 65 70 75 80 85 90 95

PLYMOUTH DUSTER 318

Manufacturer: Chrysler-Plymouth Division
Chrysler Motors Corporation
Detroit, Michigan 48231

Vehicle type: Front engine, rear-wheel-drive, 5-passenger coupe

Price as tested: $2628.50
(Manufacturer's suggested retail price, including all options listed below, dealer preparation and delivery charges, does not include state and local taxes, license or freight charges)

Options on test car: Base Duster 318, $2407.00; 3-speed floor shift, $24.35; 6.95-14 white sidewall tires, $38.50; Bucket seats, $120.25; Vinyl side moldings, $13.90; Deluxe wheel covers, $24.50.

ENGINE
Type: V-8 water-cooled, cast iron block and heads, 5 main bearings
Bore x stroke . . . . .3.91 x 3.31 in, 99.3 x 84.0mm
Displacement. . . . . .318 cu in, 5210cc
Compression ratio . . . . .8.6 to one
Carburetion . . . . .1 x 2-bbl Carter
Valve gear. . . . .Pushrod-operated overhead valves, hydraulic lifters
Power (SAE net) . . . . .150 bhp @ 4000 rpm
Torque (SAE net) . . . . .260 lb-ft @ 1600 rpm
Specific power output . . . . . . .0.47 bhp/cu in, 38.8 bhp/liter

DRIVE TRAIN
Transmission . . . . .3-speed, all-synchro
Final drive ratio . . . . .2.76 to one

Gear	Ratio	Mph/1000rpm	Max. test speed
I	3.08	8.7	39 mph (4500 rpm)
II	1.70	15.8	71 mph (4500 rpm)
III	1.00	26.9	110 mph (4100 rpm)

DIMENSIONS AND CAPACITIES
Wheelbase . . . . .108.0 in
Track, F/R . . . . .57.1/55.6 in
Length . . . . .188.4 in
Width . . . . .71.0 in
Height . . . . .53.1 in
Ground clearance. . . . . .5.8 in
Curb weight. . . . . .3055 lbs
Weight distribution, F/R 54.5/45.5%
Battery capacity . . . . .12 volts, 46 amp-hr
Alternator capacity . . . . .574 watts
Fuel capacity . . . . .16.0 gal
Oil capacity . . . . .5.0 qts
Water capacity . . . . .16.0 qts

SUSPENSION
F: Ind., unequal-length control arms, torsion bars
R: Rigid axle, semi-elliptic leaf springs

STEERING
Type . . . . .Recirculating ball
Turns lock-to-lock 5.7
Turning circle curb-to-curb . . . . .37.6 ft

BRAKES
F: . . . . .2.25 x 10.0-in cast iron drum
R: . . . . .1.75 x 10.0-in cast iron drum

WHEELS AND TIRES
Wheel size . . . . .4.5 x 14-in
Wheel type . . . . .Stamped steel, 5-bolt
Tire make and size . . . . . .Goodyear Power Cushion, 6.95-14
Tire type . . . . .Tubeless, bias-ply
Test inflation pressures, F/R . . . . .26/26 psi
Tire load rating . . . . .1230 lbs per tire @ 32 psi

PERFORMANCE

Zero to	Seconds
30 mph	2.9
40 mph	4.5
50 mph	6.2
60 mph	8.3
70 mph	10.8
80 mph	14.3
90 mph	19.0
100 mph	28.2

Standing ¼-mile . . . . .16.4 sec @ 85.5 mph
Top speed (observed) . . . . .110 mph
70-0 mph. .241 ft (0.68 G)
Fuel mileage . . . . .14.5-16.5 mpg on 91-octane fuel
Cruising range . . . . .230-260 mi

PLYMOUTH DUSTER 340

Manufacturer: Chrysler-Plymouth Division
Chrysler Motors Corp.
Detroit, Michigan 48231

Vehicle type: Front engine, rear-wheel-drive, 5-passenger coupe

Price as tested: $4213.70
(Manufacturer's suggested retail price, including all options listed below, dealer preparation and delivery charges, does not include state and local taxes, license or freight charges)

Options on test car: Base Duster 340, $2728.00; Torque-flite transmission, $208.40; Power disc brakes, $62.30; Power steering, $92.95; Suregrip differential, $40.65; Air conditioning, $353.80; Bucket seats, $120.25; Rallye road wheels, $52.80; E70-14 raised white letter tires, $37.20; Electronic ignition, $30.75; AM/FM radio, $124.55; Light package, $28.80; Custom exterior package, $19.90; Interior convenience group, $18.45; Interior decor group, $36.15; Rear seat speaker, $13.45; Tuff steering wheel, $28.00; Inside hood release, $9.50; Console, $51.00; Rear window defogger, $26.55; Undercoating, $20.25; Tinted glass, $35.85; Color-keyed racing mirrors, $13.50; Bumper guards, $24.20; Side tape stripes, $24.80; Lower deck tape stripes, $12.35.

ENGINE
Type: V-8 water-cooled, cast iron block and heads, 5 main bearings
Bore x stroke .... 4.04 x 3.31 in 102.5 x 84.0mm
Displacement .... 340 cu in, 5570cc
Compression ratio .... 8.5 to one
Carburetion .... 1 x 4-bbl Carter
Valve gear ..... Pushrod-operated overhead valves, hydraulic lifters
Power (SAE net) .... 240 bhp @ 4800 rpm
Torque (SAE net) .... 290 lb-ft @ 3600 rpm
Specific power output .... 0.71 bhp/cu in, 43.1 bhp/liter

DRIVE TRAIN
Transmission .... 3-speed, automatic
Max Torque converter .... 2.16 to one
Final drive ratio .... 3.23 to one

Gear	Ratio	Mph/1000 rpm	Max. test speed
I	2.45	9.3	48 mph (5200 rpm)
II	1.45	15.7	82 mph (5200 rpm)
III	1.00	22.8	118 mph (5150 rpm)

DIMENSIONS AND CAPACITIES
Wheelbase .... 108.0 in
Track, F/R .... 57.5/55.6 in
Length .... 188.4 in
Width .... 71.0 in
Height .... 53.1 in
Ground clearance .... 5.8 in
Curb weight .... 3445 lbs
Weight distribution, F/R 57.7/42.3%
Battery capacity .... 12 volts, 46 amp-hr
Alternator capacity .... 574 watts
Fuel capacity .... 16.0 gal
Oil capacity .... 5.0 qts
Water capacity .... 15.0 qts

SUSPENSION
F: Ind., unequal-length control arms, anti-sway bar
R: Rigid axle, semi-elliptic leaf springs

STEERING
Type .... Recirculating ball, power assist
Turns lock-to-lock 3.3
Turning circle curb-to-curb .... 37.6 ft

BRAKES
F: .... 10.8-in vented disc, power assist
R: .... 1.75 x 10.0-in cast iron drum, power assist

WHEELS AND TIRES
Wheel size .... 5.5 x 14-in
Wheel type .... Styled, stamped steel, 5-bolt
Tire make and size .... Goodyear Polyglass E70-14
Tire type .... Tubeless, bias-belted
Test inflation pressures, F/R .... 24/24 psi
Tire load rating .... 1400 lbs per tire @ 32 psi

PERFORMANCE

Zero to	Seconds
30 mph	2.7
40 mph	3.8
50 mph	5.4
60 mph	7.3
70 mph	9.4
80 mph	12.0
90 mph	15.7
100 mph	21.3

Standing ¼-mile .... 15.6 sec @ 89.5 mph
Top speed (observed) .... 118 mph
70-0 mph .... 225 ft (0.73 G)
Fuel mileage .... 10.0-12.0 mpg on 91-octane fuel
Cruising range .... 160-192 mi

dual horns and a deluxe steering wheel with three horn buttons near the rim, instead of one center button. That option lowers the "Tuff" steering wheel price by $10. An AM radio comes with the Basic group ($113), as well as 3-speed electric wipers, remote control outside mirror, day/night inside mirror and wheel covers. For an additional $65 you can have AM/FM with the Basic group or for $125 without.

Perhaps the best way to amaze your friends and neighbors is to order the Light Package for $29. The glowing halo of light around the ignition switch is worth the price by itself. It goes on as soon as you open the door so that you won't have to fumble around in the dark looking for the ignition. After you've had enough time to get the key in and orient yourself, it magically switches off. It's accompanied by lights for the trunk, ash tray and glove box, as well as a map and courtesy light. The package also includes turn signal indicators mounted on top of the front fenders.

If you can stand the $354 price tag more easily than a hot summer, air conditioning is the only way to be sure of a livable interior when the heat's on. It's not available with the 198 cu.in. six or if you specify a manual transmission with the 318. You'll be adding weight to the front wheels and diminishing fuel economy by roughly two miles per gallon but there's no other way to keep cool.

You can upgrade the Duster on the outside as well. The Rallye Road wheels ($52.80) will surpass any hubcap you could dream of in appearance and heighten the styling impact of whatever fat tires you may choose. The Custom Exterior package ($44 without the 340, $20 with) contains nothing more than shiny moldings for the roof drip rails, wheel openings and the door sills, as well as a tape stripe around the taillights. If that is your predilection, you'll love the Twister package which contains everything in the Custom Exterior package plus tape stripes for the body sides, a black paint treatment for the hood, dual racing mirrors, and for the final coordinated touch, a Twister decal for the decklid. If that $98 worth of geegaws doesn't get you the police recognition you obviously desire, you'll have to resort to fire burnouts in front of the station. But the crowning exterior group is known everywhere as the Gold Duster package. It features a vinyl roof that suggests a shortage of material in the assembly plant. Since it overlays only a part of the roof, they call it a canopy cov-

ering. It is accompanied on the inside by bench seats with pleated vinyl trim and carpeting. Larger (on 6-cylinder models) 6.95-14 white side wall tires appear on the outside with 5.5-inch wheels. The wider wheels are a must for the Turbo-flash wheel covers pirated from Satellite models. For your $115 ($127 with a 6-cylinder engine), the exterior will also be enhanced by a gold tape treatment on the lower deck and a genuine Gold Duster decal. Be the first on your block.

Now that the Duster's secrets are unveiled, you can take the basic game plan and apply it to any Ford, GM or AMC shell that strikes your fancy. Certainly Mavericks, Comets, Novas and Hornets are direct Duster equivalents. A cooperative dealer will supply the options list with prices and a key to the meaning of some of the less obvious codes. Then it's a simple matter of checking the boxes and a brief period of anticipation before the computer will transform your wishes into four-wheeled reality. ●

83

Road Test
DODGE COLT GT

A smooth and thorough blending of the small-car philosophies of Tokyo
and Detroit is unlikely to produce too many surprises

• The Dodge Colt is one foreign car that is well on its way to becoming a domestic. For the moment at least, Dodge is completely open about the Colt's Japanese origin; in fact, it seems to be the keynote of its current advertising theme. But to customers wandering through showrooms stuffed with Darts and Coronets, the Colt hardly seems alien. It could be made in Newark for all you can tell by looking. Or in Hamtramck. Or at least no farther west than, say, Torrance. The same holds true for all you can tell from driving it.

The real point about the new Colt is this: Of all the Datsun-Toyota-Subaru collection, it is the *least* Japanese in nature. Which is more of a clue to its personality than to its goodness or badness.

In design, the Colt is in no way revolutionary; it is not an automotive breakthrough on any front. If it is remarkable for anything at all, it would be for its marriage of bad traits from both Japan and Detroit. Yet despite this rather negative introduction, we think that the Colt is one of the most satisfying cars of its type. It has a feeling of familiarity to it, like we'd grown up with it, (an unmistakable Detroit flavor), and we find ourselves prepared to overlook some of its faults just as we would those of an old friend.

To start with the basics, we should enter into the record that Colts come in five models including a 4-door sedan, a 4-door station wagon, a 2-door coupe, a 2-door hardtop and a GT ... which is a 2-door hardtop with 5.0-inch (instead of 4.5) wheels, Skunk Stripe interior and a lot of exterior badges which say "GT." It is also the subject of this test.

The next thing you should know is that nothing is "GT" about the GT except for what you have just read. Nothing else is either stated or implied. So when it comes to choosing engines and gearboxes from the options menu, the GT

has no more privileges than the station wagon or the 4-door. Standard equipment is the carry-over 1600cc, 4-cylinder Hemi with a 4-speed gearbox and a 3.89 axle ratio. If you want an automatic, then you get a new 2.0-liter Hemi and a 3.55 axle, but you cannot have the 2.0-liter engine with a 4-speed. It reminds us of 1955 when the additional money for an automatic also got you a piece of chrome script on the deck that said something like "Flite-o-matic" or "Hy Drive" and a half-dozen extra horses under the hood to help you keep up with those cheapskates and their "straight sticks." Dodge's current rationale goes like this: "The 2.0-liter is a new engine this year and the plant does not have enough production volume to satisfy demand. For performance, it's the auto-

matic cars which need the most help. So they get the big motor."

Mitsubishi, the company that builds Colts in Japan, has been tooling up more than just a new engine for the 1974 model year. It has stamped out a new body as well—longer, lower and wider according to traditional Detroit practice. Taken altogether, it's very much like that of the old Colt but fatter

and sleeker, more Tina Russell and less Twiggy. And inevitably, more like those other American machines in Dodge's showroom. When you get right down to dimensions, both the '73 and '74 models have the same wheelbase. The '74s have 2.2 inches more width, 11.6 more length (mostly bumpers), a slightly wider track and about an extra 100 pounds of weight. Mechanically the new model is

84

ACCELERATION standing ¼ mile, seconds

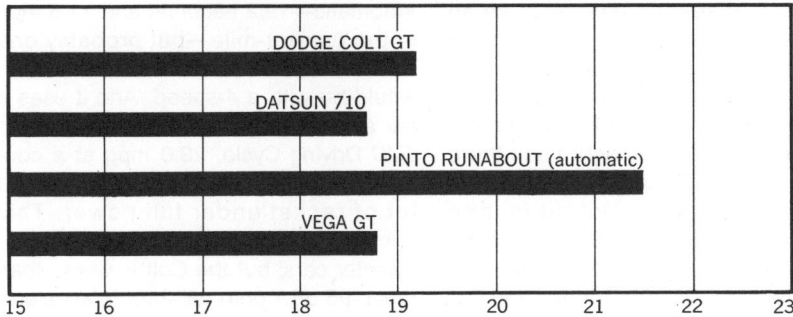

DODGE COLT GT
DATSUN 710
PINTO RUNABOUT (automatic)
VEGA GT

15 16 17 18 19 20 21 22 23

BRAKING 70-0 mph, feet

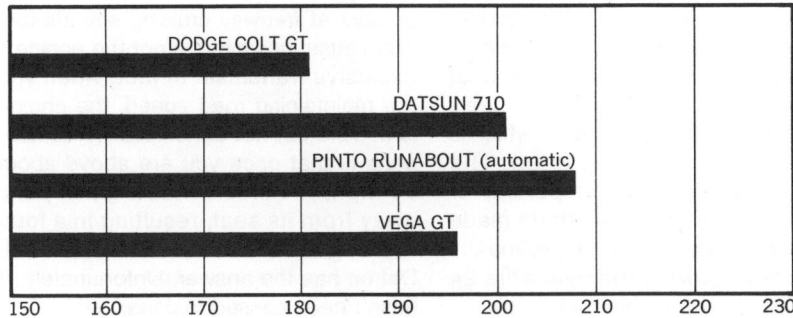

DODGE COLT GT
DATSUN 710
PINTO RUNABOUT (automatic)
VEGA GT

150 160 170 180 190 200 210 220 230

FUEL ECONOMY RANGE mpg

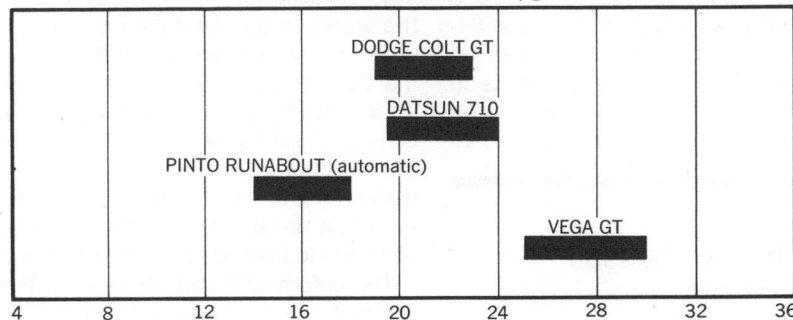

DODGE COLT GT
DATSUN 710
PINTO RUNABOUT (automatic)
VEGA GT

4 8 12 16 20 24 28 32 36

PRICE AS TESTED dollars x 1000

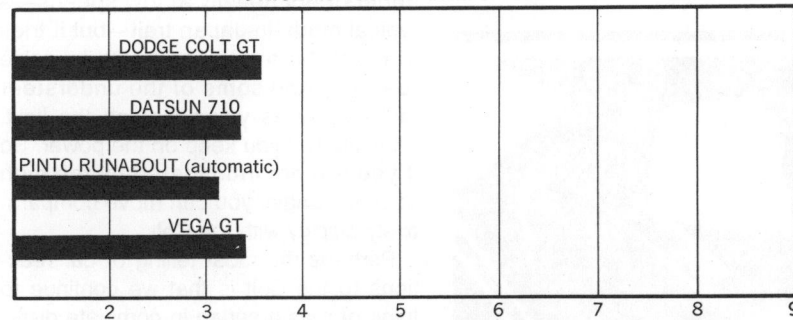

DODGE COLT GT
DATSUN 710
PINTO RUNABOUT (automatic)
VEGA GT

2 3 4 5 6 7 8 9

INTERIOR SOUND LEVEL dBA

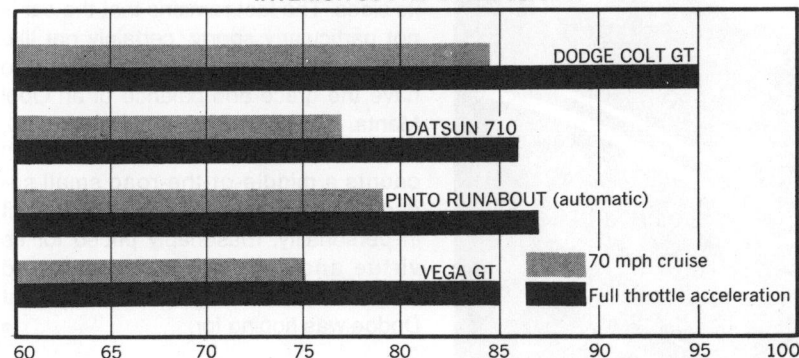

DODGE COLT GT
DATSUN 710
PINTO RUNABOUT (automatic)
VEGA GT

▨ 70 mph cruise
■ Full throttle acceleration

60 65 70 75 80 85 90 95 100

Colt GT

Importer: Dodge Division
Chrysler Motors Corporation
Detroit, Michigan 48231

Vehicle type: Front engine, rear-wheel-drive, 4-passenger
2-door hardtop

Price as tested: $3580.40
(Manufacturer's suggested retail price, including all options listed
below, dealer preparation and delivery charges, does not include
state and local taxes, license or freight charges)

Options on test car: Colt GT coupe, $3015.00; 2000 cc en-
gine, $131.75; automatic transmission, $214.15; power
brakes, $42.55; rear window defogger, $58.85; California emission package, $26.85; AM radio, $66.25; dealer preparation,
$25.00

ENGINE
Type: Four-in-line, water-cooled, cast iron block and aluminum
head, 5 main bearings
Bore x stroke ....3.31x3.54 in, 84.1x89.9mm
Displacement ....121.8 cu in, 1993cc
Compression ratio ....8.5 to one
Carburetion................................1x2-bbl Mikuni
Valve gear ....chain-driven overhead cam
Power (SAE net) ....94 bhp @ 5500 rpm
Torque (SAE net) ....108 lbs-ft @ 3600 rpm
Specific power output ....0.77 bhp/cu in, 47.0 bhp/liter
Max. recommended engine speed ....6000 rpm

DRIVE TRAIN
Transmission ....3-speed, automatic
Max. torque converter ....2.1 to one
Final drive ratio ....3.55 to one

Gear	Ratio	Mph/1000 rpm	Max. test speed
I	2.45	7.8	47 mph (6000 rpm)
II	1.45	13.2	79 mph (6000 rpm)
III	1.00	19.2	97 mph (5100 rpm)

DIMENSIONS AND CAPACITIES
Wheelbase ....95.3 in
Track, F/R ....51.8/51.2 in
Length ....172.2 in
Width ....63.6 in
Height ....53.1 in
Ground clearance..................................7.1 in
Curb weight ....2284 lbs
Weight distribution, F/R................54.4/45.6%
Battery capacity ....12 volts, 60 amp-hr
Alternator capacity ....480 watts
Fuel capacity ....13 gal
Oil capacity ....4.4 qts
Water capacity ....8.3 qts

SUSPENSION
F: ....Ind., MacPherson strut, coil springs, anti-sway bar
R: ....Rigid axle, semi-elliptic leaf springs

STEERING
Type ....Recirculating ball
Turns lock-to-lock 3.7
Turning circle curb-to-curb ....32.8 ft

BRAKES
F:....................9.0-in. dia. solid disc, power assisted
R:..................9.0x1.6-in cast iron drum, power assisted

WHEELS AND TIRES
Wheel size 5.0x13-in
Wheel type ....stamped steel, 4-bolt
Tire make and size ....B. F. Goodrich, BR70-13
Tire type............nylon and rayon cord, radial ply, tubeless
Test inflation pressures, F/R ....24/30 psi
Tire load rating ....1160 lbs per tire @ 32 psi

PERFORMANCE

Zero to	Seconds
30 mph	3.8
40 mph	6.2
50 mph	9.3
60 mph	13.2
70 mph	18.2
80 mph	25.1
90 mph	33.8

Standing ¼-mile ....19.2 sec @ 71.8 mph
Top speed (observed) ....97 mph
70-0 mph ....181 ft (0.91 G)
Fuel mileage ....19.0-23.0-mpg on regular fuel

very similar to the older version, even though many of the detail parts have been changed. The front suspension is still MacPherson and leaf springs are still used in back. The new engine is fundamentally a scaled-up version of the old one and so forth. Appearance is the big news, we think . . . and some additional space on the inside.

The Colt GT's dashboard immediately separates this car from all the other compact Japanese 4-seaters. The Colt's panel is simple and straightforward with three large round dials, one for the speedometer, one for the tach and one for everything else. The steering wheel is a 3-spoke, deep-dish design with a softly padded rim. There is a console, complete with a bin of generous dimensions, and a parcel tray under the passenger's side of the dash. All of this is handsomely styled, direct and to the point, and much more visually pleasing than the cluttered Datsun-Toyota-Subaru equivalent. The rest of the interior is more typical of its origin: heat-embossed black vinyl everywhere. Except for the Skunk Stripes, that is. This little visual kicker is a Colt original. Each black seat has a pair of narrow white stripes running down the center of the backrest and across the cushion. Drive it proudly.

The Colt's interior is plenty roomy for the two front seat passengers. As an added bonus, the front seats move through a long fore-and-aft range and they are as comfortable as those of any car in this class. The rear is another story: An adult can't sit upright back there without having his head rubbing on the roof. Here we have a Detroit feature picked up by Japan. And there is no excuse for it in a car that is 53.1 inches tall.

The Colt's admixture of Japan and Detroit is downright unavoidable from the driver's point of view. Right from the start, you are aware of the automatic transmission, the authority with which it shifts and its built-in awareness of what gear it should be in at which time. It feels like a good Detroit automatic . . . which is exactly what it turns out to be. The Chrysler A904 Torqueflite reporting for duty, sir . . . full throttle upshifts made automatically just before the redline . . . part-throttle downshifts available 24 hours a day . . . no problem at all, sir.

Well, you do have to wait for the engine. With 2.0 liters of displacement and 94 horsepower working against a 2284-lb. car, it's not quite as persuasive as the usual Six or V-8 that Chrysler bolts to that transmission. So you have to lean into the gas pedal hard to get up to

speed. Acceleration is reasonable for an automatic—19.2 seconds and 71.8 mph in the quarter-mile—but probably one second and three mph slower than it would be with a 4-speed. And it uses a fair amount of gas too: 20.0 mpg in the *C/D* Driving Cycle, 23.0 mpg at a constant 60 mph. But worst of all, it makes a lot of racket under full power. This seems to be typical of all automatic 4-cylinder cars, but the Colt is worse than most: 95 dBA on a full-throttle acceleration to 70 mph. And the sound-level meter says it's noisier than most of its competitors at freeway cruising speeds too. The cause, however, is not the engine's exclusive franchise. In fact, when you are maintaining road speed, the engine is audible but not obnoxious. What happens is that once you are above about 65 mph, the side window glass pulls away from its seal, resulting in a loud whistling sound. This is an area in which Detroit has the answer. Unfortunately, it hasn't been passed to Japan yet.

Nor has Detroit's suspension technology. Collectively, Japanese sedans are the worst on the American market for down-the-road directional stability. And the Colt is bad for a Japanese sedan. This is the Colt's single largest shortcoming. It simply won't go straight, not even on the freeway. It's the only car we've encountered that nibbles while rolling on radial tires. The result is that you have to keep steering all the time.

The unfortunate part about all of this is that the Colt is better than most of its countrymen for track-type handling. It understeers heavily at low speeds—a typical made-in-Japan trait—but it tries to resist the temptation to lift its inside rear tire. And some of the understeer melts away as you approach the limit, particularly if you keep on the power. So if you are not intimidated by the high body roll angle, you can move comparatively quickly with the Colt.

Perhaps the most telling of our reactions to the Colt is that we continue to think of it as a sedan in complete disregard for the GT emblems pasted on all its sides. The fact remains that the car is not particularly sporty, certainly not like the Super Coupes. It doesn't begin to have the grace and balance of an Opel Manta. But compared to a Datsun 710, the Colt is a real charmer. It is by all counts a middle-of-the-road small sedan, halfway between Japan and Detroit in personality, reasonably priced for its virtue and competent over a broad range. Which, we expect, is exactly what Dodge was hoping for.

●

> '
> Nothing, not even the yards of heat-embossed
> black vinyl all over the interior,
> can prepare you for the Skunk Stripes
> '

Road Test:
Plymouth
Valiant Brougham

They're swinging a little late, but when the
Plymouth product planners got the bat off their shoulders, they really uncoiled

• Leave it to Chrysler to come wandering into the market, droopy-lidded and yawning, a mere three years late. And with a 4-star cliche´ name like Valiant Brougham. How can a Valiant be Brougham? It sounds like a joke, like "Raoul of Bayonne," a furious contradiction in terms which completely cancel each other out before they reach your inner ear, leaving only a residue of mirth.

You have to make allowances for Chrysler; its product plan-

ning department has not been feeling well for the past decade . . . iron deficiency anemia or something. Always swings too late at the ball. Tried to counter the original Mustang with a fastback Valiant called Barracuda; fouled that one off. Three years late on the Camaro. Missed the Monte Carlo. Took a called strike on the Vega and Pinto market. Just introduced a new line of 4-wheel drive RVs in the middle of the energy crunch. A real hitting slump.

Luckily, this luxury compact idea is such a slow ball that even with the late swing, the Valiant Brougham looks like a base hit. Nothing big, mind you—a lazy bouncer into short right field—but it's better than that hang-head shuffle back to the dugout. The problem, once again, is that the heavy hitters have already zeroed in on this market. Ford launched the Maverick LDO and its Mercury Comet counterpart three years ago. They were compact sedans with high-class upholstery and quiet interiors—nothing more—and the buyers soaked them up. Since then, three more GM divisions have tried to ingratiate themselves with the same clientele. Pontiac's Ventura, Oldsmobile's Omega and Buick's Apollo were the lures. And the success has been modest. But the competition is turning serious now. All of the GM models will be completely new for 1975. And Ford has whipped up the Granada, a very

impressive entry in this segment of the market. Chrysler, on the other hand, will have to hang in there with the Valiant Brougham until 1976 when its new compacts are ready.

Any way you look at it, the Valiant Brougham is a couple of innings late. And it's very conservative, exactly the same format Ford used in the Maverick LDO: up-graded upholstery and a quiet package applied to an existing car. But when Chrysler's product planners get around to swinging, they really uncoil. The Valiant Brougham's interior is truly lavish. It easily overwhelms the competition, both in quality of materials used and in the tasteful way they are arranged. So the impact of the car is considerable, particularly when you remember that the basic body is virtually unchanged since 1967.

In some ways, as a matter of fact, this old body is advantageous. Back in 1967, 4-door sedans—particularly compact 4-

PHOTOGRAPHY: BARRY TENIN

door sedans—were very basic and utilitarian cars. People who wanted style bought something bigger. Compacts were strictly Transportation—value for the dollar—so they ended up being blocked-shaped cars with room for five or six passengers inside. And the Valiant was more block-shaped than most. But now with "formal" styling being all the rage, the Valiant's square corners and upright greenhouse look almost contemporary. And it's perfect for the Brougham formula. Apply the vinyl roof treatment. Slip on the color-keyed wheelcovers and the thin-stripe radial tires. Erect the obligatory stand-up hood ornament on the nose. Line each side with a long, parallel pin strips. Don't forget the "Brougham" nameplates in die-cast script. *Voila*, simulated elegance from Motor City.

All of this sounds cynical. Maybe cars *are* elegant if they look elegant. Once you are inside this particular Brougham,

The Brougham's interior easily overwhelms the competition's offerings, both in quality of materials and the tasteful way they've been arranged

sealed off from the transportation boxes and the White Hat Specials, you can believe you are in a very expensive automobile. First, there are no "Valiant" emblems to break the illusion. But even more important, everything you touch feels costly and opulent. The bench seats have heavily pleated inserts of suede-like cloth and feel like fine furniture. The floor and lower door panels are covered with a deep cut-pile carpet. The headliner is a coarse, linen-like weave. All of this blends together in delicate shades of brown and beige, the work of a thoughtful and confident designers. There are no eye-grabbing cheap shots. Fake wood is used sparingly, as an accent rather than a material, so its lack of authenticity doesn't seriously depreciate the overall effect. And there are a few first-class touches. The window sills are covered by deeply padded rolls of vinyl which are *stitched* in place. This padding adds a soft look to the whole interior and is far more pleasing than the fake wood sills in the Granada Ghia.

And though the suggestion of elegance weakens as you drive, it is not completely dispelled. Your body can't forget the softness of the upholstery and the interior is silent, better even than some Intermediates. So the Valiant Brougham remains acceptably luxurious no matter how rough the going.

But the machinery is definitely dated; the steering, the suspension and all of the controls feel one full generation removed from today's General Motors standards. Chrysler engineers have tried to save the old power-steering gear—the one that has about the same road feel as the radio volume control knob—by increasing the effort requirement. It's a small improvement; at least the steering wheel feels like it's connected to something now. But the extra effort adds a high-friction sensation rather than a genuine improvement in the road feel. The steering is really this car's weakest mechanical attribute. On-center response is poor. The car has little straight-ahead ambition—it would rather wander down the road—and it is unusually sensitive to crosswind. As the driver, you are constantly making small steering corrections.

The brakes are balky too. If you measured the components—10.8-inch diameter discs in front and 10.0 by 2.5-inch drums in back—you would say they were of more than adequate capacity for a 3372-lb. sedan. But they take forever to stop the car—220 feet (0.75G) from 70mph. There are two problems. The first is balance; the rears lock up much too soon. The second is slow response. As you press on the pedal, the system seems to slowly gather itself up, becoming more effective with time even though the pedal pressure has not changed. We would blame this on a poorly developed power booster. It's something that a driver has to work very hard to get the most out of. The result—of both the brakes and steering—is a car that's not much fun to drive.

Thrill-seekers wouldn't like the standard-equipment 6-cylinder engine very much either, but it happens to be quite a popular powerplant in a number of Detroit factories these days. The Valiant's Six displaces 225 cu. in. now . . just as it did when first introduced in 1960. And apart form certain re-calibrations necessary to cope with today's emission control laws, it's very much the same engine. In the Valiant, coupled to the 3-speed automatic transmission, it's a tolerable package. Except for a marked reluctance to stay awake following a cold start, it is generally well-behaved. And it's very quiet. The Brougham gets a special exhaust system which has a resonator in addition to the usual muffler. And the engine compartment is well insulated with underhood blankets and the like. So the humble Six's muted tones are in keeping with the Brougham's intentions. Performance, when you put it into

Text continued on page **100** *specifications on overleaf*

ACCELERATION standing ¼ mile, seconds

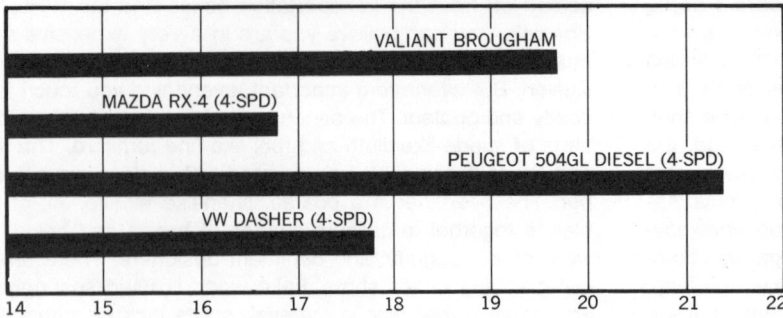

- VALIANT BROUGHAM
- MAZDA RX-4 (4-SPD)
- PEUGEOT 504GL DIESEL (4-SPD)
- VW DASHER (4-SPD)

14 15 16 17 18 19 20 21 22

BRAKING 70-0 mph, feet

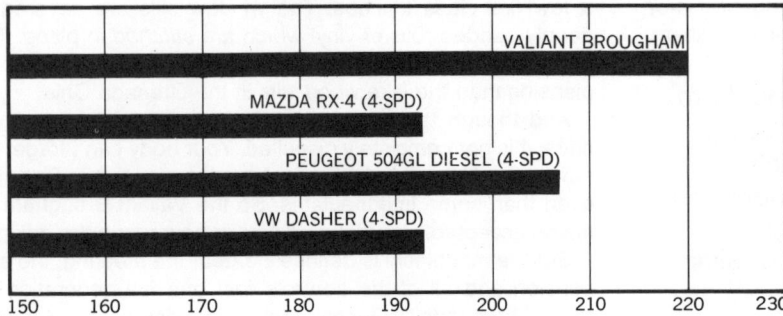

- VALIANT BROUGHAM
- MAZDA RX-4 (4-SPD)
- PEUGEOT 504GL DIESEL (4-SPD)
- VW DASHER (4-SPD)

150 160 170 180 190 200 210 220 230

FUEL ECONOMY RANGE mpg

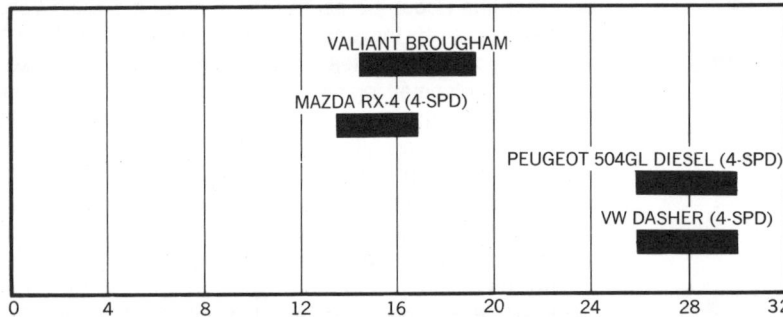

- VALIANT BROUGHAM
- MAZDA RX-4 (4-SPD)
- PEUGEOT 504GL DIESEL (4-SPD)
- VW DASHER (4-SPD)

0 4 8 12 16 20 24 28 32

PRICE AS TESTED dollars x 1000

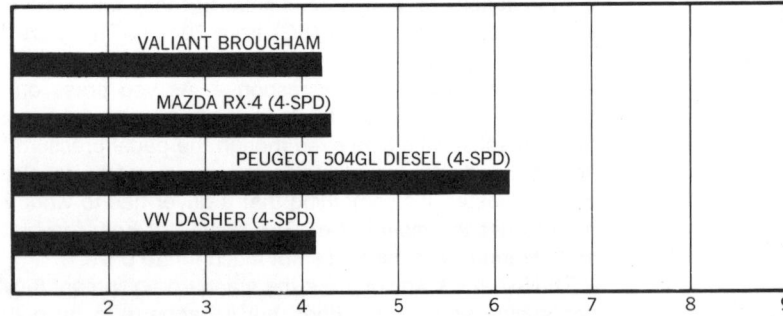

- VALIANT BROUGHAM
- MAZDA RX-4 (4-SPD)
- PEUGEOT 504GL DIESEL (4-SPD)
- VW DASHER (4-SPD)

2 3 4 5 6 7 8 9

INTERIOR SOUND LEVEL dBA

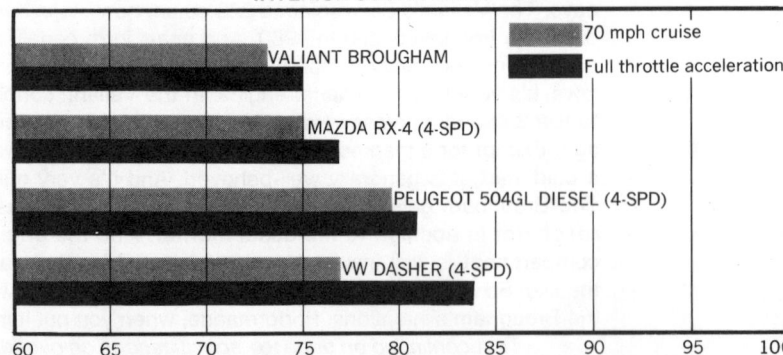

■ 70 mph cruise
■ Full throttle acceleration

- VALIANT BROUGHAM
- MAZDA RX-4 (4-SPD)
- PEUGEOT 504GL DIESEL (4-SPD)
- VW DASHER (4-SPD)

60 65 70 75 80 85 90 95 100

Valiant Brougham

Manufacturer: Chrysler-Plymouth Division
Chrysler Motors Corporation
P. O. Box 857
Detroit, Michigan

Vehicle type: front engine, rear-wheel-drive, 6-passenger 4-door sedan

Price as tested: $4215.35
(Manufacturer's suggested retail price, including all options listed below, dealer preparation and delivery charges, does not include state and local taxes, license or freight charges)

Options on test car: base Valiant Brougham 4-door, $3743; ER78-14 tires, $178.10; radial tire roadability package, $12.85; power brakes, $67.40; heavy duty battery, $14.75; rear window defogger, $60.50; tinted windshield, $28.75; AM/FM radio, $70.50; rear speaker, $14.50; delivery charge, $25.00

ENGINE
Type: Six-in-line, water-cooled, cast iron block and heads, 4 main bearings
Bore x stroke . . . . 3.40 x 4.12 in, 86.4 x 104.6mm
Displacement . . . . 225 cu in, 3682 cc
Compression ratio . . . . 8.4 to one
Carburetion 1x1-bbl
Valve gear . . . pushrod-operated overhead valves, hydraulic lifters
Power (SAE net) . . . . 105 bhp @ 3600 rpm
Torque (SAE net) . . . . 180 lbs-ft @ 1600 rpm
Specific power output . . . . 0.47 bhp/cu in, 28.5 bhp/liter

DRIVE TRAIN
Transmission . . . . 3-speed, automatic
Max. torque converter . . . . 2.16 to one
Final drive ratio . . . . 2.76 to one

Gear	Ratio	Mph/1000 rpm	Max. test speed
I	2.45	10.9	48 mph (4400 rpm)
II	1.45	18.5	73 mph (3900 rpm)
III	1.00	26.8	90 mph (3350 rpm)

DIMENSIONS AND CAPACITIES
Wheelbase . . . . 111.0 in
Track, F/R . . . . 59.1/55.4 in
Length . . . . 197.6 in
Width . . . . 71.0 in
Height . . . . 54.3 in
Ground clearance . . . . 5.8 in
Curb weight . . . . 3372 lbs
Weight distribution, F/R 55.5/44.5%
Battery capacity . . . . 12 volts, 59 amp-hr
Alternator capacity . . . . 475 watts
Fuel capacity . . . . 16.0 gal
Oil capacity . . . . 5.0 qts
Water capacity . . . . 13.0 qts

SUSPENSION
F: . . ind., unequal-length control arms, torsion bars, anti-sway bar
R: . . . . rigid axle, semi-elliptic leaf springs

STEERING
Type . . . . recirculating ball, power assisted
Turns lock-to-lock 3.6
Turning circle curb-to-curb . . . . 37.3 ft

BRAKES
F: . . . . 10.8-in dia. disc, power assisted
R: . . . . 10.0x2.5-in cast iron drum, power assisted

WHEELS AND TIRES
Wheel size . . . . 5.5 x 14-in
Wheel type . . . . stamped steel, 5-bolt
Tire make and size . Goodyear Custom Steelgard Radial, ER78-14
Tire type . . . . steel-belted radial ply, tubeless
Test inflation pressures, F/R . . . . 24/24 psi
Tire load rating . . . . 1400 lbs per tire @ 32 psi

PERFORMANCE

Zero to	Seconds
30 mph	4.1
40 mph	7.5
50 mph	9.8
60 mph	13.8
70 mph	20.0
80 mph	30.3
90 mph	47.7

Standing ¼-mile . . . . 19.7 sec @ 69.7 mph
Top speed (estimated) . . . . 97 mph
70-0 mph . . . . 220 ft (0.75 G)
Fuel mileage . . . . 14.5-19.0-mpg on regular fuel
Cruising range . . . . 230-300 mi

Preview:
Chrysler Cordoba

Further proof that Detroit-style luxury doesn't have to come in an enormous package

• Product planners are shameless men. Skilled in their craft and honest about their methods . . . but shameless. Because they do not make cars for driving . . . only for selling.

The Cordoba is a new car from Chrysler in 1975, one that has been endlessly groomed by the corporation's product planners for what they feel is an expanding and highly profitable segment of the new-car market. Its interior has been massaged and its exterior preened, all in an effort to make it irresistible to a broad cross section of buyers. While the basic automobile derives from a simple formula, every detail has been consciously planned and executed. The result is a handsome 5-passenger coupe that, when examined in concert with the product planners' story of its origin, offers a fascinating glimpse at Detroit's marketing methods.

First, you should understand that the product planners are completely candid about the lack of originality in the Cordoba's concept. It is a deliberate replica of a Chevrolet Monte Carlo. The two are virtually identical in silhouette, styling themes are similar and principal interior and exterior body dimensions do not vary more than a few per cent. Both are

primarily front seat cars with marginal room for adults in back. There is no embarassment on this issue: The Monte Carlo has been an enormous success; building a Chrysler Corporation version is simply good business.

In the product planners' view, the only real innovation is that the Cordoba is an intermediate-size car with a Chrysler name plate. Chryslers have been full-size cars for as long as anyone can remember, so the Cordoba is a significant step toward smaller cars in the luxury field. It is, the planners feel, the direction in which the market is moving. While one out of four new cars sold is still full-size, that segment has been decreasing since the late Fifties. And with the current and expected future emphasis on fuel economy, sales of big cars will continue to decline, probably at an even faster rate. Intermediates, on the other hand, have been relatively stable since their introduction in 1961—about twenty per cent of total sales. Until 1972 that is, when they moved past big cars to become the most active segment of the market.

The fascinating thing about Intermediates is that almost 75 per cent of them are 2-door models. And nearly half of the

91

2-doors are sport/luxury coupes like the Monte Carlo and Grand Prix. The product planners figure that this group will exceed one million cars in 1975 (up from only 200,000 in 1970) and they quite logically want to carve off a bigger piece than they have been able to do in the past with the Charger, the company's only previous offering in this class.

Once the decision had been made to build a sport/luxury coupe, establishing the styling theme of the car was easy. If this is to be a sport/luxury coupe, then it must have a formal appearance in the Monte Carlo idiom. There was only one other choice: It could have had a "performance" shape, like the current Matador or the Dodge Charger through the 1974 models. But Monte Carlos sell better than Chargers, so the Cordoba is a Monte Carlo . . . and so is the new Charger.

For 1975, Chrysler has completely abandoned the sleek, flowing theme it pioneered with its Charger and Road Runner Intermediates in favor of the stiff, upright shape of GM and Ford. When pressed for a reason, the product planners explain that formally shaped cars "look more expensive." This is very important to their marketing scheme because the Cordoba's customers are expected to come from two areas: big car buyers looking for luxury in a more compact package and

Intermediate buyers who will ante up a few hundred more dollars if the car shows them some class.

When product planners speak of "luxury" and "class," they are referring to external appearance and the "feel" of the interior qualities that will impress you in the showroom . . . or if you happened to ride in your neighbor's new car. It is assumed that the engineering department will make the car as quiet as possible at the price and that the ride will be soft. But what the *driver* feels—handling and the subtleties of the controls—never even enters the conversation. So it is not surprising that the Cordoba ends up being a passenger's car rather than a driver's car. In our opinion, this is the one flaw in the Cordoba's concept and the primary reason why it can never stand in the ranks of the world's great cars.

For any automobile to merit luxury status in our view, it must offer a high degree of precision to its driver. The Cordoba does not do this. Our driving impressions, which stem from a pre-introduction day session at the Chrysler proving ground, were dominated by steering column and instrument panel shake in response to road impacts, brakes that did not respond linearly and feeble acceleration. A discerning driver cannot overlook these shortcomings.

From the sumptuous interior to the bogus coin on the hood ornament, the goal of the product planners has been to create an impression of value

But passengers will be more impressed. The interior is very quiet. Chrysler has made enormous progress in damping the resonances of its Intermediate unit body and the ride is free of harshness. In terms of passenger comfort, we have no reservations about the Cordoba. It is a luxury car.

The amusing aspect of this evaluation is that the product planners who rode in the Cordoba with us were as impressed as we were with the silence and smoothness . . . and they also seemed to be somewhat surprised. Perfecting the car was an *engineering* process; since this one was one of the very first production Cordobas, it is likely that the product planners had never ridden a final version before. But their reaction suggested that a product planner's concept of luxury finds its source in headwaters other than the basic car. They maintained that surface detail has very much to do with luxury. And once the basic Monte Carlo theme was settled upon, they set out to make the Cordoba more desirable than the Monte Carlo—and hence worth its higher price—almost exclusively through the use of ornamentation and trim.

Their goal, as they proceed about their business of interior and exterior decoration, is to create the impression of value. They have two ways of doing this: One is to simulate value;

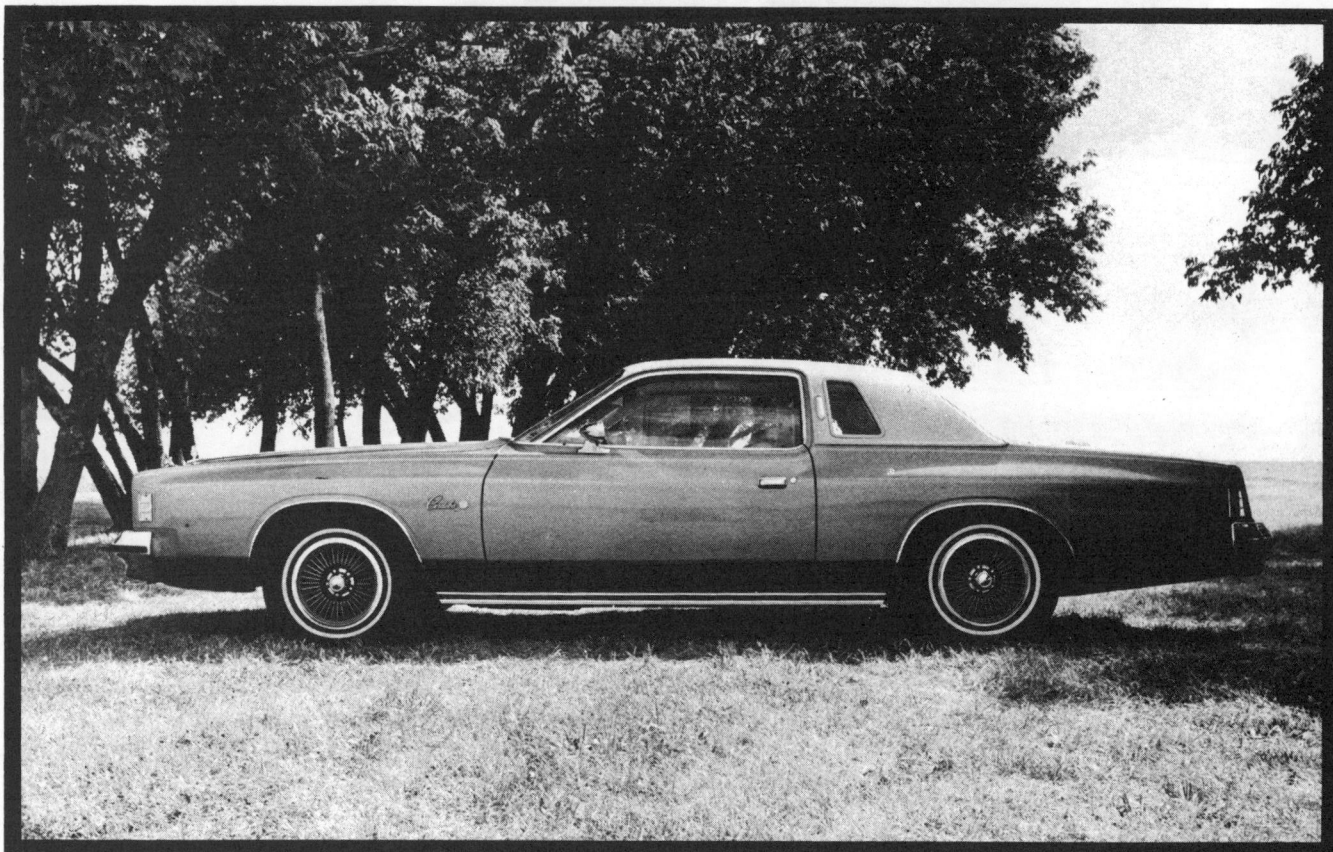

the other, to really put it in there. They do not seem to prefer one method over the other. The best example of the latter is carpeting. They have specified deep shag carpeting ("it's 25-ounce, the best we can get") for the Cordoba's floor, lower door panels and seat backs. And a more durable grade of exterior carpeting for the trunk.

They've done the right thing with the material for the upholstery too. There is leather for those who want it, crushed velour for those that don't and brocade for newly converted big car owners who may be too conservative for velour.

But there is only so much Good Stuff they can put in before they get down to precious metals for the bright work . . . which isn't going to play in the accounting department. So then they must resort to *simulations* of value and the Cordoba has plenty of these. Everybody has opera windows these days, but only the Cordoba has an opera light . . . a kind of porch light attached to the rear roof post that glows whenever the headlights are on. Then there is the jewelry-tooled filigree moldings accenting the dash board, door panels and seats which are supposed to remind you of the ironwork in Spain. And then

there are the forged aluminum coin replicas that are captured within the perimeter of the hood ornament and affixed to the sides of the front fender.

According to the product planners, Cordoba is not only a city in Spain, but a coin in Argentina. And they thought a fine detail like this would properly symbolize the car's lofty position in the sport/luxury section of the 2-door coupe class. Never mind that this coin shows a pair of Chrysler griffins facing each other over some obscure crest and bears no resemblance whatsoever to an Argentinian cordoba. The product planners reckon that you are going to take one look and say, "Well, this looks like a pretty nice car."

The problem is that the Cordoba *is* a pretty nice car for those who are warmed by Monte Carlos. But it could be a whole lot better if Chrysler spent less time designing with bogus coins and instead directed its attention to making fine cars responsive to their drivers. Perhaps we are asking for too much too soon. Maybe we should be satisfied that the Cordoba is a firm indication that luxury cars are getting smaller. That alone is damn good news. ●

CHRYSLER CORDOBA
Manufacturer: Dodge Division
Chrysler Motors Corporation
Detroit, Michigan 48231

Vehicle type: front engine, rear-wheel-drive, 5-passenger coupe

ENGINE
Type: V-8, water-cooled, cast iron block and heads, five main bearings
Bore x stroke . . . . 4.00x3.58 in, 101.6x90.8mm
Displacement. . . . . .360 cu in, 5600cc
Compression ratio . . . . .8.4 to one
Carburetion . . . . .1x2-bbl Holley
Valve gear . . . . pushrod operated overhead valves
Power (SAE net) . . . . .180 bhp @ 4000 rpm
Torque (SAE net) . . . . .290 lbs-ft @ 2400 rpm

DRIVE TRAIN
Transmission . . . . .3-speed, automatic
Max. torque converter. .2.02 to one
Final drive ratio . . . . .2.45 to one

DIMENSIONS AND CAPACITIES
Wheelbase . . . . .115.0 in
Track, F/R . . . . .61.9/62.0 in
Length . . . . .215.3 in
Width . . . . .77.0 in
Height . . . . .53.0 in
Curb weight. . . . . .4456 lbs
Weight distribution, F/R 56.0/44.0%
Fuel capacity . . . . .25.5 gal
Oil capacity . . . . .4.0 qts

SUSPENSION
F:. . . . . .Ind., unequal-length control arms, torsion bars, anti-sway bar
R:. . . . . .Rigid axle, semi-elliptic

STEERING
Type .recirculating ball, power assist
Turning circle curb-to-curb .41.2 ft

BRAKES
F:. .10.8-in vented disc, power assist
R:. . . . . .10.0x2.4-in cast iron drum, power assist

WHEELS AND TIRES
Wheel size 15x5.5-in
Tire make and size . . . . .Goodyear HR78-15
Tire type . . . . .steelbelt radial, tubeless

Road Test:
Plymouth Road Runner

BY DON SHERMAN

A former wild stallion joins the herd.

• Could it be they haven't heard? Could some cloistered sanctuary exist at the fringes of Motor City where the news hasn't seeped in? Performance—at least the quarter-mile acceleration variety—is dead and the funeral is ancient history. Yet Plymouth can't bring itself to bury the corpse. Right here in 1975, the age of pristine exhaust and improved fuel economy, Plymouth is still fielding one of its heroes from drag racing days: the Road Runner.

In its heyday, the blurry-legged bird was the star of an extensive rapid transit system, but insurance underwriters and emissions bureaucrats dismantled that scheme like kids with a new toy. Still, the Road Runner lives on, even though all the rapid has been drained from its transit. Today the car with cartoons on its doors is American graffiti right out of the 1960s when smoking tires came as factory standard equipment.

That page of automotive history was irrevocably turned with the demise of horsepower. After a peak in 1970, killer-engines quickly faded toward extinction. The Hemi died in 1972 when Chrysler realized it couldn't afford the toll of emissions certification, special assembly procedures and high warranty costs for a handful of engines. The muscular 440 Magnum was added to Road Runner option lists in 1970 and the version with three 2-barrel carburetors pumped out an incredible 390 hp. But that too was not to last; the top engine was reined back to a single 4-barrel in 1971. In 1974, Plymouth tried to twist the Road

95

Runner's performance image toward economy by adding a 318-cu. in. 2-barrel as the base engine.

For 1975, the final debilitating blow has been dealt: The 440 is gone and now the Road Runner's most powerful source of energy is a 400-cu. in. 4-barrel. Under its load of emissions hardware and breathing through a catalytic converter, this engine struggles to develop a disparaging 190 net hp at 4000 rpm. It amounts to less than half the might that came with a good-running Hemi. The Road Runner's drag racing days are truly over. Weight has gone up as horsepower has fallen off; the *C/D* test car could barely chirp a tire on the drag strip. With a payload of 4350 pounds and a Torqueflite transmission, it struggled through the quarter-mile in 17.1 seconds at 80.5 mph. The Road Runner, an

American performance classic, has deteriorated so dramatically that it now performs down with the super coupes—a Mazda RX-2 with its 16.5-second E.T. and 83.4-mph top speed will blow the Road Runner's doors off.

Even though the Road Runner name, fat tires and flat-black paint across the hood may resurrect hopes of performance, this is no longer the car's major strength. The Road Runner is now a minor sideline of Plymouth's intermediate offerings—a series that was redesigned for 1975 with performance at the bottom of the priorities list. So the Road Runner has taken on the traits of the new stars in the Plymouth intermediate squad: comfort and luxury.

The crystal balls of the Chrysler corporate marketing experts showed that the intermediate segment, particularly the specialty-car division, would be the most active automotive arena for the last half of the 1970s. So a new car was designed to make Plymouths, Dodges and even Chryslers competitive with the Monte Carlos, Grand Prixs and Ford Elites that Americans were heartily snapping up. The 4-door models were also revamped to make them fitting conveyances for the expected rush of buyers stepping down from larger cars. And just to let both kinds of prospective owners know some dramatic changes had been made, Plymouth rolled out its well-known Fury nameplate for the new intermediates. Meanwhile, the old full-size Furys were pumped up another notch with a "Gran" prefix.

For the 2-door versions of the new Fury, Detroit-style elegance was the watchword. The brutal performance look

was discarded for the "classically formal" look that has every stylist from Dearborn to Lansing in its grip. This means a grille that stands as erect—if not as tall—as a Ford Model A's. The body sides were ironed flat, and both the roofline and decklid were sharply blocked in profile. One almost expects a flat, vertical windshield for harmony. It amounts to the Gatsby Look applied to automobiles, the impression of styling culled from the past—as if yesterday's ideas are somehow better than today's.

This is a strange suit indeed for one of the few survivors of the drag racing age to be wearing. Who could have guessed that the Road Runner would fade from existence wearing "formal" sheetmetal? Luckily, the Road Runner carries insufficient rank as a specialty car to be graced with the hood ornaments, opera windows and coach lights of its more elegant Charger and Cordoba stablemates, so it meets the world in simple evening dress, wearing tuxedo-like sheetmetal but no diamond accessories.

While the formal look is at odds with the Road Runner's performance image, the styling changeover has delivered some basic improvements. A high level of comfort was essential to compete in the specialty-car sweepstakes, so the old unit-construction chassis was discarded. The new Fury has a unit body with a half frame at the front, a technique used in full-size Chrysler Corporation cars and GM compacts. The approach allows all conductors of noise and harshness in the front (the engine/transmission assembly, front suspension and steering linkage) to be mounted to a

Text continued on page 98
specifications overleaf

ACCELERATION standing ¼ mile, seconds

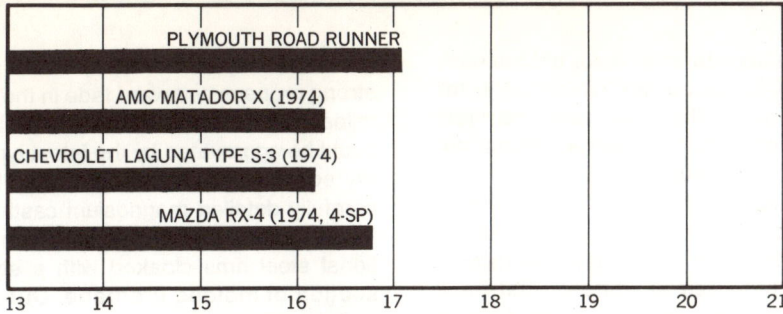

PLYMOUTH ROAD RUNNER	
AMC MATADOR X (1974)	
CHEVROLET LAGUNA TYPE S-3 (1974)	
MAZDA RX-4 (1974, 4-SP)	

13 14 15 16 17 18 19 20 21

BRAKING 70-0 mph, feet

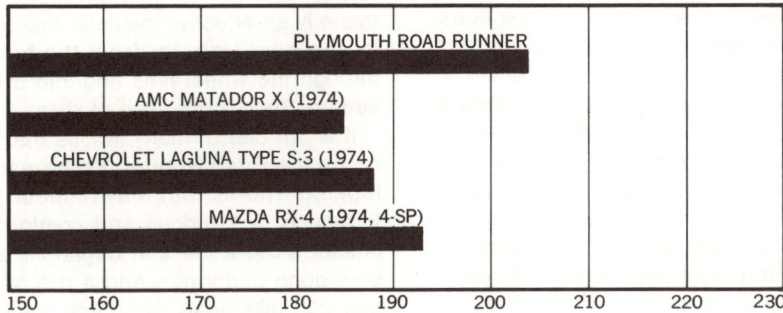

PLYMOUTH ROAD RUNNER	
AMC MATADOR X (1974)	
CHEVROLET LAGUNA TYPE S-3 (1974)	
MAZDA RX-4 (1974, 4-SP)	

150 160 170 180 190 200 210 220 230

FUEL ECONOMY RANGE mpg

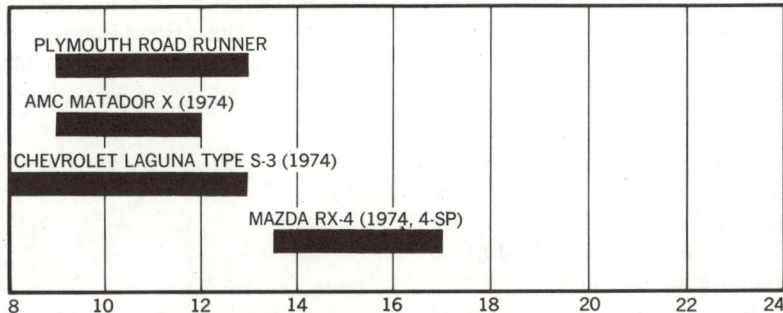

PLYMOUTH ROAD RUNNER	
AMC MATADOR X (1974)	
CHEVROLET LAGUNA TYPE S-3 (1974)	
MAZDA RX-4 (1974, 4-SP)	

8 10 12 14 16 18 20 22 24

PRICE AS TESTED dollars x 1000

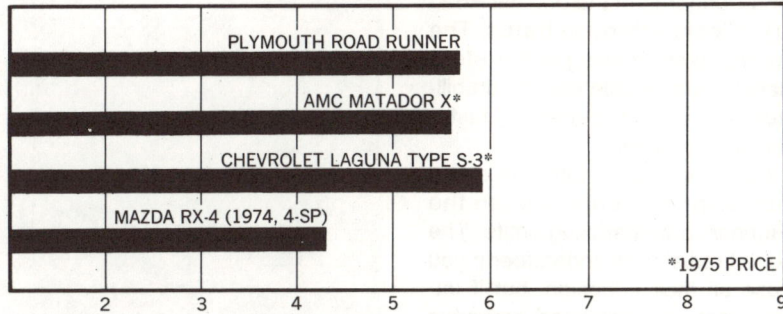

PLYMOUTH ROAD RUNNER	
AMC MATADOR X*	
CHEVROLET LAGUNA TYPE S-3*	
MAZDA RX-4 (1974, 4-SP)	

*1975 PRICE

2 3 4 5 6 7 8 9

INTERIOR SOUND LEVEL dBA

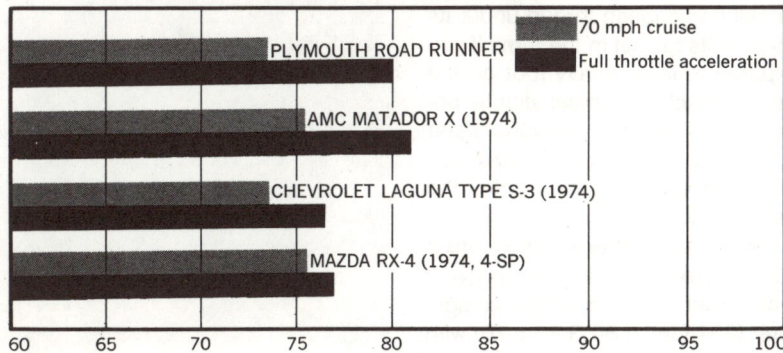

□ 70 mph cruise
■ Full throttle acceleration

PLYMOUTH ROAD RUNNER	
AMC MATADOR X (1974)	
CHEVROLET LAGUNA TYPE S-3 (1974)	
MAZDA RX-4 (1974, 4-SP)	

60 65 70 75 80 85 90 95 100

PLYMOUTH ROAD RUNNER

Manufacturer: Chrysler-Plymouth Division
Chrysler Corporation
Detroit, Michigan 48231

Vehicle type: front engine, rear-wheel-drive, 6-passenger
2-door hardtop

Price as tested: $5709.30
(Manufacturer's suggested retail price, including all options listed below, dealer preparation and delivery charges, does not include state and local taxes, license or freight charges)

Options on test car: base Plymouth Road Runner, $3973.00; 400 cu. in. 4-bbl. engine, $122.00; Torqueflite transmission, $263.85; SureGrip differential, $49.95; power brakes, $57.90; power steering, $135.55; steel-belted radial tires, $110.80; styled road wheels, $98.45; automatic speed control, $72.25; AM/FM radio and 8-track tape deck, $396.75; Tuff steering wheel, $34.25; performance hood, $26.35; tachometer, $59.25; heavy duty battery, $28.00; tinted windshield, $26.20; exterior decor package, $116.45; light package, $40.10; split bench seat, N/C; deluxe sound insulation package, $52.65; deck lid tape stripes, $16.55; bumper rub strips, $29.00

ENGINE
Type: V-8, water-cooled, cast iron block/heads, 5 main bearings
Bore x stroke . . . . 4.34 x 3.38 in, 110.2 x 85.9 mm
Displacement . . . . 400 cu in, 6650 cc
Compression ratio . . . . 8.2 to one
Carburetion . . . . 1 x 4-bbl Carter Thermoquad
Valve gear . . . pushrod-operated overhead valves, hydraulic lifters
Power (SAE net) . . . . 190 bhp @ 4000 rpm
Torque (SAE net) . . . . 290 lbs-ft @ 3200 rpm
Max. recommended engine speed . . . . 5500 rpm

DRIVE TRAIN
Transmission . . . . 3-speed, automatic
Final drive ratio . . . . 3.21 to one

Gear	Ratio	Mph/1000 rpm	Max. test speed
I	2.45	9.8	49 mph (5000 rpm)
II	1.45	16.5	82 mph (5000 rpm)
III	1.00	23.9	115 mph (4800 rpm)

DIMENSIONS AND CAPACITIES
Wheelbase . . . . 115.0 in
Track, F/R . . . . 61.9/62.0 in
Length . . . . 211.1 in
Width . . . . 77.4 in
Height . . . . 52.8 in
Curb weight . . . . 4350 lbs
Weight distribution, F/R . . . . 56.7/43.3 %
Fuel capacity . . . . 25.5 gal

SUSPENSION
F: . . ind., unequal-length control arms, coil springs, anti-sway bar
R: . . . . rigid axle, semi-elliptic leaf springs, anti-sway bar

STEERING
Type . . . . recirculating ball, power assisted
Turns lock-to-lock 3.6
Turning circle curb-to-curb . . . . 41.2 ft

BRAKES
F: . . . . 10.8-in vented disc, power assisted
R: . . . . 10.0 x 2.4-in cast iron drum, power assisted

WHEELS AND TIRES
Wheel size . . . . 6.5 x 15-in
Wheel type . . . . styled, polyurethane/steel, 5-bolt
Tire make/size . . . . Goodyear Custom Polysteel Radial, GR78-15

PERFORMANCE

Zero to	Seconds
30 mph	2.3
40 mph	3.4
50 mph	4.8
60 mph	7.0
70 mph	10.7
80 mph	16.2
90 mph	26.7
100 mph	43.0

Standing ¼-mile . . . . 17.1 sec @ 80.5 mph
Top speed (observed) . . . . 115 mph
70-0 mph . . . . 204 ft (0.80 G)
Fuel mileage . . . . 9-13-mpg on lead-free fuel

CONTINUED FROM PAGE 96

substructure isolated from the body by soft rubber biscuits. Vibration from the road stops at the subframe and doesn't penetrate the interior.

The job is well done; from a ride and noise standpoint, the 1975 version is the best Road Runner ever. The body offers a stiff barrier to unwanted noise. At 70 mph, you can cruise with an interior sound level of 75 dBA, compared to 74 dBA in a Mercedes 280. And for the first time, the Road Runner's heavy-duty suspension can be tailored for good handling without transmitting road harshness through the rest of the car. There is sufficient roll stiffness to keep the body on an even keel in high-speed turns and firm damping enhances control during sharp transient maneuvers. Even so, the ride through it all is very commendably placid.

The chassis' able handling of bumps and rough pavement is the proper base for a calm interior. You enter through long, heavy doors that provide wide access to both front and rear seats. Inside, you find a roomy compartment with rear-seat headroom most noticeably in abundance—one positive fallout from the stylists' insistence on a formal roofline. Plastic surfaces are used sparingly and the general level of luxury is well above past Plymouth intermediate fare. Points of frequent contact (the door panels, seats and top of the instrument panel) are softly padded. Supple vinyl covers the window sills as well as the seats and it needs only a pleasant aroma to compete favorably with leather.

The seats are a particularly rich-looking but simple design with a series of wide rolls marked off by straight stitching. Their most compelling feature, however, is a comfortable shape. Buckets are standard in the Road Runner, but our test car had a split-back bench arrangement available as a no-cost option. In that configuration, the seat bottom is a conventional bench, while the backrest has three sections: Bucket-seat backs on each side are linked or separated, as you prefer, by a center-folding armrest. Strangely enough, those seat backs have more curvature and are closer to a real bucket seat than anything Detroit has delivered in the past. They wrap around to match the curvature of your shoulders; stiffeners halfway up the backrest keep the edges firm to hold you in place during cornering. They're the kind of seats you'd expect to

find in a Jensen Interceptor of Mercedes 450SLC but not in a Plymouth. The full bucket seats share the same backrest design and offer a small additional degree of lateral support.

The instruments too are more driver-oriented than those of any Plymouth except perhaps the deceased Barracuda. A matching pair of white-on-flat-back speedometer and tachometer dials lie within the borders of the steering wheel rim, while four smaller instruments for fuel level, temperature, oil pressure and ammeter are grouped to the right. The driver's control module also contains a heater panel at the lower left offset by the radio on the right. The theme is strong on easy-to-read simplicity and thankfully devoid of the filigree and woodgrain distractions that Chrysler saves for more elegant intermediates.

Gaudy adornment is not the theme of the Road Runner's steering wheel either. Its lightened spokes and marshmallow-soft padded rim boldly demand an energetic driver rather than a pallid chauffeur. A discerning pilot, however, will find the Road Runner a little too bulky for comfort in the city. Part of the blame should go to the stylists who built a solid foot of dead space into the front overhang to stretch the hood toward their idea of elegant proportions. This unfortunately adds no space to the interior but does make an unnecessarily cumbersome 211.1-inch overall length (8.4 inches longer than the original Road Runner) to jockey through traffic. The extra-cost power steering is therefore necessary for reasonable maneuverability because its ratio is substantially faster than the standard gear.

This option will also help you avoid dislocated arms when you push the Road Runner to its handling limits. The steel-belted radial tires understeer if you gently use all their adhesion, but if understeer is not your preferred cornering style, there is an alternative. The Road Runner still has enough torque under its hood to slide its tail out in the turns if you are prepared to lay a heavy foot on the throttle and twitch the wheel slightly entering a corner. But you'll need the faster power steering to feed in the rapid corrections required to keep the front of the car ahead of the rear.

The new Road Runner's brakes are a good deal more mannerly than those of its predecessor. The car stops straight and short (204 feet, 0.80 G from 70) with

good stability. There was, however, a strong propensity toward fade in the low-mileage *C/D* test car. And this problem could be aggravated by the latest type of styled wheels. While they look like a carefully detailed magnesium casting fit for Le Mans, they are actually conventional steel rims cloaked with a stylish section of molded urethane. Unfortunately, there are no slots or holes through the wheel for cooling and urethane is an effective insulator that inhibits the heat transfer from the brakes through the wheel rims and into the air stream. Such is the price of style.

It is but one of many ironies that surround the Road Runner. Performance-looking wheels that may hamper performance. A luxurious and comfortable interior lining a car that began life as a bare-bone performer. And a *macho* image that falls apart when you stand on the gas. From nearly every aspect but one—acceleration—it is the best Road Runner ever. But a Road Runner without acceleration is just another Plymouth. ●

CONTINUED FROM PAGE 43

gory in an instance such as this).

Legally nothing more could be done on Sunday, the 440 Dart was a marked car. It also did a good job of marking itself for remembrance by running a 13.50 @ 106 mph on its way to a trophy run.

Naturally, when it came time to make that run, with a photographer standing by to get the winner's picture, The Incredible Disappearing Dart had done its disappearing act again.

A couple of weeks passed with nothing new being heard about the car and Dodge's New York PR man being torn between getting his car back or signing the guys who were driving it to a contract—their legal and illegal activities were doing more for Dodge's performance image in the New York area than a string of superspeedway wins. By this time, the feature editor and myself were figuring that the engine had been pulled and the GTS was lying at the bottom of the East River when, on a Sunday afternoon three weeks later, Sgt. Ligouri of the Suffolk County Police called.

"Mr. Brown, did you report a stolen car about a month ago?"

Evidently that bored-sounding cop at the 84th precinct in Brooklyn hadn't been entirely oblivious when I first reported the theft, and had actually seen fit to record my name.

"Yes, a blue '69 Dodge Dart with a 440 engine."

"Okay, you can pick up the car tomorrow. We've got the man and the car—by the way it's maroon and gold now."

Like they say, it doesn't pay to cross a man who's been crossed. Not satisfied with one near win at New York National, the Dart had showed up for another everything-but-the-trophy session and had been spotted by Ed Eaton and his scrutineering staff. Now the guys that stole the car have a very tough reputation, so Ed waited until the car made its first run of the day (a 13.3 @ 107 mph.) and had his own track security force and the Suffolk County Police stationed on the one-lane return road to the pits where they put the arm on the driver with such neatness and efficiency that no one ever noticed.

So Dodge's PR man is happy, Ed Eaton is happy, the police are happy, which leaves just the arrested driver and the feature editor and myself unhappy. The driver for obvious reasons, my co-worker and myself because the men who make the decisions that count around here have said that Brooklyn Heights is too dangerous a place to park cars that thieves might want. Right now I'm working on a test of a King Midget and the feature editor has got a Subaru 360.

Even at that, things are looking pretty bad. Last night a hairdresser kicked over the Subaru and there's been a wild band of kindergarteners casting covetous looks at the King Midget.   ●

CONTINUED FROM PAGE 49

face value and keep slamming the door the light will never go out. All this overhead console amounts to is an excuse for the product planners to hang a piece of bright work on the headliner and thereby "create the impression of greater value" when in reality it is next to useless (the Mustang and Cougar at least had a pair of map reading lights in their overhead console which worked very well). The final goodie in the SE package is a vinyl roof with a tiny back window—meant to recreate the visual ecstasy of a Carson padded top from the early Fifties. Unfortunately the normal rear window opening has been made smaller by blocking off a band several inches wide across its bottom, which means that you can no longer see any of the rear deck from the driver's seat and the Challenger consequently becomes a park-by-ear car. In all, the SE package serves to exemplify the entire Challenger approach—lavish execution with no thought to practical application.

Dodge figures it has to offer more in the Challenger because it will sell at a higher price than the Mustang/Camaro/Javelin class of sporty cars. We do find the Challenger's interior to be visually very dramatic. The inner door panels, pebble-grained one-piece molded plastic affairs, are deeply sculptured but unfortunately are as hard as a plastered wall. The door lock button has been replaced by a lever in the armrest—a lever which is cleverly positioned exactly where your elbow wants to go. Armrests are also molded into the flimsy panels that flank the rear seats but they are so high that anyone tall enough to use them comfortably won't fit into the back seat in the first place.

But never mind all of these details. If Dodge's sporty car is like everyone else's its success will depend entirely upon public acceptance of its looks. We've never accused the Mustang of being a wizard car but it sells like one and we think the Challenger has got it covered in the looks category. Still, we are disappointed that looks are awarded such a high priority over function and we think Dodge has had enough time to build a more purposeful car. It's our humble suggestion that, to avoid similar ineptitude in the future, all of the Challenger product planners fall on their swords immediately. ●

PLYMOUTH GTX

CONTINUED FROM PAGE 67

forget that you're in a Plymouth.

While the stylists were making improvements, there is another one which was probably made inadvertently. On the hardtops, the windshield has an extreme rearward slope and the pillars slope along with it. This styling quirk is just enough so that you can drive along with the side windows down at any legal speed without having your ears buffeted off by the draft.

The instrument panel layout was obviously intentional and it deserves some credit also. It manages to group a speedometer, tachometer, a full complement of gauges and a handful of knobs directly in front of the driver in a way that is both attractive and convenient. Unfortunately, the simulated replica of tree wood used to surround the dials is as bad as the instrument arrangement is good.

All in all, we would have to say that the Plymouth GTX is a step forward on a front where all others are retreating. In certain areas, styling and driver comfort, for example, it is vastly improved over the previous model and only in performance, primarily because of increased weight, has it lost ground.

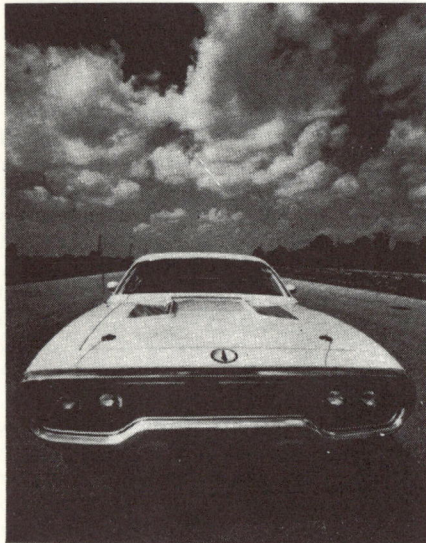

And after a brief look at history, we have no intention of crawling out on a limb and predicting the imminent demise of the performance car. Such machines have survived too many doomsday reports to roll over and die now. Cars like the GTX have too much going for them. Not only are they more capable than a normal family sedan in situations that require evasive capability but they are also more interesting and fun to drive at the same time. And these are the qualities that are central to the car enthusiast. As long as there are car nuts there will be "performance" cars. Probably the biggest difference in the foreseeable future is that Plymouth will come up with something new to supplement the GTX. In fact, Cherry said they had a couple ideas they were working on right now. ●

PLYMOUTH CRICKET

CONTINUED FROM PAGE 75

lever. The seats themselves are relatively luxuriant-looking buckets. They provide good support for long distance cruising, but not enough lateral restraint to hold you secure during tight cornering. That job is left up to the three-point seat belts. They are very comfortable thanks to the fact that the shoulder strap is properly mounted high up on the B-pillar (a distinct advantage of the 4-door sedan configuration over most hardtops). The rear seats are also comfortable, and there is both leg and headroom for a pair of passengers.

The rear seat passengers will be fairly comfortable once they get themselves stuffed into the back, but the getting there will not add to the fun. Because of its 4-door configuration, the Cricket is easier for rear passengers to enter than the competitions' 2-door hardtops, but trying to fit four doors into a 98 in. wheelbase means that each door has to be pretty small. The Cricket doors compound the problem by not opening far enough to allow you to fit medium-size packages that would otherwise fit easily into the available interior space. Wider opening hinges would help solve the accessibility problem, if not the logistics problem of fitting four where two should go.

On our test car, the optional air conditioning not only upset the balance of the engine, but also rendered inoperative both the through-air ventilation system and the defroster. Happily, the Cricket is fitted with vent windows, an amenity which has virtually passed from the domestic scene. These allow you to admit fresh air without causing either drafts or undue wind noise.

Despite its Twin Carb variant, the Cricket's prime selling point is convenience rather than performance. In that category, it has distinct advantages over many of its competitors, while in performance it is merely average. Its single biggest failing, however, is one that can be fixed or even avoided. That is the incredible audible assault it makes on you. This is more than annoying; it is aggravating and it is surround sound in the truest sense. It is up to Plymouth to make the fix, as engine mount science is beyond a normal backyard mechanic's abilities. Until they do, avoid the optional air conditioner. This will bring the price down under $2200, and thus below much of the competition. And you will not only save $339—you will end up much more serene. ●

VALIANT BROUGHAM

CONTINUED FROM PAGE 89

perspective, seems reasonable enough as well. Quarter-mile acceleration is right in there with domestic and imported subcompacts with automatic transmissions: 19.7 seconds with a terminal speed of 69.7 mph. The Valiant, however, feels much better in city traffic; in under-15-mph squirts of acceleration, you have the punch to be competitive. The Valiant's torque convertor is well-matched to the engine's output curve and the transmission is quick with the part-throttle downshifts. So the Valiant ends up short for high-speed passing situations, but it's better than automatic Pintos and the like in the city. Fuel economy is poorer than the typical sub-compact cars in direct proportion of the Valiant's higher weight. Highway driving nets you about 19 mpg if you stick to 55 mph. City traffic drops to the 14-15 mpg range. Overall averages tend to be under 16 mpg . . . a solid position in the vast middle ground between good and bad.

Despite our aversion to its name, we find ourselves applauding this automobile; we like its particular combination of excesses and economies. The interior is sumptuous . . . which seems appropriate since the owner and his guests customarily ride inside where they get full benefit. But the external dimensions are modest (almost exactly those of the Granada), which means that the car is easy to maneuver and not overly heavy, which in turn results in a certain degree of economy, both in original cost and in fuel consumption. Efficiency and comfort without ostentation. There is definitely a market for cars of this type and Chrysler is finally on the case.

The Valiant itself, upon which all this "Brougham" stuff is overlayed, is a fairly neutral car. It is a straight forward design that has been in production long enough to have its bugs ironed out, but it is not quite obsolete enough for Chrysler to replace it. Car connoisseurs will notice its deficiencies: numb steering, uncoordinated brakes and assorted clunks and creaks that are transmitted up through the unit-body. But typical motorists will think the seats are great and dismiss everything else as "just the way it is."

We see the Valiant Brougham as a veteran car—its personality fully developed—that has been dressed in a new suit of clothes. An automotive Uncle Ernie from Hamtramck. Who, according to the sales reports, just happens to be a lot of peoples' favorite uncle in spite of some of his coarse habits. ●